GOLDFINDER

GOLDFINDER

KEITH JESSOP
NEIL HANSON

John Wiley & Sons, Inc.

New York • Chichester • Weinheim • Brisbane • Singapore • Toronto

This book is printed on acid-free paper. ∞

Copyright © 1998 by Keith Jessop. All rights reserved

First published in Great Britain by Simon & Schuster UK Ltd, in 1998.

Published by John Wiley & Sons, Inc.
Published simultaneously in Canada.

This publication is designed to provide accurate and authoritative information in regard to the subject matter covered. It is sold with the understanding that the publisher is not engaged in rendering professional services. If professional advice or other expert assistance is required, the services of a competent professional person should be sought.

Library of Congress Cataloging-in-Publication Data
Jessop, Keith.
Goldfinder / Keith Jessop, Neil Hanson.
p.   cm.
ISBN 0-471-40733-X (cloth : alk. paper)
1. Jessop, Keith.   2. Edinburgh (Cruiser)   3. Salvage—Barents Sea.
I. Hanson, Neil.   II. Title

VM980.J47 J47 2001
387.5'5'092—dc21   00-043918

Printed in the United States of America

10 9 8 7 6 5 4 3 2 1

To my grandchildren Scott, Tara and Thomas,
in the hope that as they grow older,
they will read and understand a little more
about their Grandad.

CONTENTS

CONTENTS

Illustrations on pages 197–212

PROLOGUE

WE HAVE A PROBLEM

———— • ————

'The gold on that wreck is further away than the surface of the moon. It took the American astronauts two and a quarter days to travel back from the moon; it'll take seven days in decompression to bring you back just eight hundred feet from the floor of the ocean.'

I paused to let that sink in, looking around the circle of faces in front of me, twelve of the best deep divers in the world. Like everyone else on the ship, they were working under the standard terms of business for treasure divers and underwater salvage men: 'No Cure, No Pay'. They stood to gain tens of thousands of pounds each if we found the gold; if we didn't, they wouldn't get a penny. My own risk was even more extreme. True, I'd get millions if we found the gold, but if we didn't, I'd be bankrupt, saddled with debts that I'd never be able to clear.

'Don't think about the gold, keep this in mind instead. This is the Arctic, not the North Sea. If things go wrong here, there'll be no helicopters, lifeboats or rescue ships to help us out.

'We're on our own. None of us have ever dived to such depths, in such icy waters, for such a length of time before.

'This is saturation diving. Once you're inside that compression chamber, you're in there for as long as the job takes

1

– six weeks if it goes well, eight weeks or even more if it doesn't. There are plenty of people trained in first aid on board, but there's no paramedic and no doctor. Your mates in the chamber can stop minor bleeding and deal with simple injuries. They can't fix compound fractures, repair severed arteries or sew back missing limbs. If anyone's badly injured, it will take an absolute minimum of twenty-four hours to fly in a doctor and get him into the chamber with you. By that time, it may be too late.

'Think safety above everything else. We want to find the gold, but we want to bring a full dive team back with us as well. Every item of equipment must be checked, rechecked and then checked again, every time it's taken out. If the hot-water system for the suit fails, for instance, you'll be dead in a couple of minutes.

'Storms can blow up here without warning and even if the weather is kind, there is always a risk that the dynamic positioning will fail – it happened often enough in the North Sea.' There were grim smiles and nods from the divers who had worked there.

'If the DP fails, the mother ship will start drifting off station while you're still inside the wreck – a steel box full of jagged edges. If the dive supervisor tells you to return to the bell for any reason, do so at once. I don't care if you're holding a gold bar in your hands at the time, drop it and return to the bell. We can always go back for the gold later, we can't go back for you.

'We won't even be able to go back for the gold if you don't take maximum care as you work. It's stored in the bomb room, the most secure part of the ship. It's also, sur-prisingly enough, the place where they stored the bombs. If the gold is still there, it'll be surrounded by unexploded shells, bombs and ammunition. Try not to use your oxy-acetylene cutting gear on any of them.'

2

There were a few strained smiles. The tension was obvious in all of them. Even the most experienced diver is nervous before his first dive on any new job, let alone one to these depths. I knew the thoughts going through their minds only too well: 'Have I lost it? Can I still hack it?'

It was time to wind up the team talk. I nodded to Mike Stewart the dive controller. 'Okay, they're all yours.'

The shift supervisor, Derek 'Cyclops' Hesketh winked at me with his one good eye and then gave a terse briefing on the technical details of the dive. 'Right,' he concluded. 'It'll take five hours to blow you down to five hundred feet. We'll stabilise you there for six hours and then we'll go the rest of the way at half-rate, so it'll take the neck-end of sixteen hours altogether. After that we're ready to go to work. Any questions?'

They all shook their heads.

'Okay. Time for blow-down. Good luck.'

I stood at the side of the lurid orange compression chamber and shook hands with each of the divers as they filed inside. Jim Tucker was the last to go in. I knew him of old, from our days working in the North Sea together. As I grasped his hand, I winked at him. 'Don't leave any down there, Jim.'

He laughed. 'Didn't you know, Keith? You always leave ten per cent as a tip.'

The door clanged shut. A few moments later there was a high-pitched whine as gas started pouring into the chamber. The divers were now beyond recall, still on the surface but already beginning to feel the pressure of a drop into the ocean depths.

We arrived at 72.06N, 35.09W – the position of the wreck – late in the morning of 3 September. We'd left three Aquafix beacons at the wreck site when we sailed away in May, but as the captain, Ronnie Gotz, began sending out the signal to activate each one in turn, his face grew longer. The first two were dead as hammers and would not respond. Heart in mouth, I waited as he tried the third, then heaved a sigh of relief as he nodded. 'It's functioning.'

Using the *Stephaniturm*'s thrusters we began positioning the ship directly over the wreck. In the small hours of the following morning, Friday, 4 September, we were ready to lower a pan-and-tilt camera to the sea-bed to check that nothing had moved or changed since the last voyage. We clustered around the monitor screens watching the grey, spectral images as the camera explored the wreck.

A soft, silent rain of microscopic sediment and debris fell constantly in the black depths far below us, clouding our vision of the ship, which lay on its port side at the bottom of the ocean – a real lucky break, the bomb room was on the starboard side. Had the ship been lying on that side, it would have been twenty times more difficult to cut a way through the tangle of twisted steel to the gold.

Suddenly a huge feature loomed out of the murk. It was one of the cruiser's 6-inch gun turrets. There was a buzz of excitement. The camera panned on, scanning across a gaping hole in the side of the ship, blasted by one of the German torpedoes that had sunk her almost forty years before. If the bomb room had not also been blown apart, the gold lay not far from that torpedo hole.

We were now ready to begin the dives. The first job was to place two replacement transponders on the sea-bed, to help the vessel on the surface take up any position required above the wreck. The second and most vital task was to survey the bomb room area, to dispel any remaining worries that the gold had spilled out after the strike by the German torpedo. It would also help us decide on the final plan for gaining entry into the bomb room.

A few minutes before 4 a.m. the first divers transferred

from the deck compression chamber to the diving bell. There had been fierce competition among them for the right to make the first dive. An Australian, a New Zealander and an Englishman – Banjo West, John Diamond and Brian Cutler – had been given the privilege. They were three very experienced divers, all ex-Royal Navy men.

Already under a pressure equivalent to a depth of 750 feet, they crawled through the narrow trunking into the cramped diving bell. The bell was designed for two divers, but it was big by normal standards and the dive controllers had decided on three-man dives for safety reasons. There would then be two divers working in the wreck while the third stayed in the bell, ready to respond to any emergency.

The divers' umbilicals – the hoses that carry the helium/oxygen mixture they breathe, the circulating hot water that stops them dying from hypothermia and the communications cables linking them with the surface – had also been lengthened as another safety measure. Even though all the special tools and cutting equipment were lowered in a separate basket, three burly divers and two huge umbilicals, each as thick as a man's forearm, made the bell very full indeed.

Good housekeeping inside a diving bell is always essential. You must have clear access to all the dive controls and clear sight of the many gauges inside the bell. Even on a routine dive it isn't good practice to have umbilical cords in a tangle all over the place. With space at such a premium on this dive it was even more vital.

At 4.06, the bell was finally uncoupled from the chambers and the winch ground into life, hauling it off the deck. The bell rocked gently to and fro as it dangled from its lifting arm over the ship's moon-pool, then dropped slowly out of sight beneath the water. (On some ships the diving bell was lowered over the stern or side of the ship. A moon-pool enclosed within the ship's hull, gave the bell additional protection as it was raised or lowered.) The ripples from the splash subsided almost at once and there was nothing to see but the cables unwinding steadily from the huge drum as the bell made its long, slow descent into the inky darkness where the wreck lay, exactly 803 feet below us.

I scanned the horizon as the ship rocked slowly in the swell. The weather looked set fair, the wind a southerly Force 4 or 5. The moderate conditions would be a big relief to the divers. On this operation we could not use the heave-compensation system which ensured that the bell didn't rise and fall with the motion of the ship on the surface – sea-sickness in the bell can be a bit of a nuisance, to say the least. A large compensation weight was normally lowered to the sea-bed and the bell was then raised and lowered down two guide-wires fixed to the weight. Because of our exposed position in the Barents Sea, however, with no help to hand should things go wrong, the weight was to be suspended just above the highest point of the wreck, rather than sitting on the sea-bed. Then if the DP system on the ship malfunctioned and the vessel drifted off station, the weight would not foul in the wreck and become fast.

It was the safe decision, but it meant that the divers would be at the mercy of the surface sea conditions. In a heavy swell, even at a depth of over 750 feet, the bell would still be rising and falling quickly by twenty or thirty feet.

I turned to head for the dive-control shack to watch the pictures from the camera mounted on the outside of the bell. I sat next to the dive superintendent, Mike O'Meara, as the divers went through their checks at each stage of the descent. They kept up the usual stream of banter with Derek, their voices distorted into Minnie Mouse speech by the helium/oxygen mix, but there was tension and maybe just a little fear in their voices. I knew exactly what they were feeling. There is always tension before the first dive of a new operation, let alone one to these depths, but it's similar to parachuting; once you get there and step outside, the fear goes.

The diving bell came to a stop with its normal jerk, at a depth of 750 feet. In the pool of light that surrounded it, I could just make out a small part of the massive wreck below them.

'Bell checks completed.' The pressure inside and outside the bell had equalised, allowing the hatch inside the bell to be swung soundlessly upwards and locked back. The divers immediately began dumping out the heavy, coiled umbilicals to make more room inside the bell.

Suddenly there was the first warning of danger. The life-support team technician called urgently to Derek. 'CO_2's building up.'

'How serious?'

'Bad and getting worse.'

I glanced across at the gauges. The CO_2 levels were already dangerously high and still moving slowly upwards. There was no time for delay.

Derek shot a questioning look at Don Rodocker, who was monitoring the flow of gases to the bell. We were using his gas-recirculating system for the first time. The phenomenal cost savings would be no compensation if the system didn't work.

Don shook his head. 'There's no fault here. The CO_2 scrubbers are functioning perfectly.'

'So what is going wrong?' Derek asked, swinging his chair around to look at Mike.

Mike shrugged. 'I don't know. In trying to make it safer for them in the wreck, perhaps we've made it more dangerous in the bell. Too many men and too much gear in too small a space, trying to work too hard and too fast for the depth. Let's worry about it when we've got them back up here.'

Derek nodded and snapped into action. 'Abort the dive.' As he spoke to the divers, he was careful to keep his voice neutral. If they panicked they would die. 'Divers, we have a small problem up here, nothing serious, but we're aborting the dive.'

There was a long pause before a response came in. 'What was that?' Banjo asked.

The biggest danger in carbon-dioxide poisoning is that the divers themselves don't realise there is a problem until too late. They become sluggish, don't respond to instructions, and can slip into unconsciousness and possibly death in a matter of minutes.

I was now desperately worried, but powerless to intervene. I had contracted this dive team to do the job; I could not interfere now. The divers' lives were in the hands of Derek and his back-up team. I had to trust his judgement.

Mike shot another worried look at Derek and voiced my thoughts for me. 'We're losing them.'

Derek nodded and immediately thumbed his radio mike. 'Abort the dive now.'

There was no response.

'Diver, do you read me? Abort the dive.'

Still there was no reply.

'Banjo!' Derek shouted.

'Yeah, s'all right, Cyclops,' came a drowsy voice, the Minnie Mouse tones slowed almost to normal speed.

Derek immediately barked into the radio again. 'Confirm aborting dive.'

I scanned the gauges again. The CO_2 level was still inching steadily upwards. As they said on Apollo 13, 'We have a problem.' The only difference was that Apollo 13 was under just one atmosphere of pressure. The diving bell was at one for every 33 feet it had descended, a crushing total of 23 atmospheres.

Once more Derek had to repeat the command before he got a response: 'Aborting dive.'

The needles on the gauges still crept upwards. I could imagine just what it was like inside that bell, the divers in their bulky suits, with little space to move, trying as hard as their befuddled minds would allow to retrieve the umbilicals hanging outside the bell. They could cut them instead, but it would take even more energy and time than stowing them.

We could do nothing for the divers until we had them back on the surface. We could not get them there until they had secured the bell. If they did not get the top door closed, they would be dead. Without that seal to maintain the pressure inside the chamber, we could not bring the bell back to the surface. If we tried to do so, they would all die from massive attacks of the bends.

Derek now started to coax, shout and bully the divers to keep them from slipping into unconsciousness. 'Begin stowing the umbilicals immediately.'

Once more there was the same heart-stopping pause before the response 'Okay surface' came in from the bell. Banjo's voice was even fainter and weaker this time.

'Danger level.'

The life-support technician's warning was superfluous. We could hear the divers talking to each other as they tried to haul in the thick, unwieldy umbilicals. As they worked, they kept complaining of tiredness – another classic symptom of CO_2 poisoning – and their movements were desperately slow and clumsy. We sat helpless in the control shack, listening as their voices grew steadily slower and more slurred.

Derek kept up a constant dialogue with them, but each

long silence before they responded gnawed at our nerves. If they succumbed to the CO_2 poisoning, there would be no drama, no famous last words. There would just be a silence that would grow and grow until there was no longer any doubt. The seconds would tick into minutes, as we called again and again on the radio, but received no reply.

We could wait and wait and wait, but finally we would have to take the decision to raise the bell, its door still open and the umbilicals trailing below it. As it rose through the depths, every vessel and organ in the men's bodies would rupture, still saturated with helium and oxygen at the massive pressure of the ocean floor.

CHAPTER ONE

THE JAY STREET GANG

My lifelong pursuit of riches from the sea began in the least likely of places and I was the least likely of people to end up chasing millions of pounds worth of gold at the bottom of the ocean. Keighley was a nondescript Yorkshire town of fraying textile mills and worn-out engineering factories. It is about as far from the sea as you can get in northern England, though you wouldn't have known it from the aroma surrounding our house. Across the alley at the back was a fishmonger's yard strewn with fish crates and bins full of bones and skin. On hot days the stench was overpowering.

My only contact with water in my early years was the tin tubful warmed in front of the fire for the weekly hot bath on Friday night, but I was fascinated by the sea long before I first clapped eyes on it. One typically grey and wet Keighley afternoon, I and my mates were whiling away the time in the public library when I came across a picture book about famous shipwrecks and the treasures lost with them.

While my mates flicked paper pellets at each other and surreptitiously carved their initials in the tables, I sat spellbound, staring at the illustrations and poring over the stories of Spanish galleons, doubloons and pieces of eight. From then on I devoured every book about shipwrecks and pirates that I could get my hands on, and I knew *Treasure Island* almost by heart.

As soon as I learned to swim, I used to leave the jostling mass of bodies in the shallow end and dive to the bottom of the pool, imagining myself prising fabulous pearls from giant clams on the sea-bed or finding pirate treasure chests spilling gold and jewels. It was a hard fantasy to sustain at the bottom of a municipal swimming bath in Keighley, but I gave it my best shot.

In summer, we swam in the River Aire which flowed through the town and I'd scour the river-bed for treasure, emerging with an old glass bottle or a metal cigar tube, as pleased as if I'd found a gold bar.

My first sight of the sea was on a day-trip to Morecambe. To my eyes the grey ocean reaching to the horizon concealed a mountain of gold, though the only things I got from beneath the waves that day was a carton of potted shrimps and a couple of shells I found amongst the shingle. I carried the shells in my pockets for weeks and was heartbroken when I lost them.

As I grew up and left school, the dreams of buried treasure began to fade. I had other things on my mind. What spare time I had was filled with a series of progressively more dangerous sports, including cycle-racing, potholing, rock-climbing and finally diving.

My first-ever dive could have killed me, so little did I know about the sport and its dangers, but it was enough to rekindle all those burning childhood dreams. From then on, diving was my sole obsession. I and a few friends formed a local branch of the British Sub-Aqua Club and scraped together enough money for some rudimentary equipment.

My first dives in icy lakes and rivers were for my own pure pleasure, but then came one that was the last act in a tragedy for someone else. A small boy had slipped and fallen into the River Aire in Keighley and drowned. Another boy had been with him, but he'd been warned by his parents never to go near the river and was so scared of the punishment he'd get for disobeying them that he said nothing about the drowning for five days.

Knowing nothing of the tragedy, the police began a search, making house-to-house enquiries and combing waste ground and outbuildings. Volunteers helped them to scour the moors above Keighley for any trace of the missing boy, but it was only when the distraught parents made a public appeal for information that his friend broke down and told his own parents what had happened.

A police diving team then tried to find the body for a further two days without success, though they were hampered by heavy rain and flooding which reduced underwater visibility to inches.

We offered them the use of our compressor, saving them the fifty-mile round trip to Wakefield to refill their air bottles, but they snubbed us. They were even less enthusiastic when we also volunteered to help with the underwater search. I heard the words, 'Here come the glory-seekers,' as we approached the river. We ignored the insult and eventually, when they could still find no trace of the boy, they swallowed their pride and asked us if we would do a search.

The place where the boy had gone missing was known as the S-bend. I'd spent countless idyllic summer afternoons there as a kid, playing on the banks and swimming in the river. On our way down to the river, we used to go through a scrapyard and pinch spears – decorative iron railings cut down and sent for scrap to aid the war effort. Armed with these, we'd dodge the owner of the scrapyard and spend the day using our trophies to dig caves in the riverbank. Before we went home, we'd hurl our spears far out into the river.

When we began the search for the boy, the first thing I

13

put my hand on as I swam along the bottom was one of those iron spears. I picked it up, bridging twenty years in an instant. I laid it down again as we cut out towards the deepest part of the river, where my eye was momentarily caught by something white sticking out of the sand. I was just about to pass it when I realised that it was the rubber strip on the sole of a child's baseball boot. I half-turned back and stretched out my hand to pick it up. As soon as my fingers closed around it, I realised this was not just a shoe. I had found the missing child.

He was lying face down, completely buried in the sand. I pulled slowly on the exposed part of his leg. After a week in the water, it was stark white and swollen; it had a crease at the knee like a baby. I took hold of the leg and pulled again, giving an involuntary shudder at the feel of the soft, pulpy flesh.

The lower half of the body rose out of the sand. The boy had been wearing jeans and a T-shirt — any kid, from anywhere. One leg of the jeans had ridden up above his knee, exposing the bloated white leg, marked with the usual schoolboy assortment of bumps and scrapes — a purple bruise on the shin, a graze on the knee.

I took hold of the shirt and gently pulled the rest of him free of the sand. He was curled into the foetal position. There was a shiny new watch on his left wrist, a gift from his parents just a week before. I'd seen it mentioned in the story of his disappearance in the local paper. As I turned him on to his back to carry him up to the surface, I caught sight of his face. It was still contorted in its death agony, eyes staring, mouth wide open in a silent scream.

I cradled him in my arms and swam to the surface, then kicked for the bank. As I reached the shallows, I got awkwardly to my feet, still clutching the body to my chest. There were shouts from the policemen waiting on the bank.

A man walking his dog and a courting couple strolling by the river stopped and turned to see what had caused the commotion. Their faces blanched as they saw the river giving up its dead.

As I reached up to hand the body to a policeman on the bank above me I took my last look at the small figure in my arms. He could easily have been my own boy, Graham. There was a lump in my throat and tears were trickling down the policeman's face as he took the child from me and wrapped him in a blanket, hiding him from the eyes of the passers-by.

Long after an ambulance had taken the body away to the mortuary and the police had packed up and gone, I sat huddled on the riverbank staring into the water, thinking about the waste of a young life and how easily my own childhood could have ended the same way.

I was born in 1933, the depths of the Depression. My mother, Hannah, was a seventeen-year-old mill girl. I don't know who my father was – my mother never told me and I never asked, but all my childhood I had the stigma of being illegitimate, the only boy in my class without a father. Few called me a bastard to my face, however, for I soon learned how to fight; I had to, Keighley was a tough town in those days.

My mother was small and painfully thin but she was also surprisingly strong and fearsomely strict. Like almost everyone else in the town, she worked in the textile industry, as a spinner. She grafted from 7.30 in the morning until 5.30 in the evening and when she came home, she tackled the housework with a rare ferocity. Everything from the furniture to the oilcloth on the floor gleamed from daily polishing and she scoured the front doorstep so hard she almost wore it away.

We lived with my grandparents in a terraced house in West Lane, the oldest and poorest area of the town; two of the town workhouses were just around the corner. We were always skint but in those hungry years my mother thought herself lucky to have any work at all. My grandfather had known even harder times. Frail and whippet-thin, with a pair of wire-rimmed glasses perched on the end of his nose, he'd tell me of the time he'd walked all the way from Keighley to Settle – around thirty miles – in the hope of a job. They gave him a shovel and, shoulder-to-shoulder with a few hundred other hungry men, he dug the reservoir which supplies Keighley's water.

Our diet was very basic: mostly bread and jam, or if we were lucky, bread and dripping. My grandmother baked the bread and I can still remember the delicious smell that greeted me every Tuesday when the week's supply was brought out of the oven. We didn't starve, but there was no money for even the smallest luxury. Very occasionally I'd manage to wheedle a halfpenny out of my grandad for a gobstopper, but that visit to the sweet shop would have to last me for weeks.

The annual holiday was exactly that, a single day – if my mother could scrape the money together. Even Christmas brought few treats. I'd hang up a pillow case on Christmas Eve and wake the next morning to find it stuffed with old newspapers and cotton wool. Hidden inside would be a couple of tinny metal toys or whatever else my mother could afford.

My grandparents both died before I was five and soon afterwards my mother moved in with Tom Leonard, a spinning overlooker at the mill where she worked. He was a small man with wispy ginger hair and had a house near the Keighley rugby league ground.

Their relationship quickly turned sour. Tommy came in

from work every Saturday lunchtime and changed into his best blue suit with a gold watch-chain across the waistcoat. A couple of medals that he'd won years before playing football for Keighley Town hung from the chain. He'd give his gleaming brown shoes a final polish and then he was off to the Dyers' Club for the rest of the day. There were always furious arguments when he came in after closing time, full of drink. I used to curl up in bed, wishing they would stop fighting. Even when he was sober, the house was full of bitterness and rancour. If a row was not already on the boil, one was invariably about to break.

He didn't treat me badly, but there was always a barrier between us; I was very aware that he wasn't my father. Whenever I could, I escaped into the back streets of Lawkholme, in the Keighley district, with my gang of mates, the lads who lived in my very local area – the three streets surrounding my home. We called ourselves the Jay Street Gang. We felt like brothers and looked like them too, all dressed in shapeless, threadbare reach-me-downs and heavy boots or clogs, with our heads shaven like convicts. Mothers believed in getting full value for money from the barber in those days.

Only the worst weather forced us indoors and the happiest times of my childhood were spent in the streets or up on the moors. At weekends and holidays I was out of the house from eight in the morning until I ran in for a slice of bread and dripping at teatime. Then I was off out again until dark. We played piggy-stick, kick-can, football and cricket, and in between times, we fought like cat and dog with other gangs in the vicinity. The gang's cricket bat was cut from a plank of wood and the wicket was the pig-bin in the street. The pigs wouldn't have grown very fat on the scraps from our neighbourhood, but there was one on every corner to collect waste food as part of the war effort.

GOLDFINDER

I was just six when war broke out. The greengrocer came round on his horse and cart, shouting that we were going to fight Germany again. My gang thought this was great news and we invented a new set of games, using guns made out of pieces of wood. The war also added a whole new dimension to the pitched battles fought in the school playground every lunchtime.

Many of Keighley's young men went to fight and many of them – including one of my uncles – didn't return, but the war wasn't all bad news for the town. It ended the depression in the textile mills and created a new industry: munitions. There was work for everyone at better rates of pay; my mother even saved enough to rent our very first radio relay. Even rationing caused few complaints. People in more affluent areas may have complained about the restrictions, but the weekly ration was far better and more varied than our normal diet – even the notorious powdered egg was something of a treat.

The army arrived in numbers to begin training and exercising on the moors above the town, and to the delight of everyone at my school, the park opposite the playground filled up with tanks, trucks and armoured vehicles. We soon grew bold enough to walk through the lines of vehicles, chatting to the soldiers and nicking live ammunition from the piles of crates lying around. Every kid had a few live .303 rounds or the even more desirable 9mm ones in their pockets; we used them as currency. The brother of one of my mates tried to make a cigarette lighter from a stolen tank shell, however – he was sawing off the head when it exploded. I saw the ambulance take him to hospital, blood streaming from his head. He lost the sight of one eye and was disfigured for life.

It's astonishing that there weren't more disasters, for we all took terrifying risks with the stolen ammo. One of our new games was to light a fire in the cellar, throw a handful of live rounds on to the flames and then run for cover as bullets ricocheted all over the place. The trick was to keep count of the bangs and not come out until all the rounds were spent. We put new heads on the spent cases and frightened other kids senseless by hitting the caps with a nail. The faint of heart soon disappeared.

We soon found an even more dangerous game. We set off on our rattle-trap bicycles one day and had been cranking along for an hour or so when we came to some Nissen huts spaced at 400-yard intervals along a deserted moorland road. The huts had no security whatsoever, not even a door; there were just strips of canvas at the front and rear. When we lifted the canvas, we saw boxes of ammunition stacked from floor to ceiling. I instantly recognised the boxes holding the familiar .303 and 9mm rounds but there were other boxes that I'd never seen before.

We prised off one lid and found ourselves staring wide-eyed at neat rows of grenades. Luckily we talked ourselves out of experimenting with them but we couldn't resist taking some detonators we found in a metal box, even though we didn't have a clue what they were. We did recognise the firing caps on them, however, so we cut off the caps, leaving just the short fuse and the detonator. We were all delighted with our booty. Bonfire Night was looming and we reckoned we'd found a free alternative to the usual penny bangers.

Back in Keighley, our pockets full of fuses, we sneaked into a back street and jammed the top part of a detonator into a gap in the red brick wall. We tried and failed to light the fuse with a match. Undeterred, we shortened the fuse and tried again. We'd just about given up and were standing around long-faced when there was an enormous bang. Half the wall blew out and we ran for our lives through a cloud of thick, brown and very acrid smoke.

My illegitimacy had long ceased to be an issue among the members of my gang, but it was partly responsible for the difficulties I experienced at school. I wasn't thick, just rebellious. I always had plenty to say and could out-think most of my classmates, but I wasted the opportunities that came my way. My teachers saw me as arrogant, shiftless and lazy – they were probably right – and eventually most washed their hands of me, other than to cane me hard and often.

One of my teachers, 'Pop' Walker, used the ultimate weapon, a cut-down hickory shaft from a golf club he affectionately called 'GC'. Most of the school went in fear of an encounter with GC; a crack on the hand from it certainly sharpened you up for the rest of the day.

One day I found GC lying on Pop's desk in the deserted classroom. It was too good a chance to miss. I stuffed it down my shirt and into my trousers and disappeared as fast as my legs could carry me. During woodwork I planed it down and made it into one of the small wooden crosses we had to make as test pieces. I then sat in Pop's class, playing with my small wooden cross, as he told the whole class what he would do to the thief who'd stolen his beloved GC if ever he got hold of him. When I let my classmates in on the secret, my stock with them went sky high.

After years of rows with my mother about my lousy school reports, I gave it my best shot in my last year there and finished up top of the class. The headmaster wanted me to go on to grammar school, but my mother was having none of that. 'No. I've kept you long enough.'

I left school at fifteen without a single qualification and as my mother wished, I went to work in a wool mill. It was a dead-end job, but it put a few bob in my pocket. If I'd taken up an apprenticeship in a trade, I'd have earned virtually nothing for several years, but any numbskull could get thirteen shillings and sixpence a week in a mill from the word go. The work needed no skills or intelligence. It was just a dull, back-breaking grind from 7.30 to 5.30 every weekday, with a half-day on Saturday. I stayed a few months, then moved on. I changed jobs regularly, working mostly as a labourer on building and demolition sites, acquiring muscles but few skills.

I spent most of my evenings at the Keighley Youth Club, where we played endless games of table tennis and danced to a stack of worn 78s. There I met a girl called Mildred. She had beautiful, almond-shaped eyes, and when she smiled – which was often – it lit up the room. She loved dancing too, which was a serious obstacle to any hopes I had of dating her, for I danced like a man wearing a deep-sea diving suit. With a dedication born of desperation I eventually managed to learn a very basic waltz and a slow foxtrot, though the way I danced them, only the keenest eye could have spotted the difference.

Beneath the veneer of Yorkshire machismo, I was quite a shy person and it took me some time to pluck up courage to ask Mildred out. To my surprise and delight, she accepted at once. Although I didn't realise at the time, she'd also had her eye on me. I was working in demolition at the time and during her lunch-hour she used to walk down to the centre of town and watch me knocking down an old church in Cavendish Street. Whatever it was she saw as I worked on the steeple was enough to convince her that I was worth a date.

We began going out regularly, but only on weekdays; at weekends I indulged my other passion, for dangerous sports. The first was cycle-racing. I joined the Keighley velo club and soon learned about pain as I tried to keep up with the older members of the club, but I trained every night and weekend like a man possessed. I saved five bob a week out of my wages, gradually building myself a top-class racing bike.

My first race was the Yorkshire championship and I'd

already decided that I was going to win it. It started from Skipton with a massed start like a poor man's Tour de France, and halfway round the circuit everything was going to plan. I was tearing along in the leading bunch at thirty miles per hour over a newly-gravelled road, when there was a pile-up which hurled me to the ground and nearly skinned me alive. It was the end of my cycle-racing career. Apart from my injuries, my £70 bike had been wrecked and I didn't have the money or the heart to rebuild it.

I soon had other, even more dangerous crazes to keep me occupied. Every weekend would see me clinging to the pillion of my friend Arthur 'Arch' Brown's Triumph Speed Twin – *the* motor bike at the time – as we burned rubber up to Ingleton in the Yorkshire Dales, the heart of the best caving country in the North.

The appeal of crawling up underground stream beds, getting cold and wet, and skinning my knees and elbows, quickly wore off, and the potholing craze only lasted six months. Then I found a new and infinitely more exciting challenge. Just a few miles further along the road from Ingleton were the towering crags of the Lake District. One taste of rock-climbing and I was hooked.

I even switched to a Monday-to-Friday job to lengthen the weekend. Every Friday evening Arch and I would set off, laden with a ramshackle assortment of ex-War Department boots and ropes. We made the Langdales our base and scaled almost every crag in the valley, then tackled climbs in North Wales and the Isle of Skye. I lived for the excitement and danger of climbing, of testing myself against the crags.

Climbing taught me better than anything else how to make decisions. Could it be climbed at all? Could I do it without freezing in panic on the rock face or falling to my death? My unwitting tutor in that vital lesson was a man we found stuck to the face of a crag one fine Saturday morning. Arch and I had made a late start after a heavy night in the Old Dungeon Ghyll pub, and decided to spend the day messing about on Raven Crag, a few hundred feet up the hillside from Dungeon Ghyll itself.

On the way up I took a good look at the route we were planning to do and noticed a climber on a section called Holly Tree Traverse, named after the small tree that had taken root in the middle of the cliff face. At the foot of the crag we found a tearful woman. She told us her boyfriend was up on the cliff, but his rope had been hanging motionless for some considerable time and there was no response to her shouts.

I secured a rope around my waist and made a fast climb up to the traverse. The man was rigid, clinging to the rock face, too scared to move or even speak. His face was death-white and there was a sheen of sweat on his forehead. I talked to him for a few minutes, trying to get him to relax a little. 'Everything's all right now. It'll be okay. I'll fix my rope to you and then you can climb back down. I'll be holding you on the rope, so even if you slip or fall, you'll be in no danger.' He gave no sign of having heard me. I tried again, but though he shifted his gaze slightly to look at me, he was still petrified, unable to move a muscle.

In the end I called Arch, who also climbed up. We roped the man between us, then began moving him very slowly back across the traverse. It took all my strength to prise his fingers free of the rock and move them a few inches to the first handhold, but once he was moving, his panic ebbed enough for him to follow our directions. It took a long time, but in the end we got him safely off the crag and down to the waiting arms of his girlfriend. They left vowing eternal gratitude and promising to leave the price of a few pints behind the bar of the pub. I got the strong impression that it would be some time before the man ventured on to a rock face again.

It was the first time I'd ever seen someone in such a state and I took the lesson to heart. I tried to make sure I never got myself into a position on any climb where I was not in control, unable to go forward or back. Yet even though we showed maximum respect for the dangers and difficulties of the climbs we made, we were very lucky to survive unscathed. There were no more enthusiastic nor dedicated climbers, but our techniques were self-taught and our equipment makeshift; we were still using hemp ropes rather than the newer and infinitely stronger nylon.

One day Arch turned up with what appeared to be a thousand feet of manila rope, which he swore would safely lift a ten-ton truck. Elated, we gave it its first test abseiling off the Cow and Calf rocks at Ilkley. The descent included a dramatic leap out into space at the end of this wonder rope to clear the overhang on the Cow. It was heady, exhilarating stuff. The gods were certainly with us that day. The very next weekend the rope snapped like cotton, luckily when the man clinging to it was only a few feet from the ground. When we examined the rope, we found sections of it were rotten to the core.

By this time I'd passed my eighteenth birthday and two years of compulsory National Service were looming. I saw an item about the Royal Marine Commandos on a cinema newsreel, heard the words 'Every Commando is now trained in rock-climbing', and saw them shinning up and down sea-cliffs. I decided there and then that the Commandos would do for me.

When I registered for National Service, I stated my preference and was laughed out of the room. The Marines only accepted the best and fittest men, almost invariably those prepared to sign on as long-term regular soldiers. Spotty

24

youths press-ganged into two years' National Service did not fit their bill at all. Still I persisted, emphasising my fitness and climbing skills, and in the end they wearily agreed to put my name forward.

According to everyone I'd spoken to, the medical examination for National Service was a formality; if you were warm you were in. To my surprise, mine was very thorough and prolonged. After weeks of suspense I received a letter. I had been accepted by the Marine Commandos.

Friends who'd already done their National Service had filled my head with horror stories about their experiences. I turned up for basic training at Lympstone in Devon full of apprehension, but there were none of the meaningless, humiliating tasks like whitewashing coal or cutting grass with nail-scissors that recruits to the army were reputed to face. Training was hard but I relished every moment of it. My school teachers would have been surprised at how quickly I lost my resentment at being ordered around every minute of the day, but then, unlike my school, the officers never asked us to do anything that they weren't prepared to do themselves.

After basic training at Lympstone, we moved to Commando School at Bickleigh on Dartmoor. I was now able to demonstrate my skill at climbing and we did all manner of stress and stamina tests: speed-marching over the moors, bivouacking in bad weather conditions, unarmed combat, beach landings and exercises with live ammunition. The last and hardest part of our training came in the final pass-out week, when they hit us with everything, forcing us to sweat blood to earn the coveted green beret. It was then, at the worst possible moment, that I got into trouble for the first and only time during my Commando training.

For once it wasn't even deserved. A sergeant put me on a charge for having a rusty rifle. What he'd actually spotted was a trace of red lubricating oil, but recruits don't argue with sergeants, even when they're wrong. I was confined to barracks for three days and when not on duty was forced to report to the guardroom on the hour, every hour, day and night. In the middle of my punishment we had to do a forced march over Dartmoor. It was thirty miles if we got our compass bearings right and anything up to infinity if we didn't.

Battling against snow and gales, my group got it more or less right, but my limbs had seized up when we finally arrived back at the barracks. While my mates settled down for a rest, I had to report to the guardroom. It took me fully fifteen minutes to hobble the few hundred yards there and another fifteen to hobble back again, but I had to keep doing it or risk failing the course.

Having secured my green beret, I was counting on becoming a Cliff Leader, teaching rock-climbing to other Marines, and when I saw an officer strolling around the camp in a pair of state-of-the-art climbing boots, I introduced myself and told him of my ambition. He invited me to go climbing with his group that weekend. They were practising 'problems', moves carried out close to the ground, which could then be faced with more confidence when they were encountered for real high on a cliff face.

One problem on an overhang beat all of them. The move was to climb out of the mouth of a cave on to the cliff face directly above it. The crux of it – the key move – was very similar to one I'd practised a number of times back home. The thought flashed through my mind that if I succeeded where they'd failed, they might let me take the Cliff Leader's course.

I volunteered to have a go. There were a few quizzical glances from the Captain and the rest of the experts, but they stood aside to let me try. I pulled myself up on to the cave roof and jammed the fingers of my left hand into a crevice in the rock. With that as an anchor, I swung myself up and out of the cave mouth. I scrabbled for a hold above the overhang with my other hand and for a second, I thought I might fall back. Then my fingertips held on the tiny ledge I'd been aiming for and I was out and pulling myself up the cliff face.

Stung by my success, the others all lined up for another go. It was then that I made my big mistake. As the Captain battled to make the move, his face puce with exertion, I called out, 'Come on Sir, it's easy.' He didn't make it. For some strange reason I was never invited to go climbing with him again and I never did get my chance to become a Cliff Leader.

I was not destined to become a war hero either. We missed involvement in both Korea and Malaya by a month and instead were sent to join 45 Commando in Malta. After the relentless training to turn us into fighting machines, our only moment of real excitement came when we were sent to Egypt after a campaign of violence against the giant British base at Suez, stirred up by the new nationalist government. We landed at Port Said, ready to knock seven bells out of the Egyptian army, but they had all run away before we got there. Only the occasional palm tree stood in the path of our relentless advance and not a single shot was fired in anger. The only thing we actually killed was a pig which we bought from an Egyptian for a barbecue. In the end we returned disconsolate to Malta without a service medal to share between us – all that finely honed fighting potential and our only score was a pig.

After that fiasco, the officers thought up all sorts of diversions to dissipate our pent-up energy, including twelve weeks' intensive training at Taruna in Libya. The Italians had used it as a prisoner-of-war camp during the Second World War and the place was dominated by a thirty-foot flagpole, planted in the top of a twenty-foot concrete tower. The wire which winched the flag to the top had been broken for years and there was a long-standing competition between various army units to be the first to run up a flag. Many men had tried and failed, many bets taken and lost.

The flagpole became an obsession for the men of 45 Commando; officers, NCOs and other ranks alike thought of little else. It seemed as if every time you looked out of the barrack-room window, you would see someone halfway up it. To a man they failed.

I took a careful look at the flagpole one day. Most of it was steel, but the top eight feet was wood. All you could see from the ground were long cracks running the length of it, which didn't exactly inspire confidence in anyone trying to climb it. I decided that people were expending all their energy on climbing the shorter, thicker part of the pole. The answer was very simple. I borrowed a short ladder, and used it to scale the concrete tower. The ladder now helped me avoid the most difficult part of the flagpole and with a wire through my belt, I started the final stage.

The wooden pole creaked ominously as it took my weight and it was a very dodgy climb. I wouldn't have made it without all my experience in the Lake District. When I reached the top, I threaded the wire through the metal hoop and on to the roller, but in my haste to get clear of the wooden pole, I'd forgotten to unhitch the wire from the loops on my belt. I then had to climb the flagpole for a second time. I was completely exhausted when I got down, but the wire was in place.

Most of the men were away from camp on manoeuvres at the time, but I was an instant hero when they returned and saw the flagpole. The RSM invited me to hoist the flag and later that night I was invited into the holy of holies, the Officers' Mess, where we drank copiously and at length to my achievement. I was then escorted to the Sergeants' Mess, where the entire boozy ritual was repeated.

A much more significant event awaited me back in Malta. Included in the standard gear of every Commando company was some basic diving equipment: fins, mask and snorkels. Since we were spending most of our time on the beach, I asked to use them. As I put my face under the water, I entered a new world. I was mesmerised by what I saw. The sea was crystal clear in those days; pollution had yet to cloud the water and reduce visibility to a few feet. I could see a hundred feet in all directions. I had no way of gauging the depth of the water, nor the size or distance of anything I saw. A tiny fish swelled into a ten-foot shark as it cruised towards me, then shrank again as it thrashed its tail and disappeared back into the depths.

The experience was so new and unreal that it brought on an attack of nautical vertigo. It was completely illogical, but I felt there was nothing to stop me dropping like a stone all the way to the bottom. I had a slight panic attack, but forced myself to turn over and swim on my back. I stared hard at the sky and gradually talked myself back to reality.

In every other respect I found diving utterly exhilarating. At times I began to resent having to leave the underwater world where everything was quiet, clean, weightless and dream-like, to face the problems of the noisy, dirty, smelly place up top. I was so anxious to spend more time on my new craze that I offered to sign on for a seven-year stint as a regular in the Marines, providing they would let me join the Special Boat Squadron, which specialised in underwater operations.

They were happy to let me sign on, but would give no cast-iron guarantee that I would be accepted by the SBS. That wasn't good enough for me. I completed my two years' National Service and went back to Keighley.

Chapter Two

Devil's Bridge

————————•————————

Back in civilian life, fit, bronzed and feeling very much a man of the world, I waited expectantly for doors to open and things to happen. None did. I went straight back to square one, working nine hours a day, five and a half days a week, in a weaving shed in Silsden. It was dark and filthy, and the noise level was enough to reduce your ear-drums to pulp; all that for the magnificent sum of three pounds ten shillings a week.

Even so, the most intolerable part of the job was the daily journey on the top deck of the workers' special bus to Silsden. I have never been seasick or airsick in my life but the fug of tobacco smoke brought me close to vomiting on many occasions. My reaction may have been at least partly psychological, for hammering through my brain every bleak, grey morning was the thought that life had so much more to offer than this.

I was no longer a completely free agent, however. Mildred and I had decided to get married, though the date of our wedding was inadvertently set by my mother. I stayed overnight at Mildred's parents' house one night. There was nothing untoward about it – her parents were there and we slept in separate rooms – but when I went home the next morning I was greeted by my mother, standing on the doorstep with my bags already packed. 'If you prefer to stay with her all night, you'd better move out of this place now.'

Faced with the ultimatum, I took my bags and left. Mildred and I got a special licence and were married within the week. My mother didn't even come to the wedding. She had come to rely on the money that I brought in each week and saw Mildred as a direct challenge, someone who was going to take that money away from her. I was both upset and angry. While I'd been in the Marines, Mildred had cared for my mother after she had an accident at work. One of the big overhead drive-belts in the spinning mill broke and gave her a very nasty crack on her head. Mildred nursed her and helped her in many other ways, and they appeared to have become very good friends. To see my mother turn on her was a big shock, but it forced me to choose between them, and there was only one choice I could make.

I was determined that my wife and our future children would have a better standard of living than I'd had as a child and took a long hard look at myself and my future prospects. They were nil if I continued in a mill. The first step was to get out of my greasy overalls and into a suit. Within six months I had a job as a travelling salesman. A decrepit, three-geared Ford Anglia went with the job but the thrill – and the status – of having a job with a car was soon tarnished. I worked hard but my ambition and my pride were pulling in opposite directions. In the mid-1950s, down-market travelling salesmen were expected to bow and scrape to their customers, which came as something of a shock to me. Before long I was looking for a new job.

In the event I found two. For the next five years I worked in a switch factory by day and as a driving instructor at evenings and weekends. The extra money was very necessary. We'd scraped together enough money to furnish our first rented house, a one-up, one-down, in Ebernezer

Square in Keighley, but Mildred had to give up work when our first child, Graham, was born. Two others, Carol and Ian, came over the next ten years.

Working at two jobs left precious little time for recreation, but the call of the outdoors was still strong. I managed an occasional weekend climbing in the Lake District or renewing old potholing friendships around Ingleton, but diving remained in abeyance until a chance encounter one day in 1960. I met a man called Arthur, who came to Ingleton neither for the caving nor the climbing. His obsession was diving, a very exotic sport at the time. My excitement must have been obvious, for after a few beers he offered to lend me his gear.

I stood at the edge of the pool below the Devil's Bridge at Kirkby Lonsdale while Arthur helped me into the first diving suit I had ever seen. It was a two-piece rubberised dry suit, with wrist, neck and waist seals to stop water getting in. I started to strip off but much to my amazement, Arthur told me to keep my clothing on under the suit to keep myself warm. I tucked my trousers into my socks and sat down on the grassy bank while I pulled on the bottom half of the suit. It was like putting on a pair of trousers with attached feet. Putting on the top section was much harder, like getting into a tight sweater. A liberal sprinkling of french chalk helped prevent me tearing the neck and wrist seals as I forced my hands and head through them.

I had to seal the suit at the waist by rolling the rubber flanges on each half together in a tight roll. They were then held in place by a rubber cummerbund. Getting into it was the hardest part of all, like a woman struggling into a tight corset. It caused a good laugh amongst the people watching from the bridge.

I struggled into the fins and Arthur strapped on the weight-belt for me, taking a guess at the amount of lead I would need to stop me floating back to the surface. He helped me into the aqualung and I took a few nervous sucks from the mouthpiece to make sure there was plenty of air.

Still a little red in the face, I pulled on the face mask and backed slowly into the water – going forward wearing fins was not a good idea – urged on by the growing band of spectators. As the water rose around me I raised my arms above my head, allowing the air trapped in the suit to escape through the neck and wrist seals. The suit tightened around me in a vice-like grip.

I spat into the mask and rinsed it out to stop it from misting underwater, then sank slowly below the surface. The only sounds in the immediate, profound silence were my exhaled breaths bubbling slowly up towards the surface, with a ringing sound almost like music. I looked around, astonished at the clarity of the water. Weed streamed in the current, fluttering like flags in a breeze. I remained motionless for a few moments, then finned my way outwards and downwards, away from the bank, as the sound of my breathing deepened to a faint rumble, like faraway thunder.

I swam thirty feet down through the clear, cold water to the bottom of the river, where I came face to face with a shoal of salmon. The sunlight filtering through the water glittered from their scales like sparks. The experience was electrifying. I was weightless, free, totally happy again.

My euphoria vanished almost immediately, along with my supply of air. Arthur had omitted to mention that the bottle was three-quarters empty. He had also failed to let me know that rising rapidly from depth can have painful and even fatal effects. At a depth of just thirty-three feet, a diver is at twice the atmospheric pressure at the surface. If he fills his lungs with air and then begins to ascend without exhaling, the gas in his lungs will expand as a result of the drop in pressure.

Instead of coming up slowly, steadily releasing the air from my lungs to prevent embolisms, I came up like a Polaris missile. The frantic breath I had taken on the bottom had now swelled to twice the normal capacity of my lungs. That over-inflation could have forced air through the walls of the lungs. The resulting embolisms could have killed me. I could feel the air trying to force its way out of my mouth, but through ignorance and inexperience, I clenched my teeth and held it in, trying to ensure I had enough to reach the surface. Luckily I suffered no ill-effects. It was the first diving lesson I learned: always exhale continuously during an ascent.

Despite that minor problem, I was hooked. Climbing, like caving and cycling before it, was forgotten; from now on diving was to be my life.

I gradually taught myself the basics and I read voraciously, gleaning information from every book and article I could find. I also scoured second-hand shops for ex-War Department equipment. Anyone taking up the sport then had to use a real ragbag of gear. Wet suits were not available, but I bought an old navy dry suit for £5, which I wore over a pullover and jeans. The suit was badly worn and leaked uncomfortably, but it was all I could afford. I also bought my first aqualung and demand valve.

Primitive equipment and lack of knowledge made diving accidents and fatalities frequent in those days. Many top divers of the day succumbed to 'the narcs' – nitrogen narcosis – caused by an abundance of nitrogen absorbed into the bloodstream. Symptoms normally begin to appear at depths below 100 feet, but individual tolerances vary widely and some divers can work at twice that depth without ill-effects. The effect of the narcs is similar to that of being drunk or drugged. Reaction time slows, judgement is impaired and the diver become irrational and euphoric to the point where he is indifferent to his own safety. If divers fail to recognise the symptoms in time, they become ludicrously overconfident, even offering their mouthpieces to passing fish. Many good men, unaware of the dangers, paid with their lives.

I learned what I could from diving manuals and soon joined forces with four or five other divers to form the Keighley branch of the British Sub-Aqua Club (B.S.A.C.). We used the Keighley swimming baths for training and began to buy our own equipment, including a compressor, saving a 36-mile round trip to refill our air bottles in Leeds.

On weekends and light summer nights, we explored virtually every stretch of water in the North – lakes, rivers, reservoirs, mill dams and flooded quarries. In the process we cracked many myths about bottomless pools. We never knew what to expect, for we were usually the first people to explore them, but invariably the dive ended in disappointment a few feet down. All we ever found were old prams.

A dive at the Strid, a place where the River Wharfe is forced into a narrow gorge, was rather more successful. In Victorian times men used to prove their virility by jumping it at its narrowest point. It was not a great leap, perhaps eight feet, but it took a great deal of courage, for it's said that no one fell into the Strid and lived to tell the tale. They were dragged under by the current and drowned. We entered the Strid at the lower end. The depth was about fifteen feet, the bottom bare rock and visibility good. Looking up, I could see the faces of the spectators peering down at us. One of the first things I noticed was that the rocky sides were all undercut and smoothed by the action of the water over thousands of years. Anyone who tried to hold on to the sides would quickly lose their grip and be pulled down and under. The current was so powerful that it was impossible to swim against it. The only way forward was to climb along the bottom like an underwater mountaineer, holding on to any crack, fault or large boulder I could find.

In places the two opposing walls came very close together and the bottom sloped upwards, compressing the already powerful flow into a torrent as fierce as the jet of a fire-hose. To make progress I had to drag myself through the full force of the river. It was like trying to climb a waterfall. The force of the current almost tore the mask from my face and I was moving forward blind because of the turbulence. Using whatever handholds I could find, I managed to battle my way through and emerged, exhausted, at the point where the river enters the gorge.

Exploring the Strid carried just enough danger to make it exciting, but the risks paled besides those involved in cave-diving. My first experience was in an easy cave at the top end of Wharfedale. The entrance was a simple submerged walk–in, leading into a very inky blackness. We lit our underwater torches and found ourselves in a typical cave passageway. It was completely full of water, with no air-spaces at all. If anything had gone wrong with our breathing equipment we could have had serious problems.

The water was so clear that it felt as if we should have been walking, not swimming, up the passage, but when we turned to go back, we found that the action of our fins on the way up had disturbed all the silt on the cave floor. From perfect visibility we now found ourselves swimming through the underwater equivalent of a very thick London fog. Luckily the passageway was straight and we swam slowly out of the cave.

We'd climbed out of the water and stripped off our air bottles before we realised there were only two of us instead of three. Our friend was lost somewhere in the cave. Terrified that he was already dead, we pulled our diving gear back on. There was no time to check our equipment. We just had to hope there was still enough air in our bottles to make the search.

By now the water had cleared considerably and as we inched our way back along the passage we found our missing companion's weight-belt lying on the cave floor. I looked up. There, stuck to the ceiling above my head, was our missing friend, as helpless as an upended tortoise. All divers need added weight to compensate for their natural buoyancy. Without it you simply float back to the surface. He had accidentally dislodged his weight belt and without it he was plastered to the roof of the cave, unable to move.

Despite that fright, we all made another cave-dive the following weekend, in Kingsdale near Ingleton. We had heard on the grapevine that Bob Leaky from Settle had found a new underwater system called Keld Head. Much later it was to feature in a television documentary, *The Underground Eiger*. Bob was a brave lad and had done some long, penetrating swims into the cave, leaving fixed guide-wires to help him both in and out.

It was a very different proposition from the last cave. The entrance was a fissure under a small cliff, in one corner of a pool. I was the first to be ready and decided to have a quick look while waiting for the others. Before entering, I took a compass bearing on the general direction we'd been told the cave ran. I then lowered myself head first into the entrance, gasping at the shock of the icy water. Once inside, I found there was no way to turn around; I had to get into the first chamber before I could do that. As I peered back towards the entrance, I could see nothing but a dim greenish glow. I found the guide-wires and pointed my torch along them. They disappeared into the gloom in a very short distance. It was not a place for anyone suffering from claustrophobia. I knew that if I lost contact with the wires, the entrance would be impossible to find in the total darkness.

I moved hand over hand along the wire for perhaps twenty-five yards. Then it happened. In the act of turning around to go back I somehow managed to get the guide-wires caught in the diving set on my back. If panic did not set in, it came bloody near. I forced myself to take a few deep breaths, then began trying to clear the wire. By now I'd floated into an upside-down position with my fins pointing towards the unseen roof of the cave, but I still hung on to that wire for dear life, thinking, if I break it, I'll never find the entrance.

Very carefully I freed the wire, and at last held it safely in my hands again. There was now only one small problem. Had I already made the turn? Was the way out to the left or the right? The water around me was ice cold, but there was sweat rolling down my face.

It was a time for thought not panic, a lesson I'd learned during my climbing days. I checked my compass but as sometimes happens, the direction it showed felt wrong. I decided to obey it, but as a precaution I marked the wire with my knife. If I failed to find the entrance, I could retrace my steps to that point and try in the other direction. I began moving along the wire hand over hand, counting the number of hand-pulls. If I reached fifty without finding the entrance I'd know I was going the wrong way.

Inching along the wire in the blackness, I kept fighting down the fear rising in me, concentrating all my attention on the count. Forty-one . . . forty-two . . . forty-three. Nothing. Forty-four . . . forty-five . . . forty-six. Still nothing. I was about to give up and retrace my steps when my head banged against the rock. I felt the wires disappear upwards into a narrow cleft in the rock. As I looked up, I saw the dim greenish glow that indicated the way out.

Never have I been more glad to break surface. From start to finish the whole incident took no more than five minutes, but it felt like hours. It was more than enough to convince me of one thing. I hauled myself out on to the bank and spat out my mouthpiece. 'That's it,' I told my mates. 'You can stick cave-diving.' The remaining members of the team were less easily deterred, but their decision to carry on cave-diving had terrible consequences. Not long afterwards, one of them lost his life in another cave.

That event was still fresh in our minds when we began the search for the lost boy in the River Aire in Keighley, but finding the dead body had an even greater impact on me. Like most young people, if I'd thought of death at all it was as something that happened to other people. I was young and strong, as good as immortal. Being brought face to face with the reality that death could strike anyone, at any time, was a cold, hard shock. As I sat on the riverbank that grey afternoon, I resolved that from then on, I'd live my own life to the limit. When death came for me, I wanted no regrets about what might have been, no unfulfilled dreams.

I never forgot that young boy's death and whenever I think of the river, even now, it's not the happy days of my childhood but that pale, frail body that comes back to me.

The double tragedy had done nothing to dampen my enthusiasm for diving itself but it did increase my dislike of murky rivers and dull, cold lakes – a far cry from the world of Jacques Cousteau. I decided that the sea-bed was the only place for serious divers to be.

Every weekend I and four other divers began going to the coast, but whichever way we went, there were problems. The west coast had good sea conditions but its sandy beaches made for dull diving. The east coast had fine, rocky diving areas, but rough seas often made it dangerous or impossible. None the less we travelled hopefully eastwards most weekends and worked like mules to haul our equipment down the cliffs at North Landing, Flamborough Head. Often, just as we were finally ready for action, a gale would spring up and ruin everything, but even when the weather was kinder we took some terrible risks. It was only good luck that none of us were swept away to our deaths. Several divers have since perished off that coast because they lacked the protection of a boat.

The obvious danger scared us sufficiently to work hard to raise the cash to buy a club dinghy, but we also became desperate for a more reliable diving site. One weekend, two of us, Eric Capstick and I, went up to Scotland. There, on the Mull of Galloway, we found a place which offered excellent diving in all conditions, with always a lee shore protected from wild weather.

On our first dive there, in Loch Ryan, we saw a mast sticking out of the water at low tide and I dived down to my first wreck. It was an eerie but overwhelmingly exciting moment, as if I had opened a time capsule. I felt that I was the first person to lay eyes on that ship since it had sunk decades before.

We promptly organised a Keighley Sub-Aqua Club holiday on the Mull of Galloway that summer. About twenty of us took our families and towed caravans to a local site and all the talk among us was of wrecks. When we heard of one in Portencorkrie Bay, near our campsite, we hurried to investigate.

The SS *Pollux II* had been wrecked on Boxing Day 1942. It was on its way to Londonderry with 375 tons of US naval stores when a fire broke out off the Mull of Galloway. The crew abandoned ship and were rescued, but the *Pollux* drifted into Portencorkrie Bay and ran aground. The fire was still burning with such intensity that the hull plates buckled and red hot rivets were fired into the air like rifle bullets, sending the onlookers scurrying for cover. As huge gaps opened in the ship's side, the sea poured in and extinguished the fires, sending clouds of steam belching hundreds of yards into the air.

The lighter cargo began to wash out through the holes in the hull and the locals waded into the surf to rescue cans of beer and cartons of Lucky Strike cigarettes. The local coastguard, Mr McClymont, was issued with ammunition for his rifle in an attempt to deter the looters, but by his own later admission, his duties as a coastguard came a distant second to the need to get a share of the cargo for himself. Some of it was turned over to the authorities but not before every local had had his share. Mr McClymont alone claimed to have salted away over 10,000 cigarettes, which were hidden in the outbuildings of his farm. He smoked them throughout the rest of the war, complaining with appalling ingratitude that the American tobacco gave him 'terrible sore throats'.

There had been no shortage of takers for the beer and cigarettes, but the locals showed little interest in salvaging the *Pollux*'s main cargo of non-ferrous metal fittings. They went to the bottom with the blackened, twisted hulk of the ship, lying on the sea-bed in up to fifty feet of water.

Most of my diving experience until then had been in the relatively shallow waters of lakes and rivers. I still had much to learn about diving in deeper waters – both its physical effects on the body and the way that perceptions were altered by the effects of water on light and sound. Sound-waves travel better through a relatively dense medium like water; the speed of sound through water – around 3,240 miles per hour – is four times as fast as it is through air.

Ships have long used sound-waves – sonar – to detect submarines, and passive receivers were used before the First World War. Set in the hulls of ships they could pick up the sound of underwater warning bells beneath lighthouses from as far as fifteen miles out at sea. Unlike the lights, the sound of the bells was detectable whatever the weather conditions.

Since sound transfers poorly from air to water and vice versa, however, it's impossible for divers to communicate with each other underwater without the use of radio. The only exception is when two divers wearing metal helmets physically put their heads together. They can then carry on a conversation.

On dry land we detect the direction a sound is coming from because it's picked up by one ear before the other. Sound travels so fast underwater, however, that it appears to reach both ears simultaneously. Without visual confirmation of the source of a sound, a diver may literally not know which way to turn to avoid an oncoming danger. He will hear the noise of a ship's propeller a considerable distance away, but in his confusion, he may swim into its path rather than away from it.

The speed and clarity of sound transmission may also put divers at risk in other ways. The noise of operations such as drilling and blasting, which is contained within acceptable safety limits on dry land, may be so loud underwater that it causes ear damage in divers. Light is also affected by its passage through water; the effects on light-waves of refraction, absorption, diffusion and turbidity all distort what we see underwater.

Like sound, light travels at different speeds in air and water, moving about thirty per cent faster through air. When light passes through the water surface in either direction, it speeds up or slows down, and is refracted, the familiar phenomenon which makes us misjudge the position of a fish or a rock underwater and makes a stick appear to bend at an angle as it passes through the surface.

A diver's glass face mask heightens the effect; light is refracted by the water surface, then by the glass and again by the air inside the mask. Underwater objects appear to be larger – and therefore closer – by the same thirty per cent ratio. A gold bar apparently within reach is actually a few inches beyond your grasp, a shark is smaller and less threatening than it appears.

Light also diffuses in water. The diffusion reduces the available light but it also spreads it more evenly and cuts glare and deep shadow so that vision may even be enhanced. In general, however, light intensity decreases progressively with depth.

If the water is pure and clear, visibility may extend down to beyond 300 feet. If it is turbid – affected by particles of silt, algae, sewage or other pollution – the onset of underwater darkness comes much sooner. Even where light is still present, high turbidity might leave a diver swimming blind, and in urban rivers and harbours, visibility is often nil immediately below the surface.

Colour is also affected as light travels through water. The wavelengths of the visible spectrum of light are absorbed in turn, beginning with the lower-wavelength, red end of the spectrum, which disappears even in quite shallow water. At greater depth yellow is also lost. Red objects appear black and most others take on a blue tinge. Oxidised copper, for example, which is green at the surface, appears purple underwater.

Around the *Pollux*, the sea-bed was littered with brass bars, nuts, valves and fittings. We were completely ignorant of the laws of salvage and unaware that even a wreck on the bottom of the sea has an owner. All we saw was a ship that had supposedly been salvaged, surrounded by non-ferrous metal. As far as we were concerned, it was there for the taking – and there was plenty to take. We set to with a will. It brought back memories of my childhood fantasies to me, but this was the real thing, almost as good as diving on a galleon full of pieces of eight. At the end of the fortnight, we'd beached a huge pile of metal, which we stashed away beneath our caravans. When we took it down to the local scrap merchant, we discovered that we had a small fortune – £150 a man, a lot of money in those days!

As we drove home, my mind was working overtime. We had made £150 each and had taken only a fraction of the metal on and around the *Pollux*. How many more similar wrecks were lying around the coast of Britain? I resolved to find out. With the help of patient librarians in the public libraries in Bradford, Keighley and further afield, I read every book and article about shipwrecks I could get my hands on. I soon found out that there were not just hundreds but thousands of them at depths from a few feet to a few thousand feet below the surface. There were tales of the treasure ships and galleons I had read about as a kid, but there were countless modern wrecks too, with cargoes of base metals like tin, brass and copper, and of precious metals like platinum, silver and gold.

In a book of memoirs written by a Russian Admiral, I read about a cargo of ten tons of gold sunk with the warship HMS *Edinburgh* during the Second World War. Although I'd devoured books on shipwrecks as a boy, I'd never heard of the *Edinburgh* before and stared at the page for a few minutes, trying to imagine what ten tons of gold would look like. As I read further, I realised that the *Edinburgh* was the stuff of pipe-dreams. It lay on the bottom of the Barents Sea, in very deep water, far beyond the depth any free diver had then reached. One day it might be possible to reach the wreck, but that day was a long way off.

If the *Edinburgh* was an impossible dream, however, there were plenty of other, less glamorous wrecks like the *Pollux*, lying in shallow water around the British coast, just waiting to be salvaged.

Similar thoughts had been occupying the minds of two of the other weekend divers, Geoff Snow and Frank Guest. Over a couple of pints one night we decided that if we returned to Scotland each weekend we could not only enjoy our sport with all expenses paid but also show a healthy profit.

We were an unlikely partnership. We came from the same mean streets of Keighley, but otherwise had virtually nothing in common. Where I was brash and outwardly very self-confident, Snowy was quiet and unassuming. He was a self-taught motor mechanic and fanatically hard-working. The only thing he loved more than making money was not spending it, but like the rest of us, he'd had a very hard upbringing. Money was always scarce and he'd learned to value ever penny he ever made. His preferred tailor at the time was a war-surplus shop in Haworth. 'Good hard-wearing gear . . . and cheap,' as he used to tell me.

Frank had worked for a scrap dealer before becoming a coal merchant, but unlike Snowy, he was a very snappy dresser when not in his working clothes. Friday night was always a special time for him. By mid-afternoon he was washed, shaved and changed into a smart suit and tie, ready to collect the money from his coal round. After collecting his cash, he'd take up station in one of the local pubs, standing back from the bar with a cigar in one hand and a beer in the other. He always drank halves, his elbow raised to the horizontal as if he was taking the salute at a regimental march-past instead of getting another half of Timothy Taylor's down his neck. He was always quick to try to get his wallet out when it was his turn to buy a round; he liked to impress people with the fact that it was so bulging with cash he could barely get it out of his pocket.

Most weekends from then on found us hammering along the road to the Mull of Galloway. It was a long haul. At the start of the sixties there were no motorways leading to Scotland and cars were not as fast as they are today – particularly the old bangers that were all we could afford. The 200-mile trip from Keighley to Stranraer could take eight to ten hours. After the long, slow haul over Shap Fell behind the convoys of lorries, there was the crawl along the narrow bridges and single-file main street of Penrith. Carlisle was just as bad and we still had the long run out to Stranraer. We got to know every bump in that road by the time we finished.

We left home early on Saturday morning, arrived at the site in the afternoon and got straight into the water. On Sunday we were up at dawn and worked all day, then had to load our scrap and make the long drive back, arriving home exhausted, well after midnight. Another handful of hours sleep later, it was back to the day-job in Keighley. It put an intolerable strain on ourselves and our families, and it soon became obvious that something would have to give. It took me all of two seconds to make my decision.

At a time when the average wage in Keighley was between £5 and £10 a week, the rich pickings to be had pulling scrap from the sea-bed were enough to convince me to try it full time. I persuaded Snowy to join me. We reckoned we could earn a minimum of £20 a week. We would be £1,000-a-year men, the sort of money that only bosses made. The die was cast. We quit our jobs and became full-time divers – underwater salvage men.

I knew very little about Snowy and he wasn't the sort of person to open his heart to anyone. I'd first met him when he applied to become a member of the Sub-Aqua Club. He was just a young lad then and I didn't take any special notice of him at the time, other than to note that he took to diving like a duck to water. It was only when the club did our first couple of dives on the *Pollux* that I noticed what a very hard worker he was – a real grafter. That was the reason I'd asked him to join me. Working with him over the years I slowly learned a bit about his past and I grew to have a great deal of time for him.

He was a very valuable member of the team, looking after the compressor, keeping the cars running and doing all the 101 jobs we needed to keep the show on the road in those days. He could strip down a car engine – or anything else for that matter – put it back together again and have it working like new in no time. He was almost a diesel mystic; he could sometimes tell you what was wrong with an engine just by sniffing the oil.

He had the ability to fix anything mechanical, but paperwork or research was beyond his capabilities. He just wasn't interested. He once took great umbrage at a story in the *Sunday People* which described us as office pals 'working at our desks' as we planned another salvage dive, because he didn't want to be known as a person who worked behind a desk. He took great pride in being an outside worker, a grafter, a man who got dirt on his hands.

At first the pair of us didn't realise how lucky we'd been to find a wreck loaded with a cargo of non-ferrous metal. The *Pollux* had also had a part-cargo of ship's bells, but they were long gone. I'll never understand why those divers only took the bells. There were gullies full of non-ferrous nuts and bolts, bronze ingots, brass bars and valves that weighed fifty or sixty pounds. We used crowbars to get it all free. When we started, all we had to do was sit on the bottom filling a bag or a basket with nuts and bolts and then try to swim across the bottom to the shore, dragging half a hundred-weight of scrap.

A diver adjusts his buoyancy in the water by the use of lead weights. The amount is an individual thing. One person may need over twenty pounds of lead, another as little as two.

You adjust your buoyancy by removing or adding weight until breathing in causes you to rise from the bottom and exhaling makes you sink slowly back. Attempting to pick up a heavy piece of scrap in this weightless state is almost impossible. All you can do is drag it across the bottom.

Our first recovery vessel was a humble one – an old inner tube from a tractor tyre, anchored to the sea-bed by a rope and fitted with a basket into which we tossed the scrap metal we scavenged. When I had an armful of the scrap fittings that littered the bottom, I struggled across to the rope, hauled myself up with my free hand and tipped the scrap into the basket. The bigger bits, like the bronze valves, were two-men jobs. We dragged them across the sea-bed, then I held on to the rope with one hand and the valve with the other, while my mate helped to push me up the line, both of us finning like mad. When we got to the surface, there was a final exhausting struggle to get the valve up and over the inner tube and into the basket.

One of the drawbacks of the system soon became apparent. If someone dropped just one piece of scrap too many into the basket, it sank. As I struggled up the line, I sometimes found the basket coming down to meet me. On good days it would simply sink to the bottom and then rise slowly back to the surface after we'd lifted out the excess pieces of scrap. On bad days the basket would snag a rock on the sea-bed, tip over, spill its load and then shoot up to the surface like a cork, leaving us to begin the whole back-breaking process all over again. Landing the basket on the rocky shore was also a problem. The sea always appeared to get up as we were trying to do so and many times the surf threw us on our backs and scattered our precious scrap among the rocks.

Sometimes we found very heavy brass bars and bronze ingots on the sea-bed weighing a hundredweight or more. There was no way that we could get them up to the basket, no matter how hard we finned. Instead two of us dragged them along the bottom all the way to the shore. On one surreal occasion we took off our fins and walked across the seabed with a long brass bar on our shoulders, like two men carrying a plank on dry land.

Even with the rich cargo from the *Pollux*, our talk of easy money was quickly silenced. There was no certainty of a regular weekly wage, let alone the quick fortune that we had been secretly hoping for, and the work was cruel. Even though the metal was there all right, getting it out fast enough with just two pairs of hands – three when Frank Guest joined us as a third partner, though he wisely kept his coal round to fall back on – was back-breaking work.

We started at first light and spent so much time in the water that we had to fill our air bottles sometimes three or four times a day. We dragged ourselves out of the sea at the end of the day numb with cold and exhaustion, but still had to find the energy to load all the scrap into our Bergens (rucksacks) and carry it over the rocks and up the cliff to the car.

From time to time, Customs and Excise officers would come to the site, have a look at what we were bringing up from the *Pollux* and then leave without comment. Only afterwards did we learn that we should have bought the wreck from the legal owners. Just because a ship sinks, it doesn't mean that anyone can come along and help himself. Eventually we made a deal with the owner of our caravan site and he bought the wreck.

We existed on next to nothing as we gradually stripped the wreck of its cargo, living in my caravan and only returning to our families at weekends. We built a trailer and often towed the scrap back to Keighley for the weigh-in, to get a better price, but we soon learned from bitter experience that there were tricks of the trade at weigh-in time. Until we grew wiser, we were cheated by having bronze weighed in as brass and even robbed ourselves on one occasion by asking, 'How much for this piece of brass?' In fact the brass was gunmetal, commanding a much higher price.

Scrap dealers used another trick when weighing in copper piping with brass flanges on the ends of the pipes. We soon realised that we got considerably less for the pipes, which were classified as contaminated copper because of the brass flanges. From then on we cut off the flange ourselves with a hammer and chisel, and got the right price for both the copper and the brass.

In brass-type metals, copper is the base metal and the more coppery the metal looks, the higher the value should be. The copper content in gunmetal is obvious from its colour. Manganese bronze, which most propellers are made from, is a very pale yellow and the cheapest of these metals because of its high steel content. Another way to get an indication of the value and content of the metal was to scrape it with a file. If a magnet attracted a lot of steel filings, I knew it was manganese bronze.

Not all the fiddles were perpetrated by the scrap dealers. During our very early days the sea taught us a good lesson. Many a length of bent copper piping was half-full of sand and weighed in very nicely. Once we caught on to this, we sometimes helped nature to do its job.

When we'd weighed in, we'd drive to a quiet spot for the share-out. First would come the expenses, recorded on grubby bits of paper. What was left was then shared out equally. After that we went home to pass on some of the money to our wives, had a drink to celebrate and then immediately began planning the next trip.

Our earnings were wildly variable. Sometimes we came home with our pockets stuffed with fivers, but there were plenty of other times when we were beaten by the weather and came back cold and tired with nothing at all to show for the trip. It put a lot of extra strain on Mildred and my popularity with her was at an all-time low, particularly when money became so tight that she had to take a job as a machinist in a factory. In the early days she was as much the breadwinner as I was; many times her earnings were the only money we had. At times she begged me to give it all up and get a 'proper job', and we had many fierce arguments, but deep down, she wanted to help me succeed. When times were hard, we tightened our belts and carried on.

I was determined not to quit. Despite the hardships, I knew that I would never return to wage slavery in Keighley. My destiny was in my own hands; I was a free man, not just another sallow face on the smoke-filled top deck of the 7.20 Workers' Special to Silsden.

We certainly succeeded in making a better living than was available to us in the textile mills, but it was hard and very cold work. Despite the name, the dry suits of this era were never dry; the million and one sharp edges on a wreck soon turned them into very wet and cold suits. Even if you managed to avoid ripping them, the seals always leaked. I usually wore a sweater and a set of long johns under my dry suit, but in winter another layer was essential. A string vest was not a good idea, as the pressure of the water on a deepish dive tattooed the outline of the vest on to the skin.

My first suit was a one-piece, a second- or maybe tenth-hand, neck-entry, ex-Royal Navy suit, and an absolute pig to get into. There was an air escape valve in the hood which made venting the suit relatively easy and it also had another highly useful valve, enabling the wearer to have a run-off (pee) without getting out of the suit. It came in handy at times, but you always had to remember to tighten down the valve after use. Failure to do so could lead to a particularly terrifying peril of the deep as the ice cold water flooded in.

Neoprene wet suits made dry suits redundant except for work in dirty or contaminated water. They were a major advance, bringing a previously unknown freedom of movement into diving, though they were still very difficult to get into. In the first suits we had the open-cell neoprene gripped the body and refused to slide. Liberal use of french chalk helped, though we ended up looking like ghosts. We tried washing-up liquid instead, which worked fine, but we had more bubbles floating around than a washing machine and we were heartily glad when suits of nylon-backed neoprene finally became available.

When you entered the water, a thin film of water leaked into the suit. Body heat warmed it and the neoprene insulated you from the outside water temperature. It was just like a warm bath – until working on a wreck took its toll. Seams started to split, knees and elbows wore thin and holes appeared. As you moved about on the bottom, the flexing of your muscles pumped cold water continuously into the suits through every nick and hole. In those conditions, you soon started to feel the cold.

At the start of a new day it was not too bad, but as the dive progressed, the cold started to penetrate the body. Our fingers became numb and useless and our hands could only be used like dishpan lids. When we ran out of air, it was back to the surface, scrambling over the rocks and up the steep cliff to get our diving bottles on the compressor. While they were filling, we'd put Bergens on our backs and go back down to begin hauling our scrap up the same murderous climb to the top of the cliff. In no time at all we were back in the water again.

By the time I'd finished my third, or even fourth dive of the day, I was cold to the bone. My whole body temperature had dropped and it took many hours to regain its normal temperature. The pleasure had gone from diving, now it was strictly work. Money was the driving factor and time spent in the water was the only way to earn it.

Chapter Three

The Black Pig

When everything loose had been recovered from the *Pollux*, we turned our attention to what was left of the ship itself. We wanted the big pieces of non-ferrous metal – condensers, propellers, pumps, bearings and engine-room fittings – and even some cargo buried deep in the holds. For those jobs we needed something more powerful than muscles and crowbars.

Explosives were far less carefully controlled in the days before the IRA bombing campaigns and it was relatively easy to obtain a licence. An instant-usage licence allowed you a stated amount of explosive for a named job, but we needed a continuous licence and for that we had to have a secure magazine. We bought three tons of plaster gelatine explosives, submarine detonators and many rolls of primer cord, and stored it in a magazine borrowed from the explosives company.

Three tons of explosives would have comfortably re-landscaped a large part of the west coast of Scotland and since we were complete novices with them, we came close to doing exactly that. We needed some advice but though several people could tell us how to use explosives on land, few knew anything about their use underwater.

As a former Commando, I'd assured the police that I'd

been schooled by experts, but in truth, the only experience I'd had was when burning lumps of plastic explosive to heat our mess tins for a brew. It was no preparation for underwater demolition and there was no instruction book to help us. We learned by trial and error and were very lucky not to blast ourselves into oblivion in the process. As we eventually discovered, the trick is to know how much to use and where to place it. Too much and a big bronze pump was scattered across the bottom like a packet of crisps; too little and all we did was polish the metal until it gleamed.

Our first effort with explosives was quite a local event. The word had got out that the mad divers were about to blow themselves up, and a large and appreciative audience turned up to watch from a safe distance. The company which had supplied our explosives sent one of its employees, Brian Greenland, to teach us how to handle them. After that we were on our own. Brian showed us all the basic moves of how to link the charges with primer cord, which looks like plastic clothes line but is filled with explosive, and fires a whole string of charges from one detonator. He taught us to thread the primer cord through the five-pound sticks of explosive with a brass rod to avoid the risk of sparks. He also told us to use gloves when handling explosives – not to evade police forensic squads, but because any trace on your hands is a sure-fire guarantee of a blinding headache.

To begin with we handled the charges as if they were boxes of eggs; you are just a little nervous at first. We swam out to the site with the charges while Brian paid out the primer cord behind us. We placed them around the engine block and then returned to shore. Brian helped us fix the detonator to the primer cord and connected the electric firing cable to ensure we did not get a short. We paid out the cable back to a suitable spot and he demonstrated how to do a final check with a circuit tester. Next came the fixing of the electric cable to the single knock box – a small generator. One good twist of the handle sent an electric current to fire the detonator, the primer cord and the charges.

Playing the crowd a little, Brian asked if everyone was ready, then fired the charge. There was a dull bang and a water spout erupted. It was all over in a splash. As the water settled down, I could smell the oily, seaweed stink of the explosives. It was soon to be as familiar as the salt tang in the sea air. So ended our first and only lesson in the use of explosives. We were now experts, our licence attested to that.

After the water cleared, we dived down to the wreck and found the engine block split apart, with lots of bronze bearings showing. A large spanner was also lying on the bottom, shining like new. It must have been very close to the explosion and received a thorough polishing in the blast. It fitted all the main bearing nuts, so we put it to good use.

With practice we became very proficient with explosives and could remove a ship's propeller from the shaft without leaving an awkward piece stuck inside the boss. There was no room for overconfidence however. We all knew the tale of an Italian salvage company clearing First World War wrecks from the approaches to the harbour of St Nazaire. One of them had been carrying ammunition. The Italians laid a series of charges over a number of days, trying to detonate the cargo. Each time they pulled off a distance of two miles before firing the charge. There was never any secondary detonation and eventually they decided that the ammunition was inert.

They began using charges to cut the wreck to pieces, gradually reducing the distance they withdrew. Two months later, they laid a final charge right under the stern. By now they were only pulling off a couple of hundred yards. When they fired the charge, the ship's cargo went up with it. A waterspout erupted several hundred feet into the air. The salvage ship toppled into the vortex and was swamped. It went to the bottom, killing eleven of the eighteen-man crew. We had no wish to emulate them, but the need for caution was always tempered by the harsh realities. As far as earning money was concerned, time spent on safety was time wasted.

We had a few scares but our local reputation as explosives experts remained undented. I was approached by a farmer one day who wanted me to remove a rock which he was convinced was the tip of an underground mountain. Every spring he forgot the position of the rock and wrecked his plough, and every autumn he broke his harvester. I accepted the challenge, despite only having worked with explosives underwater, never on the surface. The difference is crucial; you tend to use far larger amounts underwater.

When I arrived on site, the farmer was there with some of his friends to watch the free show as the expert went to work. My idea was to dig a trench around the rock to a depth of a couple of feet, then place a necklace of small charges around it. It would be like taking the top off a boiled egg.

In fact the rock was only a couple of feet deep anyway, but rather than disappoint my audience, who by now had taken up a secure position behind a wall 100 yards away, I placed the charges, fixed the detonator and ran out the wire back to them. Now for the moment of truth. I fired the charge and there was a deafening bang. The rock came out of the ground like a guided missile and sailed right over the wall and on to the beach. I became an instant star with the farmer. Not only had I removed the rock, I'd even blown it out of his field in the right direction.

Explosives enabled us to break up some of the heavier scrap metal – propeller blades, condensers and heavy pumps –

lying on the sea-bed, but we still had to find a means of getting them ashore. We had outgrown the tractor tube and one incident finally convinced us of the need to get a boat. In wild weather we allowed our rubber dinghy to get caught in a terrifying tidal race during a big spring tide and were bounced helplessly around a headland at a rate of knots. We realised that our only option was to go over the side and swim for the shore, dragging the dinghy behind us.

We could easily have been swept away, but luckily the sea hurled us up on to a very steep and rocky headland, a considerable distance from our starting point. We had a long, hard and dangerous journey back to base, carrying all our gear – and our precious scrap metal – over treacherous rocks and up steep cliffs, as rain lashed us and the wind shrieked around us.

We decided then and there to go and buy ourselves a boat. Armed with some highly optimistic projections of our future income, I went to see my bank manager in Keighley and emerged triumphant with the promise of a loan. After scouring the docks from Whitby to Girvan, we ended up at the Jubilee Pier in Fleetwood, a kind of elephant's graveyard where old trawlers go to die. There was nowhere else to go after the Jubilee Pier, except straight to the bottom of the ocean. Even the jetty the boats were tied to was rotten.

We spotted a small Scottish trawler, about thirty-five feet long, fitted with a winch, a radio and a three-cylinder Russell–Newbury diesel engine, started by a couple of old car batteries. The boat was covered in oil and obviously on its last legs, for it appeared to take on water with the rising tide and then drain off again at low water, as it came to rest on the bottom.

Despite its many flaws, we reckoned that it would meet our needs; all it had to do was stay afloat and lift our scrap. We bought it for £1,200. It had *The Braw Lad* painted on the side facing the pier, but when we looked on the other side, it was called *The Braw Lass*. Both sides were soon reunited in a new name: *The Black Pig*, partly in honour of the pirate ship in Captain Pugwash and partly because it was bulging in the middle and smothered in filthy black oil. We began trying to scrub off some of the oil, but it was a hopeless task, though it did give us something to do while storm-bound in port for a week, along with the entire Fleetwood fishing fleet.

We were desperate to get back up to Galloway and start earning some money to pay off the debt, and when the weather began to ease we prepared to launch the *Black Pig* on her maiden voyage under new management. There were just a few minor problems to face, not least that none of us had ever sailed a boat before. We managed to find out how to get a radio fix by chatting to the local fishermen in the pubs and after we had bought some charts, we began to feel like real navigators, although we still hoped that when we first sailed her we would be able to see where we were going.

While having a meal in the Seaman's Mission that night, we heard the locals planning to sail before dawn the next morning for a fishing ground off the north coast of the Isle of Man. Since this was only twenty miles from the Mull of Galloway, we decided to follow them to the Isle of Man and then cut across to the Scottish coast. What could be easier?

We were at the docks before dawn the next morning to make sure we didn't miss the departing fishing fleet. Our first surprise was waiting for us. Someone had stolen all the bulbs from the navigation lights and the wheelhouse during the night. Next Frank refused to sail with us. If we'd been on the high seas I could have hanged him for mutiny. He preferred to drive up to Galloway, but unfortunately without the trailer which was left sitting on the dockside. There was a thirty-foot tide that night and the remaining three of us had to lower the trailer laboriously the thirty feet to the deck.

By the time we'd managed that, the trawler fleet was already sailing down the channel. We set off in hot pursuit. Since I'd been in the Marines, I was elected skipper, with Snowy as mechanic and Big John, who had just joined us as a potential investor, as deck hand and cook. In fact, my only knowledge of the sea was that it was wet and frequently stormy and while the fishing fleet steamed up the right-hand side of the channel, I steered a course up the left, trying to make it appear that we weren't following them.

It was like driving the wrong way down a motorway. I was about to execute a smart turn to port at the entrance to the estuary when I found myself face to face with a huge Icelandic trawler, bearing down on us, horns blaring. Somehow we avoided each other and, chastened, I carried on in pursuit of the fleet.

Out on the open sea, visibility was about five miles and the wind was blowing at Force 4, a light breeze to real seamen, but gale-force to us. We crossed Morecambe Bay without further alarms, but as the fleet turned to the west, some of the fishing boats started to lower their trawls and began to fish, miles short of the Isle of Man. As we pondered this, the engine began to splutter, firing first on two cylinders and then only one, spewing out oil at the same time. We now realised why everything was covered in it.

We didn't dare stop the engine in case it never started again – one cylinder was better than none at all – but our progress was so painfully slow that we were even being overtaken by trawlers with their nets down. We were reduced to throwing bits of wood over the side to see if we were making any headway at all. The fishing fleet slowly disappeared over the horizon, leaving us totally alone in a strange and terrifying world. There was no land in sight, no other boat, just the *Black Pig*, labouring in the grey ocean swell. I had to rely entirely on a radio navigation signal to get us across to the Isle of Man. I set a course and hoped for the best.

Nine hours later, we could see the lighthouse at Maughold Head, south of Ramsey, but it was six more before we managed to limp into harbour and tie up at the pier. Never before or since have I been so relieved to feel dry land under my feet. We had been taking it in turns to pump the bilges all the way across. Snowy pumped them one last time, covering the pretty little harbour in an oil slick. Then we leapt off the boat, black from head to foot, and hurried to the first pub we could find to wash away the traumas of the day.

We were still sitting there an hour later when an irate harbourmaster put his head around the door and barked, 'Which bastard filled my harbour with oil and left that heap of shit dangling from the pier?' We'd forgotten about the falling tide and returned to find the *Black Pig* hanging at a crazy angle from the pier. It was a perfect end to a perfect day.

We decided it would be wise to leave Ramsey as soon as possible. The next morning dawned fair, with visibility so good that we could see Scotland from the quay. Astonishingly the engine roared into life, firing on all three cylinders, but before we set out we agreed among ourselves that if any of them so much as missed a beat, we would turn back.

We didn't get the chance. We were a few miles out when the engine suddenly stopped dead. We dropped anchor and Snowy, who after all was a mechanic by trade, set to work on the engine. He eventually discovered that the filter pads were clogged, starving the engine of fuel. With two removed, the engine started first time and ran like a dream. Some hours later we finally reached Scotland, after a further interruption to our journey caused by the top-speed arrival of a coastguard cutter. The coastguard had been alerted by Frank Guest, waiting on dry land, who had given us all up for lost, drowned at sea.

It was an entirely reasonable belief. We'd only managed to reach Scotland safely thanks to a generous helping of beginner's luck. A crew-load of incompetent sailors and navigators should never have been out on the high seas at all, least of all in a rusty, leaking tub like the *Black Pig*.

In retrospect the risks we took were insane but we were divers after all, and divers regard risk as an inevitable part of daily life. Facing continual danger together should have forged us into a loyal band of brothers – a united team – but it didn't work that way. There was little concern shown for the underwater welfare of the next man. If you got into trouble down there it was generally regarded as your own stupid fault. You had to look after yourself; we were all working as individuals and there was no love lost between us.

In between the arguments, we set to work with a vengeance to clear the wreck of the *Pollux*. The boat made our working life much easier, but we had to find a safe anchorage for it. The nearest harbour, Maryport, was tidal and dried out at low water, so we moved the *Black Pig* up to Port Patrick, where there was an inner and an outer harbour. The entrance from the open sea was narrow and guarded by a large rock, called a tidal stone, at the south side, which stood clear of the sea at low water. Once you had negotiated the entrance, you then had a smart turn to port to get into the inner harbour. There were two leading lights to guide you through the narrow entrance at night, one on the harbour wall, and one up the main street. The only thing to watch in the inner harbour was the lifeboat, tied up in the centre of the harbour.

We awoke one morning to find half a gale blowing. I called the local coastguard who told me, 'Stay in bed today lads, it's going to get worse.' I passed the news on to the team and the usual argument followed. Frank had come up for a few days and was eager to get into the water. Snowy and I were somewhat less keen, but agreed to give it a go.

On our way out of harbour we were flashed red by the coastguard. The message was simple, 'Don't go out.' We knew better. It was a rough, uncomfortable three hours' passage to the dive-site, where we were working very close to the cliffs. The sea was in turmoil. As a rule we never used an anchor, for it tended to get fast in the wreck. Normally we fixed a rope to the wreck but because of the sea conditions, Frank came up with the bright idea of tying a large piece of scrap from the hold on to the line to do the job of an anchor. It held for a short time.

Suddenly the block and tackle on the derrick came loose and started to swing wildly about. Snowy saw the block coming straight at him and ducked. Frank, who was behind Snowy, looked up, and caught the swinging block on the forehead, knocking him out. On regaining consciousness he gave Snowy a right bollocking for ducking. Then the anchor-line parted and we were loose and drifting, minus one large piece of scrap. Even Frank was forced to admit that diving was impossible and we called it a day. By now a full gale was blowing, and the winter darkness was closing in fast. By the time we reached Port Patrick it was completely dark.

The sight that greeted us through the storm and the spray was not pleasant. Big rollers were rushing through the harbour entrance and to make matters worse there were no leading lights to guide us. Someone had turned them out.

We could only guess the position of the tidal stone. To come down on it in such a sea would certainly have put paid to the *Black Pig*. In pitch darkness, in the teeth of a howling gale, we held a hasty conference on whether to risk attempting to get into the harbour or do the run up to Loch Ryan for shelter.

I knew what the answer would be. 'You've had the most experience Keith. You take it in.'

'Not fucking likely,' I said, but in the end I agreed, though I knew full well that I'd be blamed if I hit anything on the way in. Such was life in this team.

I sent Snowy up to the bows, to guide us along the middle of the channel by hand signals. As I brought the vessel closer I could see the size of the waves rushing through the narrow entrance. The *Black Pig* had little power; even at full throttle forward or astern you just had to wait for it to happen. Once in those waves, we would be picked up like a surfboard and sent on our way with no control whatsoever. I got into the best position I could find to start the run, then shouted to the lads, 'Here we go.'

As we reached the harbour mouth I felt the *Black Pig* being picked up by the following wave and we surfed through the entrance. As I battled to stop the boat from going sideways or capsizing, we were swept into the outer harbour. I threw it hard to port, and waited for the worst or best to happen. The bows came around very slowly. After requiring every ounce of power and speed, I now had to lose it pretty damn quick. I just missed the lifeboat and with the engines full astern, the boat finally came to rest against the tidal meter tube, in the corner of the harbour.

'Could you not see the fucking tidal meter?' was Frank's first and only comment.

Chapter Four

The Zaffaris

B y late 1965 we were in trouble. The *Pollux* and its cargo was long finished and there was nothing much left on any of the other wrecks in the area. We had to find another wreck quickly. If we didn't, it was back to the mills of Keighley. Despite the cold water and the incessant pleas from Mildred to 'get a proper job', I just didn't fancy that.

Even when we found a workable new wreck, it was only the first step towards earning some money. We then had to buy the rights to it. Many times we traced underwriters and made an offer, only to be told, 'It's not worth our time and effort to uncover the paperwork.' I understood that, but it was very frustrating to do a volunteer salvor's job which entailed holding the cargo until we'd made a deal with the owner. If no one came forward, it became ours outright after a year and day, but it was a long wait for our money, particularly when the scrap we'd recovered had a habit of disappearing from the storeplace.

Snowy and I still kept diving full time, but Frank went back to his coal business to earn his living, though he still put in an odd few days when we had a wreck to work. We had a particularly hard time of it during the winter. Getting in a couple of dives produced enough scrap to keep my wife and kids fed and watered for two or three weeks, but even when we'd managed to find a wreck to work, prolonged gales and storms meant we couldn't get into the water to earn money.

As we drove up to Scotland one day, we passed John Brown's shipyards on the Clyde, where the QE2 was taking shape. Its new aluminium superstructure towered high above the shipyard buildings. Stuck in an enormous tail-back of traffic, I watched the ship's massive bronze propellers being transported to the yard. I fell asleep that night dreaming of finding them lying on the sea-bed.

The dream did not come true. We were rapidly running out of work and taking more risks as the wrecks became less and less productive. By the middle of the winter I was absolutely broke. Late one night, Frank Guest got a phone call from a Scottish farmer, Bobby Ramsey. A Greek freighter, the *Zaffaris*, had gone aground on the Mull of Galloway. The others decided to share it between them and set off for Scotland leaving me asleep in bed with Mildred.

They returned a few days later with their trophies of sextants and chronometers and made some feeble excuse to me. It was the last straw for the 'Braw Lads'. I told them that I was calling it a day, and took a job at a local factory, just to pay the bills. I told myself that I'd have another go at diving for a living in the summer, but in reality there was little chance, because I didn't even have the price of an air compressor to fill my diving bottles.

Things have a strange way of working out, however. A few weeks later, I got a call from Bobby Ramsey, telling me that he'd bought the rights to the Greek ship, now fully submerged on the bottom. Could I help him to salvage it?

Bobby was a kindly man with a round, weather-beaten farmer's face. He lived at Cadryne Farm, overlooking the sea, and ran another two farms as well, but he was a farmer who loved the sea more than he loved his land. He was out every day in his boat catching lobsters and saw salvage as another good way to spend time messing about in boats. He wasn't a diver, however, and if we were to salvage the *Zaffaris*, I needed someone else to dive with me. Luckily a friend from my Sub-Aqua Club days was working in the same factory. Peter Sellars, a draughtsman by trade, was about ten years younger than me, quiet and studious, with mournful brown eyes. He also had a longing to try diving for a living and we came up with the idea of building ourselves a low-pressure compressor instead of buying a costly high-pressure one.

Without high-pressure air, we could no longer use our diving bottles, but we improvised a supply with air pumped down to us from the surface. We used a scrap compressor from an old fridge, after Peter assured me that the delivery rate of air would keep two divers happy at thirty feet. We took an engine from an old lawnmower to run the compressor and fitted a filter, layers of pads interspersed with activated charcoal and silica gel. The diver's mouthpiece was the second stage of a two-stage demand valve. With two sixty-foot airlines we were ready to go.

We started work in early spring. The *Zaffaris* had been pounded by the winter storms and was now broken up on the bottom, its cargo of grain scattered on the beaches for miles around. The wreck itself was in about twenty-five feet of water. The biggest obstacle to us was the four-knot tide running constantly from the north.

Our two main targets were the main and spare propellers, which were made of manganese bronze and would give by far the best and quickest return. Each one weighed two and a half tons and my job was to blow the main prop off its shaft and then split the propellers into four with explosives for easy lifting, using Bobby's small boat.

Our first dives with the new compressor showed that feeding air to two divers was a little ambitious. One diver got the air, the other got nothing. From then on we could only have one diver in the water at a time. If anything went wrong, you had to sort it out yourself or drown. Fragments of charcoal also kept escaping from the filter and coming down the air line straight into our mouths, but using this primitive method we nevertheless managed to salvage the propeller blades.

Their sale gave us enough money to buy new equipment: a Zodiac inflatable boat, decent wet suits, diving bottles and last but not least, a brand new Dunlop high-pressure air compressor. We formed a company, Solway Salvage, and began to look for other wrecks.

When I read in the press that a small coastal tanker, the *Eileen M*, had run aground and sunk on Islay, we left for the island at once. My first sight of Islay was a memorable one. As we sailed towards the island on the ferry, an endless stream of wild geese that had migrated from Greenland and Iceland passed overhead, then circled and landed to rest and feed. When we drove around the coast early the next morning to try to reach the *Eileen M*, the fields were still packed tight with geese. They took off in their thousands, almost turning day into night.

If the island was a birdwatcher's dream, it also turned out to be a salvage man's paradise. After chatting to a few islanders, we made contact with Jim McCauley, a local grocer whose hobby was tracing the story of the shipwrecks around Islay. It was a life's work, for the rocky coasts of the island were littered with them. We sat open-mouthed as he reeled off a list of them, all apparently untouched by salvage men. Apart from the *Eileen M*, there was the *Rothesay Castle*, a big refrigeration ship wrecked on the northern tip of Islay, the submarine HMS *Graph*, the *Otranto*, an armed merchant cruiser wrecked during the First World War, and a host of others. Best of all, he told us that the bronze propeller of a

Second World War merchant ship, the *Floristan*, was actually sticking out of the water. A quick trip to the west coast confirmed the story.

We returned to the mainland at top speed, desperate to set the paperwork in motion to buy the wrecks before my late friends in Keighley got to hear about them. The Lloyd's agent in Stranraer supplied the names of the interested parties and we sent off a number of offers.

While waiting for the replies we went back to Islay to try to land a few loads of scrap before winter set in. The east coast of the island was relatively sheltered, with small sandy beaches and rocky coves, and wooded slopes giving way to moors thick with grazing deer. The west coast was another world: wild, rocky and almost treeless because of the violent Atlantic storms sweeping in from the west. Its sheer cliffs, reefs and rocks had made it a graveyard for many ships.

The contrast in the weather on the island could be equally marked. There was no point in ringing up Port Ellen on the east coast to ask about sea conditions, for they could be completely different over on the west coast. Several times we set off in perfect weather, only to find a big Atlantic swell rolling in and the surf pounding the rocks. In the relatively shallow waters of the west coast, the conditions made diving impossible.

We also had to learn to decode the shipping forecast. Islay is in sea area Malin but we soon discovered that a quiet forecast for Malin didn't always mean safe diving for us. A storm way out in sea area Rockall would send massive rollers pounding on to the west coast of Islay. Even in good weather, it was an extremely difficult place to work and just to reach the west coast by boat at all we had to face the terrible tides around the Mull of Oa and the Rhinns of Islay at the south of the island, or the equally fierce ones in the Sound of Islay if we went north.

At the start of operations, we made Kilchiaran Bay our
base. It was about the only place on the west coast where
you could launch a small boat. There was nothing outside
the bay but ocean for the next 3,000 miles. Diving from the
bay was as safe as anywhere on that coast which compared
to almost anywhere else, was not very safe at all.

Kilchiaran Bay had another attraction for us however; the
Floristan lay submerged across the entrance to the bay. At the
time of her stranding, it was rumoured that there was gold
on board. We took those stories with a pinch of salt; its
seven-ton bronze propeller would do very nicely for a start.
It was too late in the season to salvage it that year, but we
could make life a little easier for ourselves and a little harder
for any potential competitors by blowing the propeller apart.
It would make it easier to lift once we owned the rights and
in the meantime it would put it safely out of sight beneath
the waves.

Before we started the job I arranged to get some extra gear
flown up from Glasgow. The only airport buildings on Islay
were a lock-up garage for the fire tender and a wooden hut
which doubled as the airport office and passenger waiting
room. The runway was tarmac, a rarity for the islands where
most were grass strips or a sandy beach, but when I got there
to meet the morning flight, it was completely covered by
what appeared to be a hundred sheep, basking in the sun. I
could hear the aircraft coming in from the east but there was
no sign of movement from the sheep. Then a fireman drove
out to one end of the runway in his Land Rover, with his
sheepdog in the back. The dog raised its head in a weary sort
of way and gave a few half-hearted barks, whereupon the
sheep just got up and walked to the side of the runway.
When the flight had come and gone, they all wandered back
on to the tarmac and lay down again. I didn't know whether
to be more impressed with the sheep or the dog.

I went back to Kilchiaran with the gear and we paddled out to the wreck in the Zodiac. I perched on top of it, wrapping my legs around the prop-shaft and holding on with one hand to keep myself upright while I fixed the charges with the other. There was a long swell rolling in from the west which made life even more difficult. One minute I was high and dry, the next I was buried by a swirling mass of water. Eventually I fixed and linked all the charges. There were quite a few because I was aiming to blow the propeller from the shaft and split the four blades apart at the same time.

When I fired the charges, a waterspout rose into the air, a vertical column of water eighty feet high with a mass of kelp perched on the top of it like a flat cap. The sound of the explosion boomed and echoed around the cliffs and probably gave half the sheep on Islay a miscarriage, but the explosives did their job. We split the engine block apart in the same way, then reluctantly left the metal lying on the bottom until the next spring.

Peter and I managed to scrape through the rest of the winter doing odd jobs for Bobby on his farm on the Mull of Galloway and getting an occasional load of scrap from Islay when the weather was favourable, but all my thoughts were fixed on spring.

We'd been pressing the Lloyd's agent for an answer on the *Floristan* but kept being told by the insurers that all the paperwork was missing and the owners couldn't be traced. After a council of war with Bobby and Peter, we reached our decision. If the owners couldn't be traced, they certainly weren't going to be hanging around the west coast of Islay to complain if we lifted the *Floristan*'s propeller blades. If they came forward at a later date, we'd give them a fair price for the wreck; if they didn't, we'd have an even better return on our labours.

As soon as the fine weather came we hired a trawler

belonging to Bobby Ramsey's brother-in-law, Hughie Campbell, to raise the scrap. I stood on the beach as Hughie brought the boat into Kilchiaran Bay on a perfect morning with a flat, calm sea. I went on board and gave him the position and depth of the propeller blades. He then told me where to fix lines to the bottom to stop the boat being dragged into the shallows by the weight of the metal being lifted as the strain came on the winch.

The lift went like clockwork and in no time we had Hughie's boat loaded to the point where even he conceded there was enough on board. He sailed up to Crinan to unload and then return for a second lift.

It was a fine start to the season but it was a struggle from then on. Bobby hit problems on his farms and had to return to Galloway, leaving Peter and me to carry on. The small Zodiac we were using was far from perfect for landing scrap, but hiring Hughie's boat was out of the question unless we had a load as valuable as the *Floristan*'s propeller to lift.

It was a deeply frustrating time. We were working a coast we knew was littered with wrecks but because of our limitations of manpower, capital and equipment, we were barely scratching the surface. After years of back-breaking effort, I was still living hand to mouth. Whatever surplus we made was quickly swallowed by the cost of better equipment. The main problem, as always, was that wreck diving was either feast or famine. Good earning periods were always followed by bad ones when the weather turned ugly.

The only way I could see to change things was to find the *Otranto*, the biggest and most profitable wreck off Islay. The 12,000-ton ship was a cruise liner built for the Orient Steam Navigation Company in 1909. It had been converted to an armed merchant cruiser at the outbreak of the First World War and sailed from New York on 24 September 1918, in convoy HX50, bound for Glasgow and Liverpool. During

the course of the voyage, the ship's complement was augmented by the unfortunate crew of a sailing ship, the
Croisine. Sailing without lights, the convoy had ploughed
straight through a fleet of French fishing ships and the
Croisine was run down and sunk by the *Otranto*.

The thirteen-ship convoy – ten merchantmen carrying
almost 20,000 troops, escorted by three US warships – sailed
on in six columns. The *Otranto* was the leading ship in the
third column; the next one to its north was led by the SS
Kashmir, a 9,000-ton liner of the P & O line. As they
reached the North Channel, they were hit by a ferocious
storm. Poor visibility had prevented any sightings being
taken for several days and the convoy had been navigating
by dead reckoning.

On the morning of 16 October, the captains of both vessels spotted land. The Captain of the *Kashmir* correctly identified it as the coast of Islay, but the Officer of the Watch on
the *Otranto* thought the land he could see was Inishtrahull.
Both men put the helm hard over, battling the mountainous
seas as they tried to steer away from trouble. There was one
small problem; while the *Kashmir* turned to starboard, the
Otranto turned to port. At 8.45 that morning the *Kashmir*'s
bow smashed into the port side of the *Otranto*, gouging a
huge hole.

Badly damaged, the two ships drifted apart and lost sight
of each other in the spray and towering seas. Pounded by
mountainous waves, the *Otranto* shipped more and more
water through the hole in its side. The engine room flooded
and with both engines stopped, it drifted helplessly towards
the coast of Islay.

Its SOS calls were answered by a destroyer, HMS
Mounsey, which reached the stricken ship at 10 a.m. The sea
conditions made a rescue almost impossible. One minute
the destroyer's deck was rearing upwards, the next it was

plunging down, burying its bows in the next massive wave as tons of green water roared over its decks. Despite the risk to his own ship, the *Mounsey*'s captain, Lieutenant F.W. Craven, repeatedly brought it alongside the badly listing liner. In calm water, the destroyer's deck would have been thirty feet below the liner's. In such a storm, the waves would raise it almost level with the *Otranto* for a fraction of a second, then cast it down into a trough sixty feet below. American troops lined the deck of the doomed liner and as the two ships were hurled together by the swell, they began trying to jump across the gap. Four times the *Mounsey* crashed into the side of the *Otranto* as hundreds of men jumped for their lives. Many fell into the sea and were drowned or crushed between the ships' hulls. Many more were killed or badly injured as they plummeted on to the deck of the destroyer, but a sizable number were saved.

With almost 600 men now on board, the *Mounsey* was itself dangerously overloaded and in grave danger of being swamped and sinking. It pulled off and steamed away, labouring in the swell. The thoughts of Captain Davidson and the over 400 men still remaining on the *Otranto*, as they watched their last hope of rescue sail away, can only be imagined.

It grounded half a mile from the shore and began to break up. The captain gave the order to abandon ship, but only sixteen men managed to survive the swim through the terrible seas to the shore. The bodies of the dead, including Captain Davidson, were washed up right along the west coast of the island. In all, well over 400 men were drowned. A simple cemetery, containing the British war graves, looks out across the site of the disaster. All the American bodies were returned to the States for burial.

Searching through contemporary newspapers for information, I was amazed to find no reference to the sinking. It showed the grip the Government had on the press in those days; it's hard to imagine a similar catastrophe being hushed up today, even in wartime.

Admiralty charts placed the wreck in Machir Bay on the west coast of Islay, and with the help of the locals we managed to trace a very old man who had watched the *Otranto* breaking up on the reef. By the time he got there, the pounding of the massive waves had broken the vessel in two and bodies were washing ashore. By nightfall the *Otranto* had disappeared below the surface. He took us to the exact spot where he had stood all those years ago, watching that terrible scene being played out below him. I could see a few tears running down his cheeks.

In late summer I found a trawlerman from the Isle of Man who was having a thin time at the fishing. After a great deal of persuasion and not a few glasses of whisky, he agreed to work with us 'on spec' for a couple of weeks while we searched for the wreck. We used towed searches across the area to find it. Neither of us enjoyed it; it was always much colder being towed than swimming because so much more water got into your suit. We took turns behind the boat holding a heavily-weighted line and another one attached to a buoy. If one of us found the wreck, he could let go of the towing line and fix the buoy to the wreckage, making sure we did not lose the site.

I took the first turn myself. As the boat moved off, I slid down to the end of the line near the weight, which helped to keep me near the bottom. Without it, I would have been pulled to the surface. Four long, cold days of tows across the sea-bed followed. By the end of the fourth day even I was getting despondent. How could we be missing a 12,000-ton wreck, 535 feet long? The weather had been kind to us up to then but it was bound to change soon and Islay was no place to be diving in bad weather.

I had just finished another tow, very cold and disappointed, and Peter was about to start his turn on the end of the line, when a small trawler came into the bay. I recognised the boat. It belonged to Lachy Clark, who had fished the lobsters for many years on Islay and many of the other islands. He had a reputation as a quiet, Bible-reading man. I hailed him as he came alongside, and explained our problem. He thought for a while, then said, 'Follow me.'

He led us a fair distance to the south of our position, then gestured into the depths. 'I've lost a few pots in these parts, I suggest you try here.'

Peter was quickly into the water. No sooner had he disappeared below the surface, than he was back again. 'It's here.'

I was back in the water, the cold forgotten, just as soon as I got a set of bottles on my back. What I saw would have gladdened the heart of any salvage diver. Here was a ship built by a company who believed in putting the best available materials into their vessels. An engine block the size of a house stood proud of the sea-bed. I swam right through it. Big connecting rods led to huge bearings, there were two large condensers, and bronze pumps and large-diameter copper piping lay strewn all over the sea-bed. I swam to the stern of the vessel and found the massive three-bladed bronze propeller. What a find!

We recovered a few lengths of thick copper piping, just to cover the expenses of the day of celebration that would follow, but before we sailed back, I also took a few moments to take some markers of our position. There was no way I was going to lose this wreck-site.

When you want to mark your position at sea, you look towards the shoreline and pick out two objects in line, like a tree and a house, or a church spire and a feature on the skyline. You then look in another direction and do the same, which gives you a good cross-bearing. My markers for finding the *Otranto* were the roof of a croft which aligned with a small V in the hillside, a black gully that lined up with a telegraph pole on the hill, and three brown patches which we termed rabbit holes and which aligned with a peculiar rock on the foreshore. These gave me the perfect fix and with the bearings in line I could put us on any part of the wreck.

We returned to shore ready for the mother of all celebrations, but before I touched a drop, I arranged for a letter to be sent to the Ministry of Transport War Risks Insurance Office to make sure that the *Otranto* was for sale.

The restrictions imposed by the drinking hours on Islay, where the pubs closed at 10 p.m. sharp and all day on Sundays, could have put a damper on our celebrations, but luckily there was a ceilidh that night. At some ceilidhs people got together for an evening of song, story-telling and temperance, which was a little on the quiet side for the diving fraternity. To our great relief, that night's ceilidh was a less restrained and much more well-lubricated affair.

Islay depends almost entirely on the production of whisky and, despite the best efforts of the distillery owners, a fair amount of raw whisky straight from the still, along with stuff they call the wash, finds its way into the hands of the locals. If whisky-drinking ever became an Olympic sport, nine people out of a team of ten, including women, would come from Islay. Even when celebrating a windfall like the *Otranto*, it was wise to approach the whisky with caution. A few glasses of the white stuff – 120 proof – would have been enough to curtail our diving activities for a good few days. I stuck to beer and let an aspidistra have the benefit of my whisky. The sight of less prudent individuals after a night on the white stuff was not a pretty one.

The dancing at the ceilidh was almost as dangerous as the

whisky. The general idea seemed to be to spin your partner off his or her feet. A superb specimen of Scottish womanhood led me to the dance floor. As the music started, she clasped my head to her ample bosom. The room went dark and then began to spin. My feet didn't touch the ground for a considerable length of time and in the end I was forced to request rather urgently that she put me down. Peter and a few other outsiders also tried a few eightsome reels with the local Amazons and without exception they found themselves skidding across the dance floor on their backsides.

Chapter Five

The *Otranto*

———————•———————

After a long, anxious wait through the winter months, I received a letter from the War Risks Insurance Office accepting our offer for the wreck of the *Otranto*. It was ours for £200, plus a share of the proceeds from the sale of the – as yet unseen – starboard propeller, buried under the wreck. It sounds a trifling amount of money now, but in 1968 it was a substantial sum, and certainly far more than I could lay my hands on. I'd assumed that between us we would scrape the money together somehow, splitting the costs and the profits three ways, but when I told Peter and Bobby the good news they made it quite clear that no money would be forthcoming from them. From now on, I was on my own.

We were all in dire financial straits, but while Peter was back at his old job as a draughtsman and Bobby had his farms on the Mull of Galloway, I had nothing to fall back on. I was working night shifts at Peter Black's textile mill in Keighley to make ends meet and not enjoying it one bit.

I was desperate to find the money for the *Otranto* from somewhere, scared that word of the find would get out and someone else would step in and buy it. In the end I approached the metal brokers who had bought the propeller blades from the *Zaffaris*. When I told them of the expected returns from the *Otranto*, they agreed to loan me the money against the first big recoveries.

I completed the purchase, but with Bobby and Peter now out of the picture, I needed help; I couldn't work the *Otranto* alone. I asked Snowy if he wanted to join me again. He was very keen but to my surprise, he asked if Frank could be brought back as well. Reluctantly I agreed. The old team was back in business.

It was still too early in the spring to book a vessel to raise the first load of scrap, but just as we had done with the *Floristan*, we used a couple of clear days to prepare the easiest and most profitable pieces of scrap for lifting. Frank and I dived down to the wreck and swam right along its length to the stern. We got ready to blast the starboard propeller from the prop-shaft and split it into three.

The day we'd found the *Otranto*, I'd scratched the propeller blades to check they were bronze. While fixing the charges around the prop-shaft against the boss, I got the awful feeling that I'd made a terrible mistake. I'd been diving long enough to know the difference between non-ferrous and ferrous metal. On older wrecks it's easy enough to check. I took out my knife and gave the boss a good crack. There was a cloud of black dust, like smoke in the water. It was a sure sign that I'd hit iron. There was a sick feeling in my stomach. I couldn't understand how I could have made such a mistake.

I swam out along one of the blades, which stuck out some ten feet beyond the boss. Heart in mouth, I scratched it with my diving knife. There was no black dust, just the yellow gleam of bronze. I heaved a huge sigh of relief. Until then I'd never seen or heard of a propeller with bronze blades inserted into a cast-iron boss. They were held in place by huge brass nuts, hidden under a dome of concrete.

After firing the charges, we dived back down to the

wreck. The three massive propeller blades lay neatly separated on the sea-bed, surrounded by the brass nuts that had held them. We also blew a giant condenser into manageable pieces. All we had to do now was wait for the last of the winter storms to abate. After days of staring morosely at the wind and rain lashing the coast, we at last got a decent weather window. A big high-pressure zone came in and gave us the chance to make the lift.

I contacted Ross & Marshals in Glasgow, who ran a fleet of vessels known throughout Scotland as 'puffers', later immortalised in the television series *Parrahandy*. They agreed to have one of their vessels, the *Stormlight*, on site within two days. It was capable of lifting at least three tons, my estimate of the weight of each of the propeller blades on the *Otranto*. It failed to put in an appearance on schedule but after several more days of increasingly angry phone calls, we were promised it would arrive early the next morning, without fail.

The next day dawned clear and calm, with just the hint of a swell coming in from the west. We drove across to the west coast and used the Zodiac to get out to the wreck-site. Our lifting vessel arrived late. We made it fast to the wreck, then climbed on board. It was immediately obvious from the state of the three-man crew that drink had been taken the previous night. The skipper was a wizened little man who looked as if he could have done with being put through the washing machine and the engineer and deckhand were much the same.

It was going to be a long day and we decided to have our breakfast before starting. The crew had brought no food of their own, but generously helped us eat ours. As I briefed them on what we expected, nervous glances passed between them. The vessel was without ballast and riding high in the water, and because of the tide we were lying across the slight swell, which gave it quite a roll. There was only one hatch, with steel covers set on rollers. When the winchman released them, they rolled back at an ever-increasing speed, then turned on end and stacked vertically with a deafening clang. For some reason the skipper was standing on top of the hatch when the winchman freed the covers. I had visions of the biggest meat sandwich in history with the skipper as the filling. I stood watching helplessly. There was nothing I could do, no way to stop the covers once they started rolling. At the last moment, old and hungover though he was, the skipper made a flying dive that Mark Spitz would have envied and clung to the derrick support. He missed death by inches. The three crew members went into an immediate huddle and emerged with a request for a few extra pounds in cash. Hands tied, we agreed. It was the first of a number of such requests during the course of the day.

Our first lift was one of the propeller blades. We made it secure to the winch, which had just about enough cable on the drum to reach the bottom. This caused us endless extra work, as we had to reposition the vessel for each lift.

Worse was to follow. It soon became obvious that the winchman had no experience. He lowered the derrick to help us secure the blade to the cable and when he attempted the lift all that happened was that the vessel moved to the blade and then began to tilt over. A lot of shouting by the skipper soon put a stop to that operation. The winchman raised the derrick until it was at an angle of about forty-five degrees, then started the lift again. All went fine until the blade cleared the water. Then it began to swing. Each arc brought it closer to the side of the vessel and soon it was crashing into it with quite a bang. The blade was soon dropped back into the water and the winchman then moved the derrick to almost vertical so that the blade came up alongside the vessel.

Another disaster was in the making. Instead of dropping it straight into the hold once it was clear of the side, the winchman again allowed the blade to start swinging. Within seconds it was once more going through forty-five degrees, at a steadily increasing velocity. Panic began to take hold. Three tons of propeller blade swinging free soon starts to make its mark. The stanchions that secured the mast and derrick began to bend and the welding started to crack. It was frightful to look at. Lowered slowly it would have punched a hole through the side of the vessel. The winchman did the only thing possible. As the blade came to the far end of its swing, off came the brake and the blade went back to the depths with a tremendous splash.

Another conference was followed by a few more quid changing hands, and after much hard work we finally got the blade inboard. As soon as it cleared the side of the ship, before it could start to swing, the winchman dropped it into the hold with a crash. On the next lift, he promptly forgot everything he'd learned on the first one and allowed a condenser end-plate to swing free. It wasn't such a problem as the propeller blade; the end-plate only weighed about half a ton. After a few more dents in the side of the ship and a few more ominous creaks from the derrick, that too found its way into the hold.

The whole day went on in much the same vein and what should have been an easy day for us turned out to be one of the longest and most arduous I can ever recall. The vessel had to be constantly repositioned – by the divers, not the crew. Their ropes were old and rotten, and broke repeatedly and there were constant cock-ups. We were also short of food; the crew had made sure of that.

After thirteen hours of hard work and stomach-knotting tension, at last the day was done. One glance into the hold told me that all the trauma had been worth it. Some sixteen tons of prime non-ferrous metal lay in the hold, enough to clear my debts and make me the outright owner of the *Otranto*.

The *Otranto* alone carried enough non-ferrous fittings to keep us going for years, but on days when sea conditions made it impossible to work the wreck – and they were frequent – we could pull scrap from the *Floristan*, which was in a less exposed position.

We worked from Kilchiaran Bay, using the Zodiac to get out to the dive-site. At first we changed on the beach at the head of the bay, near a small cliff with a waterfall which was very handy for washing the salt out of our diving suits. A small cove at the seaward end of the bay, sheltered from the west by a line of rocks, made a much better base for operations however. The only problem was that we needed a four-wheel-drive vehicle to reach it.

Driving down to Portnahaven on the south-west tip of the island one day, we noticed a derelict Land Rover in a field next to the road. Most of the paint was missing, showing its aluminium body, and it had a well-knackered canvas back and four flat tyres, but it hadn't been stripped for spares. We had a quick chat with the farmer, a few pounds changed hands and it was ours. A coat of green paint, some second-hand tyres, a change of oil and we had it running in no time. It served us well over the coming months, but it carried so much weight that in the end we broke its back.

The track around the top side of Kilchiaran Bay leading to the cove had been constructed by the Army many years before. The line of it could still be traced easily enough, winding around the steep cliffs, sometimes reaching fifty or sixty feet above the bay, but time and the weather had taken their toll. As we made our first journey along it, the Land Rover leaned at an ever crazier angle, the wheels inches from a sheer drop. We were forced to hang on to the uphill side, like the crew of a racing yacht, to stop our prized new possession from rolling over and crashing on to the rocks below us. The last turn into the cove was over a deep gully, spanned by a small dry-stone bridge. What was left of the bridge could only be negotiated with extreme care. There was nothing to spare at all, both sets of wheels were no more than two inches from the edge.

The effort was worth it, however, for the cove was an ideal place to work from, only 100 yards from the wreck of the *Floristan*. The boulder-littered beach sloped up to a small grassy bank where the remains of a lifeboat from the wreck had been washed up. It became our base.

We found plenty of non-ferrous metal on the *Floristan*, including a part-cargo of twelve-foot brass tubes, some full of sand. It was an awkward cargo to handle from the Zodiac, so we built a raft out of scaffolding tubes and forty-gallon oil drums and fixed a line from the shore so that we could pull ourselves out to the wreck-site. One of us stayed on the raft stacking the tubes, while the other two passed them up from below the water.

On calm days it was a pleasure to take my turn on the raft. I used to sit there daydreaming as I waited for the tug on the rope that signalled that the diver below had fixed a load to the line. The big transatlantic jets, outward bound for America, used to pass directly over the middle of the bay. I'd watch them trailing vapour as they sped towards the horizon to the west. I dreamed of being on one one day, until a sharp tug on the line would bring me back to reality, straining and heaving at the rope and wondering what they had tied on this time.

We soon discovered the carrying capacity of the raft. A few tubes too many and it slowly started to sink. That was the signal for the diver to jump into the water. Without his weight the raft was buoyant enough for us to pull it into the shore and unload the tubes. When we'd finished with it and were ready to start for home, we simply removed the drums, and let it sink to the bottom, ready to be retrieved for our next operation.

We were at work on the *Floristan* one day when we noticed a group of five men making their way around the bay towards us. As they came closer, we could see by their clothes that they were locals, not tourists. They were rough-looking lads and had obviously not walked all that way for a picnic. They looked to have trouble in mind.

The leader shouted, 'I want to talk to you.'

Rather than pull the raft in to the shore, we decided to swim in, making sure we all had our diving knives with us. We landed a distance away from them, giving us time to strip off our fins and get ready, just in case. We were an awful long way from the nearest police station and there were no witnesses in this lonely spot. As we walked towards them, I recognised the leader. He was the local coalman, Willy Burke, who also dabbled in scrap metal. He was quietly spoken, but a hard-looking man and he constantly glanced behind him as he talked, as if expecting an attack. He'd been pointed out to us before as someone to steer well clear of.

What he said was brief and to the point. He owned the wreck that we were working and produced the documents to prove it – the paperwork that we'd been assured could not be traced. Things were a little ugly at first, but when we all calmed down we sorted out an agreement that was a true British compromise; we got to keep the wreck, but we now had a new partner, Willy Burke. As I got to know him better I found I rather liked him. He was a rough, tough character with some gypsy blood in him, but he was direct and straightforward and lived by a simple set of rules that I found it hard to disagree with.

With our new partner's blessing, we moved all the tubes we'd collected back around the bay in our old Land Rover and stacked them by the road. Then we booked a lorry to come over and collect them. It completely blocked the narrow road, but no one appeared to mind; life was very steady on the island.

It was only when we started to load the tubes that I realised just how many we'd collected. Loading them was endless, the piles never seemed to get any smaller. It took so long that by the time we'd crossed to the mainland on the ferry and driven down to Glasgow, the metal dealers' yard had closed for the weekend.

Next came the really good news. Our lorry driver had to get back to his base and refused to go any further. What the hell could we do with a load of brass tubes in Glasgow on a Friday night? If we dumped them at the roadside there'd be none left in the morning. We tried and failed to hire another lorry, but we did manage to talk our driver into going down the road to the first transport café south of Glasgow. There we found someone willing to run the tubes down as far as Carlisle. Already knackered from our long day's work, we began transferring the brass tubes to the other lorry.

We repeated the whole sequence in Carlisle, getting the driver to take us to the first transport café down the A6, where we found another two lorry drivers going to Manchester. They agreed to run the tubes down to Keighley for a few pounds.

'Are there any steep hills on the way down the A65?' one asked.

'No,' I said. 'Why?'

'Oh, it's just that we're already carrying over thirty tons of steel plate.'

Close to exhaustion, we transferred the tubes again,

praying it would be the last time. Dawn had broken, the birds were singing and all was going well, until just to the south of Kendal we came to a short, sharp hill. The first lorry got stuck on a bend halfway up. The road was completely blocked. We managed to get both lorries to reverse back down the hill and once more moved the tubes from the first one to the one in the rear, which was carrying less steel plate. This time they both managed the hill – just.

We finally arrived in Keighley, where once again we had to transfer the tubes, this time to Frank's coal lorry. We'd moved the whole stack of tubes six times in the course of the journey down from Islay.

At the weigh-in on Monday, we found we had over five tons of brass – or at least, most of it was brass. We knew there was a fair amount of sand inside the tubes, but in getting them out of the sea, the water had washed it out of the ends, so none was visible. We took the money and ran.

It was some time before we called on that particular dealer again. He broke into a smile when he saw us – always a bad sign in a scrap dealer. 'Lads,' he said. 'Come and look at this lot.'

He took us round the back where he had a fair old collection of sandbags full of sand, some seven hundredweight in all. 'It came from those tubes you sold me,' he said. There was no doubt it was our sand – I could smell the sea on it, and after a token protest we allowed him to knock a percentage off the load we were just weighing in.

Back on Islay, we found that our new partner had invested in a 25-foot launch to speed up the work of bringing the scrap from the *Otranto* ashore. The second day we used it was a reasonable one for the west coast – a bitterly cold north-easterly, blowing about Force 3 or 4 – and for a change, the sea over the wreck was almost flat calm. As dusk fell we listened to the shipping forecast; the wind would remain easterly, backing a little further to the north-east and increasing marginally. It was just a fresh breeze for that coast. With most of our diving gear on board however, we played safe. Before we went back to our digs for the night, we made the launch secure in the cove with six lines.

The first indication that something was wrong came in a phone call the next morning from Willy. 'You'd better come across, we've a problem with the boat.'

I noticed a change in the wind direction straight away – it was now in the west and blowing hard – but that didn't prepare us for the sight that met our eyes at Kilchiaran Bay.

The cove had been completely transformed. The day before the beach had been littered with huge boulders; now not one could be seen. All had gone, replaced by an unbroken stretch of pure golden sand. Where the sand came from I do not know; there is none at all in the area.

The launch had been reduced to matchwood; we collected the bits and made a bonfire of them. The two largest items we found were the fuel tank tossed up on the grass and the engine block resting against the cliff. It had been battered by the sea into a smooth, rounded shape. Then one of the lads noticed the winch. It was an ex-War Department type, and weighed about eighty pounds plus the weight of the cable. We had left it the previous night with its cables secured under the launch and another forty feet of cable inside it. Three strong men could not have lifted that winch and its dragging cable, entwined with kelp. Yet it had been thrown up on to the cliff, higher than I could ever have imagined the sea reaching.

I stood on the cliff-top looking at the weather. It was a bright sunny morning and even though the wind took our breath away and the waves outside the bay were all ten-foot white-tops, our small cove was relatively quiet. The launch would have been fine had the shipping forecast been accurate but instead of a Force 4 north-easterly, the bay had been hit by a Force 12 westerly. Neither the launch, nor the diving gear had been insured. We had learned the costly lesson once again of what an implacable and unpredictable enemy the sea could be.

After clearing the rest of the *Floristan*'s cargo, we turned our attention to the *Otranto* again. To make the recoveries from that exposed site we needed something much more substantial than the Zodiac and our scaffolding-pole raft. We eventually found an ex-army bridging pontoon at a government-surplus sale in Yorkshire. It was old but solidly built of marine ply, about 14 feet long by 7 feet wide and 4 feet deep. It even had a handrail round the outside that proved ideal for divers to hang on to. We bought a Seagull eight-horsepower outboard motor to power it through the water and Snowy built a trailer big enough to carry it.

We towed it to Scotland behind Snowy's Morris Traveller, setting off in the early hours of the morning to avoid any trouble with the police about the trailer's lack of brakes. We then hitched it to the Land Rover for the last perilous couple of miles to the cove at the end of Kilchiaran Bay and launched it into the water. It travelled through the waves with all the speed and grace of a bathtub full of concrete but it got the job done and that was all that counted.

There were still many days when sea conditions were too rough to get out to the *Otranto* and even with apparently calm and flat seas, the wreck was no picnic to work. If you did not know what to look for you could miss the long, low swell coming in from the west. But once underwater you were driven backward and forwards over the sea-bed by the action of the waves. Below sixty feet you were in the quiet zone, where surface turbulence had very little effect, but the general depth of water over the *Otranto* was only between thirty and forty feet. Hanging on to a piece of wreckage was like streaming from a lamppost in a hurricane, with the added problem that the wind reversed direction every few seconds.

You also had to be very careful which piece of wreckage you took hold of. What looked like inch-thick steel plate could crumble in your hands and leave a jagged knife-edge to rip you and your suit into ribbons. An apparently substantial bolt could also break away, leaving a needle-sharp point.

We travelled over to Kilchiaran every morning from our digs in Port Charlotte and steered the pontoon out to the wreck site. We dived solo; if anything went wrong on the bottom, the diver had to fix it himself. The water was gin clear and I could see the *Otranto*'s massive engine block as soon as I put my head below the surface. From above I could see how the ship had wrapped itself around the reef on that terrible day so many years ago and broken almost in half; the bow section lay at an angle of 120 degrees to the stern. I could follow the line of the twin shafts from the rear of the engine all the way to what was left of the propellers at the stern, pointing in towards the shore. There were eleven large boilers strewn at different angles around the wreck and looking down between the sections as I swam towards the bow I could see stacks of large brass shell cases, loaded with cordite. Swimming above the wreck was like looking down on a vast scrap yard.

We rigged a lifting device – a Tirfor, which the Americans call a 'walky-dog' or 'come-along' – to the pontoon to help us lift the pumps and bearings, plus larger pieces of metal weighing anything up to half a ton. We tied the scrap to the steel cable from the Tirfor and raised it by cranking a long lever. Unable to get the heavy pieces inboard, we sailed them back into the shelter of the cove, suspended below the pontoon, and pulled them out at low water.

Sometimes we tried to raise pieces that were too heavy or were still attached to the hull of the wreck. Raising the *Otranto* itself was well beyond the lifting power of the Tirfor. Instead one end of the pontoon would begin to sink beneath the waves and the other swing wildly in the swell. Sometimes this solved the problem by breaking the load free from the wreck below us, but in most cases we only had a few seconds to drop the load before the pontoon joined the piece we were trying to lift on the sea-bed.

When we'd cleared all the loose non-ferrous metal — which took some considerable time — we began to use explosives to blast the rest free. Whenever possible we made that the last job of the day, allowing the water to clear again overnight. We had considerable experience with explosives by now, but every now and again we were given a reminder of how dangerous the least inattention while using them could be.

We were working on the *Otranto* one day when the conditions were marginal. There was a nasty choppy swell and a stiff breeze, and it was pouring with rain as well. I'd been down on the wreck laying a number of large charges, fixing the detonators and tying off the firing cable to prevent them from dragging from their set positions. As I was about to get back on board the pontoon, someone on deck cast off the anchor. Before they had a chance to start paying out the firing cable the pontoon started to drift with the swell. I lunged for the rail, pulled myself clear of the water and hung there as it picked up speed. No one had made any connection to the battery with the firing cable but in the panic to pay out the cable it shorted and detonated the charges. Had I still been in the water rather than hanging on to the side of the pontoon, I would have been killed instantly by the shock wave through the water.

Although the seas around Islay were full of life, the hard work of hauling scrap left little time to admire it. Sometimes I'd notice a sudden darkening and look upwards to see a great shoal of fish, but much passed unnoticed. Conger eels and lobsters were an exception, however. You need to get your eye in to find lobsters, for they're very well camouflaged and know just how to tuck themselves away out of sight, but sometimes I chanced on one just waiting for the pot. Before putting my hand or arm into a dark hole or pipe, I always had a good look first, in case it was the home of a big conger eel or a large lobster; both can give you a very savage nip. I always paid very close attention to conger eels. They love wrecks and can be a nasty handful if provoked. I have never seen a lobsterman move as fast as when a conger eel came up in a pot that had just been lifted on to deck.

Once we had just detonated a charge on a wreck. After the explosion up came a number of fish and a fair-sized conger eel, belly uppermost. It looked well dead, but I remembered a couple of stories I'd heard in the past. One was about a cat that had been nosing around a rubbish tip where some fishermen had dumped the head of a conger eel a couple of days before. The eel grabbed the cat and there was one hell of a struggle to get it free. There was also a tale about a conger biting the heel off a fisherman's wellington boot.

When Snowy told me to get hold of the conger eel, I remembered the stories. 'Get stuffed,' I said. 'You do it.' He gave me a suspicious look and then poked his diving knife into its mouth. Its jaws clamped shut like a steel trap. Snowy hurriedly jerked his knife clear.

Another time I had to place a set of charges in the opening of a large condenser. Every time I approached, out would pop the head of the largest conger eel I'd ever seen, deep purple in colour, with big dark eyes that gave the unmistakeable warning, 'Keep away.' In the end I shoved the charges into the opening any old how, keeping my hands well out of the way, and then put some distance between myself and the condenser as quickly as I could.

CHAPTER SIX

YELLOW SUBMARINE

Until we found the *Otranto* I'd never really had the chance to look to the future. I was so obsessed with earning the money to feed my growing family and pay that week's bills that I never sat down and planned what I might be doing in a few months, never mind a few years, hence. But as I stumbled down the beach through rain, sleet and snow to begin another day's back-breaking work on the wreck, I kept thinking, there must be better things to look for than scrap metal.

Unearthing the documentation on the *Otranto* had fired my interest in research. I discovered that I was good at it and soon it became a passion. Whenever the weather turned sour, and during the long winter months when very little diving was possible, I took to studying old nautical records. I also began a dialogue with the Salvage Association that continues to this day. My interest in historical wrecks wasn't entirely romantic; any metal carried on them was likely to be far more valuable than brass or copper. I'd heard the local fishermen's handed-down tales about the Spanish Armada galleons wrecked around the coasts of Scotland and Ireland and I collected information on the more promising of the thirty or so wrecks.

The Armada was a fighting force not a treasure fleet, but

some of the ships carried valuables. Paymaster vessels had silver and gold coins to pay the soldiers and crew, and some of the 1,500 Spanish nobles sailing with the Armada were so confident of victory that they brought their own personal chests full of money and valuables.

The defeated Armada's retreat through the Channel was cut off and the surviving vessels were forced to make the 2,000-mile journey right round the coast of Britain and Ireland to reach safety. Few of them made it. Fierce storms drove many of the ships on to the wild, rocky coasts of Scotland and Ireland. Those who escaped drowning were often butchered when they struggled ashore.

I soon decided that the only wrecks of interest were off the Irish coast. One of the paymaster vessels, the *Santa Maria de la Rosa*, lay in the Blasket Sound. According to contemporary reports, 'Having broke its anchor in a great gale, it drifted across the Sound and struck the rock called Stromboli; it then disappeared.' Many attempts had been made to find the wreck, but I'd neither read nor heard of any cargo being recovered.

The wreck of the *Gerona*, a galliass that foundered on the north-west coast of Ireland, was of even more interest. Along with other Armada vessels, the *Gerona* had sought shelter in the harbour at Killybegs, and when it was found to be the soundest vessel, most of the nobles transferred themselves and their valuables to it. It proved to be a mistake. The *Gerona* ran aground and sank soon after setting sail.

Although it was not entirely clear whether the Spanish or British government held the title to Armada wrecks in United Kingdom waters, I was confident that having wrecked on the Ulster coast in 1588, when Britain and Spain were at war, the *Gerona* could only be classified as a war prize, and therefore the property of the UK government. I unearthed every scrap of information about the wreck, ploughing through mountains of contemporary documents and tens of thousands of words for the chance remark, the tell-tale detail, the unconsidered item, that others before me might have missed.

The massive bound volumes of the Irish and British State Papers contained most of the available information but I also wrote to the Spanish archive in Seville and found a friendly college professor from Leeds to translate the photocopies they sent. The crucial piece of evidence was in the Irish State Papers. It was late on a cold and dark afternoon, and I had been poring over manuscripts all day. My head ached and my eyes were bloodshot from deciphering archaic scripts and fading copperplate handwriting. I was ready to pack it in for the day, but decided to give it another half-hour. As I turned another page, a phrase leapt out at me. 'Close to and hard by the Castle of Dunluce, it struck the rock called Bunboise and sank.'

I could not wipe the smile from my face. The description was as good as a grid reference. I was now more than confident that I could find what was left of the *Gerona*. My confidence was increased when I studied the 1:25,000 Ordnance Survey map of that area of the coast. Below one steep cliff was a prominent rock named 'Rock of the Spaniards'. The distance from Islay to the wreck-site was no more than forty-five miles, just five hours by boat. I tried to convince Frank and Snowy that we should at least give it a week down there to see if we could find the wreck, but I found myself in a minority of one. The invariable answer from the others was, 'Stick to the *Otranto*, lad. Bird in t'hand is better than two in t'bush.'

I should have stuck to my guns, broken away and set up a new team. Instead I capitulated, though I was less than pleased about it, having spent a lot of time and money on the research. I was even less happy a couple of years later when I saw television pictures of the Belgian diver Robert Stenuit coming up from 'my wreck' with a big gold money-chain around his neck. I was mad with anger and frustration for days afterwards.

Finding a wreck now can be a hugely complex logistical operation, involving months or even years of research in libraries and record offices, and millions of pounds' worth of up-to-the-minute technology: satellite navigation and dynamic positioning to hold station over the wreck, radar, side-scan sonars and submersible remote-operated vehicles (ROVs) to survey it. But in those early days of my diving career, it was rather less complex. Most of the ones we found were close inshore and the research often involved nothing more than buying the local lobstermen a pint. They'd point out sites where they'd lost lobster pots, a good indicator of something unusual on the sea-bed. The local lifeboat station and the farmers whose land abutted the sea were other useful sources of information. As we moved further offshore, fishermen became our prime sources. Wrecks and lost nets go together, so we used to help the local trawlermen recover their nets or clam dredges and in return we got priceless information.

Sometimes even the name of a landscape feature could give a clue to a wreck-site. Years later I was to reflect rue-fully on the number of times we had sailed past Frenchman's Rock on the Rhinns of Islay, without giving it a second thought. Only when I heard that a diver had brought up cannon from a wrecked French man-of-war did I reflect on the origins of the name.

Once we'd worked the easily identifiable wreck-sites, research became the vital factor. I was our nominated researcher – the easy job, according to the other team members. I discovered the prime sources for information on wrecks and read all I could. I soon learned that finding the approximate locations of wrecks was relatively simple. Lloyd's of London had produced the definitive book on the subject: *The Directory of Disasters at Sea, 1900–1965*. It included details of the name, size, weight and brief description of every wreck and the approximate location where it sank. If it was carrying a special cargo, there was also a brief description of that.

Older shipwrecks were covered in the Lloyd's records held in the Old Guildhall in London. Every insured wreck as far back as the 1670s was documented in the Loss Books, a painstaking accumulation of human disaster on an almost unimaginable scale. In the five years between 1864 and 1869 alone, thousands of insured vessels had sunk, 1,000 of which disappeared without trace.

Having chosen a promising wreck from the basic information, I then had to do the detailed research, slowly bringing it to life. Sometimes a chance remark in a book or the files of a local newspaper would set me on the trail. Some vital information was contained in general books – biographies, war histories and so on – but most was buried in the Public Record Office at Kew and the Naval Records Office at Taunton. I always found it a great thrill to get hold of the original papers, sometimes going back two or three hundred years, and read the beautiful, freehand old English script. The Salvage Association in London and the War Risks Insurance Office – which looked after all government-owned cargoes lost during the two world wars – could also supply details of any wreck that was not included in the secret list.

Amongst those wrecks was HMS *Edinburgh* and its cargo of gold, lying inside the Arctic Circle, hundreds of feet below the surface of the Barents Sea. I remembered the name well, for I'd read about it in my earliest days as a diver.

I daydreamed for a few minutes about being the man to find and recover that fabulous cargo, then reluctantly pushed it from my mind. At the time the wreck might as well have been on the moon, for the diving and search technology to reach such depths was just not available. I logged it for a later date and turned back to the humbler rewards in the inshore waters of the west of Scotland.

I spent weeks and sometimes months poring over dusty documents − charts, bills of lading, copies of signals. The most important document of all was usually the captain's report, which contained details of the sinking, including his estimate of the ship's last known position. That was often well wide of the mark however, and no matter how good the documents, they never told the whole story. Having read and researched everything, I then had to talk to survivors and witnesses, if any, and go to the area, gradually building up a picture in my mind that would give us the best approximation of the site of the wreck. Only then would the diving begin.

Sometimes the wreck-site would be immediately obvious; swimming over a wreck that had been well broken up by the action of the sea was like a bird's-eye view of a junk yard. At other times, only an unusually straight line on the sea-bed, an unfamiliar pattern of seaweed or a momentary glint of metal told us we had found it. After a while we learned to read the markings on the ocean floor − rust stains, the scrapes made by trawler otter-boards − and developed an almost instinctive feel for anything unusual about the sea-bed.

It was hard, often frustrating work but there were ways to make the search a little easier. We could do a towed-diver search, or we could get a local trawlerman to do a bottom search with his depth sounder. If he was doing well enough to have a Decca navigational system, it also helped us fix an accurate position.

Even the best available information and equipment was not always enough, however. Wrecks were often simply not where the records or witnesses suggested they should have been and sometimes we found a wreck only to discover that it had already been stripped by pirate salvors. Even when we found an apparently workable, shallow-water wreck, we had to use great caution when approaching the site for the first time. Trailing cables, abandoned fishing nets and collapsing structures were all highly dangerous, and many wrecks carried toxic or unstable cargoes.

Although there were many disappointments, there were plenty of successes too, and being hungry divers we seized any chance of salvage that came our way. When we came upon the wreck of a U-boat in water so shallow that the coning tower occasionally showed above the surface, we decided it was well worth a look. That submarine, U-570, had been ill-fated from the moment it was launched. It ran aground off Iceland and then surfaced off the coast of Britain just as a Sunderland flying boat was passing overhead. To the pilot's astonishment, the U-boat captain promptly hoisted the surrender flag, the only time in history that a ship has been taken prisoner by an aircraft. The crew subjected the skipper to an impromptu court martial at their prisoner-of-war camp because of his cowardice and sentenced him to death. The authorities got to hear of it and moved him to another camp before the sentence could be carried out. His second-in-command was then ordered to escape and salvage some honour by scuttling the U-boat, but was shot dead by the guards as he made the attempt.

U-570 was renamed HMS *Graph* and pressed into service with the Royal Navy after a refit at Barrow. At the end of the war, in a fitting end to an inglorious career, HMS *Graph* broke its tow-line in bad weather as it was being towed away to be scrapped. It went aground near Coul Point in a very exposed position. There it lay for the next twenty-five years. A very nasty reef and a big Atlantic swell running on to the shore made Coul Point look a forbidding place. Admiralty divers had decided the sub was irretrievable, but after our experience in the wild waters of the coast, the tides around Coul Point were child's play to us.

Frank and I dived down to take a look at the submarine; one look was enough. The prow had been smashed open by the pounding it had taken from the sea over the years and there seemed to be bronze torpedo tubes all over the place. We walked back to the car with a spring in our step. The *Otranto* was forgotten for the moment; those torpedo tubes could not be allowed to lie there a moment longer.

When I'd first arrived on Islay the U-boat had been among the list of wrecks we'd offered to purchase. In due course the owners replied. We could buy it for the princely sum of £100. Despite the low price, the others argued that as it was just there for the fish anyway, why pay good money for it when we could have anything worth salvaging for nothing, with no one any the wiser? I hesitated, then gave in.

Willy borrowed an ex-army breakdown wagon with a powerful winch. We got it as close to the *Graph* as possible, then pulled out the winch cable, including extensions, all the way to the site. Our first move was to put down a couple of charges just to loosen things up. Instead of the usual small splash, a water spout twenty feet high erupted from the site. We thought for a moment that a live torpedo had been left on board.

We recovered the tubes over the next few days, and even though the conditions were calm, the shallow water near the wreck made the work very difficult. One minute you were clear of the water altogether, the next a lazy six-foot swell bore down and you had to hang on to any outcrop you could find, before you were washed head over heels on to the rocks. With all three divers tugging, we managed to get the tubes out of the gully where the *Graph* was lying but then the really hard part started, hauling them over rough ground with the swell running over the top of us.

It was all done quite openly and we even stored the tubes next door to the police station. Unknown to us however, Mr Scott, the manager of the Ardbegg Distillery on Islay, who fancied his chances in salvage, had acquired the rights to the *Graph*. He promptly lodged a complaint with the police.

We went straight up to see him and paid him £400 – four times the price of the wreck in the first place. Well satisfied with his effortless profit, he agreed to withdraw his complaint, but the police insisted on taking us to court. We didn't take the case too seriously, but our co-conspirator, Willy Burke, saw it in an entirely different light and retained Joe Beltrami, one of Scotland's leading criminal lawyers. It proved to be a mistake; if Joe Beltrami left Glasgow on a case, the Scottish press sensed a story and followed him.

A couple of days before our court appearance, my next-door neighbour in Keighley asked me, 'What's this about you and this U-boat, Keith?'

'How do you know about that?'

'It's in this morning's *Express*.'

It turned out that all the national papers had covered the story. The Beatles' *Yellow Submarine* was top of the charts at the time and the press had a field day. I tried to smile as everyone I met around the town that day came out with the same joke: 'How about a sub, Keith?'

We stayed overnight in Tarbert on Loch Fyne. The hotel was packed with reporters on their way to Campbelltown. As we drove down the next morning, I turned on the radio. Even Jimmy Young was discussing the trial.

GOLDFINDER

We met Joe at the door of the court. He had already spoken to the Procurator Fiscal and the judge. 'You can fight the case,' he said. 'But it'll last about twelve days and at the end of it, you'll be found guilty and fined £50. Alternatively, you can go in and plead guilty, in which case you'll be out in ten minutes with the same £50 fine.' It didn't take us long to make up our minds. The Sheriff's Court was packed to the rafters. We took our place in the dock, pleaded guilty and Joe put forward our plea in mitigation.

After the sentence – the £50 fine – we were the first to be let out of court and the first thing on our minds was a drink. We were halfway down the main street when we heard a commotion behind us. A whole host of reporters and photographers were chasing us down the street. We dived into the first bar we could find and sat in the darkest corner. No pleading by the press could get us to move, but in the end we decided the only way we'd be able to finish our drinks in peace was to go outside and let them take a few pictures.

The newspaper billboards we passed on the way home told a changing tale the further we got from Campbelltown. In Glasgow we were still 'hero divers' who'd gone wrong, but by the time we got to Keighley we were the worst kind of villains.

A while later, in a memorable piece of poetic justice, our old adversary Mr Scott also finished up in the dock at Campbelltown. The instrument of his downfall was the *Agious Minas*, a Greek vessel loaded to the bridge with Russian timber. It ran into the cliffs just north of the Rhinns of Islay, despite a sea so calm you could have sailed paper boats on it. It lay there below the cliffs, just like a parked car. How a vessel with radar and all the other wonders of modern navigation could do this was a mystery. As the old saying in the fishing industry goes, 'Johnnie Walker must have been at the wheel.'

It ran aground in winter, normally a time of ferocious gales, but the weather remained calm for several weeks. Scrap dealers and timber merchants arrived by the score, offering silly money for the cargo and the wreck, but we bided our time, knowing that the first big blow from the west would put the ship under the water and into our domain. In the end Willy Burke bought the hull and fittings, while Mr Scott got the contract to remove the timber.

He began winching it up the cliffs and carrying it across the moor to the road, but the farmer who owned the land wasn't one to look a gift horse in the mouth, and he promptly started charging Scott a fee for each load he carried across his land. It was proving an expensive operation for him, because to get his timber off the boat, he also had to tie his ropes to the forward mast. That belonged to Willy, who made him pay heavily for the privilege.

Mr Scott had one further price to pay. One night I was approached in the Islay Hotel by his foreman, who'd just lost his job after a big row with his boss. He told me that while removing timber from the *Agious*, Mr Scott had also taken the radio equipment and the tools from the engine room. They were hidden behind some cupboards in his office.

'Will you stand up and be counted?' I asked.

'You can count on it, Keith.'

I got into my car and drove straight to the police station in Bowmore, where I told the desk sergeant the story. Then I decided to wait outside for a few minutes. It was well worth it. There was not much crime in the islands and the police were probably bored out of their minds most of the time. Faced with the chance of some proper police work for once, half a dozen of them came rushing out of the station like Keystone Cops, pulling on their jackets as they ran. They jumped into their Land Rover and tore off to Ardbegg Distillery, where they marched into Scott's office, removed the cupboards and found the radios. Scott duly had his own fifteen minutes of fame with an appearance at the Sheriff's Court.

He also lost his chance of any further profit on the wreck. He had only removed part of the timber when a gale from the west came at last, sinking the wreck and scattering the cargo far and wide. Gullies up the west side of Islay and the other islands were crammed with timber. The locals took full advantage, taking it away by the tractor- and trailer-load, just like the scotch in *Whisky Galore.*

Our first trip down to the vessel was on a stormy day. We walked along the cliff-tops and stood looking down on to the wreck sixty feet below us. The *Agious* was in a sorry state. It was smothered in weed and the No. 3 and 4 holds were under water, and what remained of the bridge section was just showing. The bow section around the No. 1 hold had been driven so far on to the rocks that it couldn't sink.

We climbed down a rope to a ledge on the cliff and then crossed to the bow section of the ship by a ramshackle makeshift bridge – a series of planks from the cargo lashed together with rope. The handrail was another rope from the mast to the shore.

The seas pounding the hull made the ship shift to and fro with a grinding, rumbling sound, which in turn rocked the plank bridge. The sea below it was boiling with white foam. As I put my weight on one set of planks, it dipped alarmingly. Holding my balance became a work of art, especially near the centre, where the hand line was down around my knees.

After all the effort and danger of getting on to the ship we found the amount of scrap to be recovered was very small. The *Agious* had obviously been built to the tightest of budgets and her propeller and most of her pump work was near-worthless cast iron. The No. 1 hold was still full of timber, however. It was too dangerous to get to by boat and the farmer was licking his lips at the prospect of another substantial windfall from his impromptu toll-gate, when I said to Willy, 'If the sums work out, why not try a helicopter?'

He duly hired one. It carried loads of a quarter of a ton, hovering over the hold with its fixed wire hanging down. On grabbing the cable to attach the load of timber, you also got a tremendous shock from the static electricity discharged by the helicopter. Dropping the cable brought the usual cry of 'Soft bastard'.

Removing the timber was like one of those fairy tales about a magic goblet that never empties. The hold was full of water and the level of timber always remained the same, the next layer floating to the surface as the previous one was removed.

CHAPTER SEVEN

TARF'S TAIL

———————•———————

Despite the bad press from my courtroom appearance, after years of wheeling and dealing on the margins of the salvage industry I felt I now had the experience and the confidence to take on more substantial contracts. Knowing that the Salvage Association was desperate to boost competition in an industry dominated by one giant company, I kept pestering them for the chance to prove myself.

Finally it paid off. In the autumn of 1968 the manager, Mr Smith, gave me a piece of paper with three words written on it: '*Johanna Thorden*, Swona', and told me, 'Go and find this or don't come back.' I hurried to begin the research. Over the next couple of weeks, I gradually pieced together the story of the wreck.

A Finnish ship of 5,500 tons, the *Johanna Thorden* was returning from her maiden voyage to New York in January 1937. On board were the young wife of the chief engineer and their six-year-old son. A Danish engineer also had his wife and three-year-old boy with him. Six days out from New York, north-westerly gales blew up. Battered by the wind and heavy seas, the little ship entered the notorious passage through the Pentland Firth. At 4.30 on the morning of 12 January, a few miles from the Pentland Skerries, she was hit by the full force of a southerly gale.

Captain Simola and his Finnish crew may not have been aware of a new light erected at Tor Ness on the island of Hoy while the ship was in New York, or the sheer force of the gale may have pushed the ship too far to the north. Whatever the case, at 5.45 it struck the rocks with a juddering, grinding crash. The impact was so violent that the wireless mast was smashed and swept away. With no means of signalling for help, the crew fought desperately to save the ship and passengers. They collected clothes, soaked them with petrol and set them alight. Forty distress rockets were also fired, but the rain, driven by the howling winds, obscured them.

The storm ground the *Johanna Thorden* relentlessly on to the reef and the captain gave orders to abandon ship. In pitch darkness and towering seas twenty-four people, including the women and children, climbed into one lifeboat, while the captain and the remaining crew clambered into the other.

About eleven o'clock that morning, their lifeboat came ashore on South Ronaldsay. It upended three times in the breakers as it was driven on to the shore and five of the crew were thrown to their deaths in the boiling surf. The survivors staggered to a nearby farmhouse. The first that anyone on the islands knew of the tragedy was when a farmer's wife heard a knock on her door. She opened it expecting to see a neighbour but found instead eight drenched and shivering strangers, some almost naked. She raised the alarm and a search began but there was no sign of the other lifeboat carrying the women and children and the rest of the crew. It eventually came ashore, empty, at Deerness. Dead bodies from the disaster were washed up on five different Orkney islands. The previous night a woman had dreamed that she saw the body of a slim, lovely girl lying among the rocks on South Ronaldsay. Next day, the body of the wife of the

Danish engineer was discovered there.

The survivors told the Receiver of Wrecks at Kirkwall that they had foundered on the Pentland Skerries and that half the broken ship was later carried to Swona by the sea, but the islanders were unanimous that the ship had actually wrecked on Lowther Reef on Swona.

When she broke in two and sank, a cargo which included 100 cars, hundreds of radio receivers and 250 tons of copper went down with her. On 14 January the Lloyd's agent at Kirkwall reported that a small portion of the bows was still showing above water, but there was no sign of the stern portion of the ship containing most of the copper cargo. The relentless gale had driven the wreck on to the Tarf's Tail on the south side of Swona, some four miles from the reef. Part of the wreck could still be seen with huge seas breaking over it.

Then on Monday 18 January, a huge wave lifted the entire bow and swivelled it around. The ship remained poised on the rocks until the next big wave swept her away. Hides, fruit, raw tobacco, paraffin wax, motor tyres and other cargo were washed ashore, but the copper remained buried beneath the waves. In 1969 copper was worth more than £500 a ton, valuing the *Johanna Thorden*'s cargo at £125,000. There was only one problem. Despite the value of the cargo, every salvage company had turned down the chance to work the wreck, for it lay in a dangerously exposed position in the centre of the Pentland Firth, swept by its ferocious tides.

I carried the piece of paper Mr Smith had given me around for quite a while, then travelling back from Islay on the ferry one day, Frank got talking to a coastguard officer who was doing an inspection tour and who had at one time been stationed in the Orkneys. We told him that we'd soon be paying a visit to the island to look for a sunken wreck and he mentioned a few people who might be of help. Robert Swanney, the son of the owner of the Point of Ayre hotel in Kirkwall, had got himself involved in a bit of salvage work on the blockships which had been sunk in the passages into the fleet anchorage at Scapa Flow to stop enemy U-boats from getting through. Ginger Brown from Stromness had worked for Cox and Danks, the company that had bought and lifted a part of the German battle fleet that had scuttled itself in the Flow just after the end of the First World War. The coastguard officer also mentioned the Rosie family of South Ronaldsay. Mac Rosie lived at Sandwick Bay and fished the lobsters around the island of Swona. His brother, Jimmy, lived right down on the tip of South Ronaldsay. He had also been involved with wrecks in the past. There was also another Jimmy Rosie, no relation to the others, who actually lived on the island of Swona with his sister. That made my ears prick up. The third of the three words on my scrap of paper was 'Swona'. By this time I had done a con-siderable amount of research on the *Johanna Thorden*, and I knew that if the ship and her cargo had survived their battering by the sea, they would be found somewhere off the southern tip of Swona.

We made our first trip to Orkney soon afterwards, flying up from Glasgow; how the times were changing. We hired a car on the island, booked in at the Point of Ayre Hotel and set about making contacts. Robert Swanney, who ran the hotel, still owned a few of the blockships in Kirk Sound – the one used by the U-boat U-47, which sank the *Royal Oak* in the fleet anchorage on the night of 13 October 1939. An Orkney man was turning his car round by the commu-nity hall that night when his headlights picked out the shape of a submarine. He assumed it was British and went home to bed. Two hours later the *Royal Oak* exploded and sank.

Robert Swanney told us he would pass on his rights of

salvage in the blockships for a consideration and we set off in good spirits for our next visit, to Ginger Brown at Stromness. He was a little stooped, with thinning hair and watery eyes, but you could tell he'd been a powerful man in his youth. He had a great fund of stories about the raising of the German fleet and told us about a large propeller still attached to one of the sunken blockships. He let us know that he wasn't averse to recovering a bit of scrap himself. There was plenty around, for the Orkneys had been the main British naval base through two world wars.

Ginger owned a small stern-type trawler, the *Three Boys*. It had a forward wheelhouse, leaving lots of deck space at the rear, ideal for lifting a bit of scrap. Would he be interested in a 'no cure, no pay' deal, using his trawler to lift a nice little cargo? He would. All we had to do now was find the wreck.

Next we went to see Mac Rosie, who lived in a small croft at the head of Sandwick Bay. From his front door there was a spectacular view over the Pentland Firth. Right in the middle was the island of Swona. It was a little over a mile long and barely half a mile wide, and slightly crescent-shaped, with the two tips of the crescent facing the west. Mac was a small wiry man with a strong liking for a dram and a permanent twinkle in his eye. His silver-haired wife Maggie was twice his size and ran the croft with a rod of iron, but she was warm and kind-hearted and there was always a kettle bubbling on the peat fire, ready to make a cup of tea for visitors.

Our first meeting with them was altogether different from the one with Ginger. They were very cautious at first; after all, we were strangers. After hours of polite chat, punctuated by long silences, we finally got around to our interest in the wrecks around Swona.

'That may be a problem,' said Mac. 'Jimmy Rosie owns

the island and thinks he also owns all the wrecks around it.'

I had to stifle a smile. 'All the wrecks' was music to my ears.

I realised that if we were going to get anywhere, it would be better to show some trust in them, so I named the wreck we were interested in and told Mac that if we found it there would be a season's work in it for him. That seemed to remove most of his lingering doubts and a trip to the island suddenly became a possibility. He had a number of places in mind for us to search, where he had lost lobster pots in the past.

He knew of one wreck near the southern end of the island, which he called the Marmalade Boat, after a part-cargo it had been carrying. The islanders of South Ronaldsay had collected a lifetime's supply of marmalade from the beaches. I didn't recall any on the manifest of the *Johanna Thorden* and pressed him for details of other wrecks. I soon learned that most of them were named after their cargoes. The SS *Politician* on Barra was known as the Whisky Boat and the *Agious* on Islay had already been rechristened the Timber Boat.

Just around the coast from where the *Johanna Thorden* sank was a wreck Mac's brother Jimmy called the Cornflake Boat. He told us the story at his small croft right on the southern tip of South Ronaldsay, looking out over the Pentland Skerries. A Swedish ship, the *Gunnaren*, ran aground on Swona one summer night. Jimmy was one of the men appointed by the local customs officers to mount guard by day to ensure that no one helped themselves to the cargo. Jimmy had other ideas. During the night, he and a couple of friends sailed across to the island, climbed on to the *Gunnaren* and after rummaging through the hold in the dark, came away with their small boat loaded down to the gunwales.

The following morning he turned up as usual to do his day's duty. 'We must have had a right bunch of lunatics on board last night,' the customs officer said. 'Just look at this.' He showed Jimmy the hold he had scavenged the previous night. There were boxes and boxes of brand-new Remington typewriters, still stacked up, untouched. 'Look,' he said. 'All they took were a few boxes of cornflakes.'

The story inevitably got about and Jimmy had to endure a good deal of leg-pulling, but whenever he was asked, 'Why the cornflakes Jimmy?' he had the perfect answer: 'You can't eat typewriters.'

It was too late in the season to begin the search for the *Johanna Thorden* but before we parted company from Mac, we arranged that he would ring us in spring as soon as the conditions were right for us to return to Swona. We went to bed that night happy men. Before we left the islands the next morning, we went to look at the *Irene*, a wreck that cost the lives of the crew of the Longhope lifeboat as they went to its assistance. On seeing it for the first time I was staggered; the crew could almost have stepped ashore from the wreck at low water. To get on board we simply walked down to the beach and climbed up a rope ladder. The Longhope lifeboatmen lost their lives trying to save men who could have saved themselves without risk to anyone.

We went south to begin our winter routine. We stayed in Keighley, listening to the shipping forecast and poring over the weather charts. Whenever a clear, calm spell of weather was forecast or a period of easterly winds that would flatten the seas on the west coast, we made the dash from Keighley to Islay to grab another load of scrap from the *Otranto*.

One bitterly cold morning, having driven all night, we arrived at Kilchiaran at first light. A stiff easterly was blowing down from the hilltop. Getting into a cold, damp wet suit was not the ideal way to start the day after a sleepless night, but I just had to grit my teeth and get on with it. Getting into the water took even greater determination, though it was actually warmer than the air temperature.

We worked all day, getting colder and colder, but the worst part came when we had to come out of the sea. A full snow storm was blowing as numb with cold, we stripped off our suits and began making feeble attempts to dry ourselves with a towel that was already three parts soaked. The only thing that kept us moving was the sight of the fire Willy had made from the timbers of the old lifeboat. He had a skillet full of steaks cooking over it. The next morning, gleaming among the cold ashes from the fire were the hundreds of copper nails that had once held the lifeboat together. We gathered them up and found we had another half-hundred-weight of copper to weigh in.

As the days began to lengthen again and the weather started to improve we waited with growing impatience for the call from Mac to return to Swona. Finally it came. We returned to the Orkneys within days, with all our diving gear. Frank had decided he would do a dive in Hoy Sound on one of the blockships to look for Ginger's propeller, while Snowy and I went with Mac to look for the *Johanna Thorden*.

I arrived at Mac's place feeling rather apprehensive. I'd been doing a lot of reading about the terrible tides in the Pentland Firth. In certain places, the spring tides could reach as high as thirteen knots. As we waited for Mac, we watched a big ship attempting to make the passage through the Firth. It appeared to be moving at a fair speed from the bow wave it was creating, but we realised it was making no headway at all, held stationary by the power of the onrushing tide. After a time there was a puff of black smoke from the funnel and the ship fell away back down the tide to await slack water or take the longer route up and around the islands. Mac had been sailing the Firth all his life and explained that we had to work with the tides; the ebb took you across to Swona, the flood brought you back.

His boat was home made, about seventeen feet long and very beamy (wide). He'd also built the slipway on which it was pulled out of the water every night, using an ingenious pulley system he'd invented. The boat had a lugsail and a small Ford side-valve engine. On seeing it for the first time, Snowy and I were even more nervous; the tiny engine didn't look as though it would get us anywhere.

Mac's partner in his lobster business, Murdo, was also on board. He was Mac's opposite. Mac was thin and elfish-looking, but Murdo carried a bit of weight and had a round, ruddy face. Before we got into the boat they took on a fresh load of lobster bait from a barrel of the most vile, stinking dead fish imaginable. A few scoops of this evil brew were transferred to a container on the boat. Mac assured me that the lobsters liked the smell, but one whiff would have made half the so-called sailors I knew at the time run for the side.

Snowy and I got ourselves and our gear into the bows of the boat and away we went. Instead of heading straight for the island, Mac set a course a little to the north, to catch the last of the ebb, taking us across quicker and saving petrol. As we came close to the island, he cut across the clearly visible current and got the boat into the flow that ran down the east side. It swept us down to the Haven, a small anchorage where Jimmy Rosie of Swona kept his boat.

I now found out that Mac was not only the lobsterman but the island postman and delivery man as well. Mail and provisions were handed over to Jimmy, while Mac and Murdo took delivery of a few bottles of Jimmy's home-brewed beer in return. It looked horrible stuff and smelt almost as bad as the lobster bait. A sip of it later in the day was enough to convince me to leave it well alone in future, but Mac and Murdo seemed to love it.

After the two lads had had their drink it was slack water and we got down to the serious stuff, moving slowly down the east side of the island towards the Tarf's Tail, where the wreck had foundered. I had no idea what a tarf was but it must have been a pretty unpleasant creature, judging by the sharp rocks and fierce seas that lashed around its tail. Mac suggested a couple of places for us to dive where he'd noticed that the lobsters were often rust-coloured, suggesting iron-staining from a sunken wreck.

The visibility underwater was good – up to eighty feet – but we could find no sign of wreckage whatsoever. I was beginning to worry. Had the fierce tides carried it away into deep water? Then on our next dive we saw it, lying in about sixty feet of water. The whole bow section of the ship had been broken up by the surging tides, but I could see coils and coils of copper wire lying in what had been the forward holds. We paid scant attention to the wreck's position or anything else. We had found it, that was enough. All we wanted to do now was get ready to start diving for metal.

Before that, we had to learn our first lesson about the tides in the Pentland Firth. The incoming flood tide sweeps up the Atlantic from the south towards the British Isles. The main wave carries on up the Irish coast at a far greater speed than the part that splits at Land's End and goes up the English Channel, where the narrow Straits of Dover restrict the flow of water into the North Sea.

All through the ebb, however, the North Sea has been emptying itself at its northern end. By the time the new flood tide reaches the north of Scotland, having travelled unimpeded up the west coast, the sea level in the North Sea is many feet lower than the inrushing tide. That imbalance produces the terrible tides in the Pentland Firth, as the sea roars through the narrow passage between the Orkneys and the north coast of Scotland. On the ebb, the returning tide rips back into the northern reaches of the Atlantic with the same frightening velocity.

Even after checking all Mac's lobster pots around the island, we still had time to kill waiting for the flood tide to run off a little and take us back across the Firth. He put us ashore for a look around, whilst he and Murdo sank a few more bottles of Jimmy's home-brew.

There were steep cliffs on the east side of the island, but the land sloped down more gently towards the rocky fore-shore to the west. A few sheep were grazing the coarse grass-land and we saw many eider ducks nesting amongst the tussocks of grass. A community of small crofts and even a school had once survived on Swona but now only Jimmy Rosie and his sister remained. We passed a number of ruins and empty crofts, but the main one was easily recognisable by the smoke coming from the chimney. Already briefed by Mac, Jimmy invited us in.

Going through the door was like stepping back in time. I'll never forget the sight of his sister sweeping the ashes from the hearth with a raven's wing. They lived a life as simple, hard and frugal as any monk, but wanted no other. They could both walk among the seals on the beaches of Swona as if they were members of the tribe. If I tried, the seals either attacked me or ran away.

I got to know Jimmy well while we were working off Swona, but his sister was much less approachable. When she saw the boat coming, she usually disappeared and stayed in hiding somewhere until we'd left the island.

Jimmy was happy to talk about the wreck of the *Johanna Thorden* and even brought out some local press cuttings. They told the story of the wreck and showed an aerial view of the ship stranded and breaking up at the place we had just

118

dived. We were definitely in the right place, on the right wreck.

As we started back to the boat, we saw that a change in the weather had taken place. A cold easterly breeze had sprung up. It meant nothing to us until we reached the bay where Mac and Murdo were waiting. Instead of the relatively calm sea we had left as we set off to explore the island, the boat now appeared to be in an eddy. What was going on outside it did not bear looking at. A raging torrent was hitting the west side of the island and coming around the southern end at a speed I would not have believed possible if I hadn't seen it with my own eyes. As he got ready to cast off, Mac told us that the build-up of the flood tide from the west raised the water level on that side of the island some three feet higher than on the east. The easterly wind into the tide was not making our passage back to the mainland look any easier. How the hell were we going to get back through this devil's cauldron?

While we'd been exploring the island, Mac and Murdo had been polishing off the home-brew. They were in fair form and didn't even seem to notice the sea conditions. I had eyes for nothing else. To make matters worse, when he cast off Mac appeared to be steering the boat in completely the wrong direction. Instead of north-east, we were heading south-east, directly towards the Pentland Skerries, a place that any sailor knows to avoid at all costs. We sailed down the edge of the tidal race, which was worse than anything I'd ever seen. It was like a river in flood within the sea, with giant waves towering above us. I tried not to look too closely at it. Both Snowy and I were prepared to swim if we had to, but we wouldn't have lasted long in that hellish tide.

After what appeared to be hours but must have been ten minutes, Mac changed direction, hoisted the lugsail and away we went, skimming over the waves into the bay and home. We were drenched to the skin and freezing cold but mightily pleased to be safe on dry land. Mac had used the edge of the flood tide to get him to the point where part of it was hitting South Ronaldsay and being diverted up towards Scapa Flow. It carried us all the way back to the jetty and safety. It was clear we had an awful lot to learn about the local sea conditions.

I now had to go back to the Salvage Association and give Mr Smith the good news about the *Johanna Thorden*. I also had to decide the percentage we'd offer the underwriters on a 'no cure, no pay' contract for the right to recover the cargo. The British & Foreign Insurance Company had covered the copper for £17,000 in 1937. It was now worth ten times that amount. I'd heard plenty of complaints about greedy salvors and I resolved to offer the underwriters a good enough return for them to be eager to find me more work.

A short time later I was told that we'd got the rights. The agreement was signed on 27 May 1969. I was on my way. An overdraft was arranged with a bank in Keighley to cover the time until we could sell the copper – there were still mouths to feed. A couple of weeks later, we arrived back in Orkney to start work on the *Johanna Thorden*.

Ginger's son, George, was the skipper of the *Three Boys*. He kept the boat in Stromness and though working from there meant a long sail across Scapa Flow and back every day, he didn't seem to mind. He just wanted the *Three Boys* safe in Stromness harbour every night.

We quickly dropped into a routine. At the start of the day George would come over from Stromness and pick up Mac, Frank, Snowy and me from Mac's place. Mac was our pilot. His job was to show us how to work the tides in the area of the wreck and without him we would have had big problems. He told us that we could only work the wreck during the flood tide which hits the west side of the island and swirls around it, creating a giant eddy at the southern end, right over the place where the *Johanna Thorden* lay. 'Once the ebb tide starts to run there's no chance at all of diving,' he said. We nudged each other thinking, 'What does he know about diving?' But we were soon to learn that he was right.

As Mac had planned, we arrived on our first day on site just as the last of the ebb tide was running away. The sea in the area of the wreck was flat calm. You could have paddled a bathtub around the Tarf's Tail. That didn't last long and the flood tide was soon roaring around the point.

On the first dive we did a quick survey of the wreck. It was lying in a steep gully. The bows were pointing towards the shore, about thirty feet down at low water. The seaward end of the wreck was a further sixty feet down. The whole of the stern section of the vessel was missing, but we would worry about that later. We had No. 1 and 2 holds to work first.

The wreck was partially shielded from the flood tide by a ridge of rock that ran out from the island. Only the protection of the ridge enabled us to work it at all; without it, the cargo of the *Johanna Thorden* would still be lying on the bottom. We secured a chain to the wreck and fixed the largest orange buoy we could find, two feet across, on the end of it. The force of the ebb tide took the buoy right to the bottom, but once the tide ran off, it popped up again like magic, signalling that it was time to start work.

Diving on the *Johanna Thorden* was unlike anything I had ever experienced. It was a pig to work from start to finish and very frightening. It was plain suicide to enter the water during the ebb tide, which ran straight across the wreck-site at a terrifying speed. But diving over the flood tide meant working at depths varying from a reasonably safe fifty feet down to a potentially lethal 120 feet.

I knew that it was possible to get scuba divers down to almost 200 feet, but the limited time they could spend there didn't compensate for the long periods they had to spend in decompression afterwards. Even at 100 feet, the recommended working time was a paltry twenty minutes. Any longer and decompression was necessary. I knew precious little about proper decompression procedures, but despite the dangers, I made countless dives to 120 feet looking for the stern section. We gradually employed extra divers with us, again on 'no cure, no pay' terms, but I was the only member of the team prepared to work that deep.

My only knowledge of the techniques associated with decompression had been gleaned from hearsay and the British Sub-Aqua Club Diving Manual. Now that I was diving regularly into the danger zone, however, I began to take a much more active interest in the subject. I studied every text I could get my hands on, including the US Navy Diving Manual, which had the most up-to-date information. I also began trying to learn more about the physics of diving, for men plumbing the ocean depths need at least a working knowledge of it if they are to survive.

Dimly remembered names from school science lessons – Boyle's Law, Charles' Law, Dalton's Law – suddenly assumed a vital interest for me that even the most charismatic of physics teachers could not have induced. The consequences of changes in pressure, temperature and volume on gases were no longer academic; they could make the difference between life and death. If a diver cannot make the necessary allowances for temperature and pressure when reading the gauges of his breathing equipment, or cannot assess the capacity of a compressor to deliver the necessary air to a given operating depth, or is unaware of the effects that changing pressure will have on the gas in his lungs, his next dive into the depths may be a one-way trip.

Boyle's Law states that the pressure and volume of a gas are inversely related – the higher the pressure, the smaller the volume. Descending from the surface to 33 feet doubles the pressure and halves the volume of any quantity of gas. The change in volume is directly proportional to the change in pressure and consequently its effect is most dramatic near the surface. A cubic foot of gas at surface pressure – one atmosphere – occupies half a cubic foot at 33 feet – two atmospheres – and one third of a cubic foot at 66 feet, when the pressure is three atmospheres. The implications for divers of this apparently arcane law of physics are crucial. The volume of gas in a diver's blood increases more in the reduction of a single atmosphere of pressure during the last 33 feet of an ascent than in all the atmospheres of pressure that preceded it, whatever the total depth. The result is the opposite of what a layman might expect; a sudden change in depth while in shallow water is far more dangerous than in the deeps.

The tissues of the human body can withstand enormous pressures. Men have dived well beyond 1,000 feet below the surface without ill-effects, but the problems for divers begin with the effects pressure has not on the tissues but on the gases filling the natural air spaces within the body. High-pressure gas trapped inside poor dental fillings can produce blinding toothache and changes in pressure can also cause serious pain or permanent damage to a diver's ears if they are blocked by wax or the effects of a cold or infection. My eldest son Graham's active diving career was to be cut short and the quality of his life blighted by tinnitus – a permanent ringing in the ears caused by damage sustained on a dive – but there are also other, far more deadly perils awaiting divers.

The more I understood about the physics of diving, the more horrified I was by some of the risks I had already taken.

I could easily have died from an embolism on my first-ever dive and I could well have poisoned myself in the early days through breathing contaminated air. It was a miracle too that I never suffered a bend when returning from the depths, particularly on the *Johanna Thorden*, where I regularly bent the rules of safety to breaking point. I knew enough to realise that the short-cuts could only go so far, however. All divers are governed by a set of physical laws that they transgress at their peril.

Hypoxia – shortage of oxygen – is an obvious potential killer for a diver, but it is equally unsafe to breathe pure oxygen below twenty-five feet, where the greater absorption of oxygen under increasing pressure makes it a poison, not a life-saver. Divers almost invariably breathe a mixture of gases; either normal air, a mixture of roughly 21 per cent oxygen, 78 per cent nitrogen and one per cent other gases, or an inert gas such as helium or neon, acting as a carrier for the oxygen.

Another of those barely remembered physics theorems, Dalton's Law, proves that as depth increases, more molecules of each constituent gas are compressed into the same volume. A diver breathing a normal air mixture under five atmospheres of pressure is inhaling more oxygen than if he was breathing pure oxygen at surface pressure. Absorption of oxygen at surface equivalents of greater than 1.6 atmospheres will lead to oxygen poisoning, which attacks the central nervous system even before it has a noticeable effect on the lungs. A high level of CO_2 in the gas mixture, whether from exertion or contamination, greatly increases the toxicity of the oxygen.

The first symptoms of oxygen poisoning are often involuntary twitches of the facial or other muscles. Tunnel vision, dizziness, headaches, nausea, confusion, lack of co-ordination, extreme fatigue, difficulty in breathing and convulsions will follow. If the oxygen level is not reduced, the diver will die. Similarly, air containing two per cent CO_2 – which is perfectly breathable on dry land – is the surface equivalent of ten per cent CO_2 at five atmospheres of pressure, enough to kill by carbon dioxide poisoning.

Even with the right gas mixture for the depth of the dive, divers must also undergo the correct decompression when returning from the deeps. A balloon full of air taken down to depth will contract to the size of a ping-pong ball and then spring back to its normal size as it is returned to the surface. Human lungs and body tissues do not have the flexibility of a rubber balloon. They act as permeable membranes, diffusing the gas that the diver is breathing throughout his body. Some gases are more readily absorbed than others; nitrogen, for example, is five times more soluble in body fat than it is in water, hastening the possible onset of the narcs – nitrogen narcosis. For this reason, helium or neon is normally used as the inert gas in deep diving.

Once the body is saturated with gas, it will remain in solution within the body as long as the external pressure is maintained. When the diver begins his ascent to the surface however, the dissolved gas will begin to re-emerge from solution. If his rate of ascent is carefully controlled by the lengthy process of decompression, the gas absorbed into the tissues under the pressure of the depths will be returned in the bloodstream to the lungs and safely exhaled. But too swift or too short a decompression causes bubbles to form from the dissolved gases and become trapped in the small blood vessels, causing intense pain in the joints – the bends. If uncorrected, the diver will suffer progressively worse symptoms of decompression sickness. They usually begin during the ascent, but may not be detectable until some time after reaching the surface.

Skin bends occur when gas bubbles form just below the

skin, leading to burning sensations and a vivid red rash or mottling of the skin. The initial hit or bend usually shows itself as a stabbing pain in the arm or leg, however. The pain seems to come from deep within a joint or bone and begins as a slight ache but rapidly becomes unbearable. It often occurs at a previous weak point. I once playfully punched a diver on the upper arm during a test dive in a decompression chamber to 200 feet. On the way back up he took a hit from the bends at the exact spot I had punched him.

In a minority of cases – around five per cent – more severe symptoms may occur. These include the staggers (attacks of severe dizziness), the chokes (inability to breathe), paralysis and unconsciousness. Returning to depth or increasing the pressure will normally alleviate the bends, but seriously ill divers will require more intensive treatment.

Gas embolism is a related but even more serious problem. Gas retained in the lungs during an ascent, either because the diver's air passages have become blocked or because he is holding his breath deliberately or in panic, can kill. The best analogy I could find was a bottle of lemonade with the cap screwed on. If the cap is released, lowering the pressure on the lemonade, the gas in solution in the liquid immediately forms bubbles. The quicker the cap is released, the bigger and faster the bubbles are formed. Rising from the depths too fast is like unscrewing the lid of the bottle. The gas forced through the walls of the lungs by the increase in pressure forms bubbles that may block the arteries, the spinal cord or the brain, or damage the function of the vital organs. Pressure from gas around the heart can slow or stop it altogether, and gas pooling in the chest cavity may cause the collapse of one or both lungs.

Symptoms may not appear until the diver has surfaced, though he will feel a pain like a punch in the chest if one of his lungs ruptures. Within seconds of reaching the surface, however, he may suffer vertigo, blurred vision, difficulty in breathing, cyanosis and partial paralysis. He may collapse and even stop breathing. Any gas embolism will almost invariably disrupt the blood supply to the brain and spinal cord; without prompt treatment, including immediate recompression, the inevitable result will be paralysis, brain damage or death.

My increased knowledge made me a little more wary, but only a little. No sane diver would deliberately risk an attack of the bends but when it came down to it, there was a job to be done and mouths to feed. If there was metal to be salvaged at 120 feet or even deeper, someone had to go down there. There were few volunteers.

To get to the wreck we went down the chain from the buoy hand over hand. All the time the current would be ripping and tearing at us. To let go would have meant being swept off the wreck-site and down the tide towards the Pentland Skerries. Even if I'd shouted my head off after reaching the surface, no one on the boat could have heard me above the noise of the tide.

I clung to the chain until I got into the shelter of the reef. Then all was peace and calm, even though a ferocious tide was rushing past just a few feet above. At times I used to have to look the other way and pretend it wasn't there, but we had a job to do, and the coils of copper were soon coming to the surface.

Long immersion in sea water has little effect on copper, apart from encrustation by barnacles and kelp, and the metal we began recovering was in very good condition despite lying underwater for thirty-two years. Some of it was easy to reach but much of it was trapped beneath other cargo like the old car engines and ships' plates, and we had to blow away the obstructions with explosives.

While we were gathering the copper from the bow

section of the wreck, we also had to give some thought to finding the stern section, where half the cargo had been stowed. Over 100 tons of copper ingots had gone with the stern when it broke away and drifted over a shelf into deeper water. Any search for it could only be done at slack water on neap tides. On spring tides there was no such thing as slack water. One day when the main dive was finished and we had our load for the day, I set off with Mac in his lobster boat. He lowered a line over the side with a very heavy weight to keep it vertical in the water. I then swam down the line. If I spotted anything I could swim over to it and tie off the line as a marker.

There was a very short time – around ten minutes – before the tide started running and dragged me back to the surface. In any event, at this depth I only had a little over ten minutes diving time without having to do decompression stops on the return.

As I clung to the line I could see the direction the stern section must have followed, from the bits of steel plate and the odd copper ingot scattered across the sea-bed, but there was no sign of the section itself. It was also getting steadily deeper the further I got from the island.

Using this method, I carried on the search over a number of days, with Mac using his land markers to put me back exactly where I had finished the day before. On the fifth day I came across what looked like a huge pile of bars. The distortion of colours underwater made them look purple, but I knew that out of the water they would be a vivid green, the colour of copper stained by long immersion in the sea. I swam over and found a mountain of copper ingots, many tons, just lying there on the bottom. They had obviously spilled from the wreck as it broke in two and drifted down the tide. I had one small problem; on this day of all days I didn't have a buoy line with me. I was too far from the ingots to tie the downline to them. I would have had to drag the dinghy over to the ingots and with the tide just starting to run, it was a non-starter, especially at this depth.

I decided to head straight to the surface to let them know what I'd found and to make sure they didn't allow the heavily weighted downline to drag. Trying to control my impatience, I waited while they found a buoy line. Just before I disappeared under the surface again I looked up and said to Murdo, 'Don't let any weight come on to the line.'

'Don't worry yourself about that,' he said, but I noticed him relax his hands and I saw the line zip over the side by a couple of feet. When I got back to the bottom there was no sign of the ingots; we had drifted away from them. That was the end of the dive for that day. We searched and searched for that pile of ingots but never found them again.

After a few more fruitless searches for the stern section from the downline, I swam down to the sea-bed and began following the signs across the bottom, a trail of solitary ingots and coils of copper wire. I had gone some way when I suddenly noticed that I was getting out of the shelter of the reef. The tide was picking at me, trying to pull me from the sea-bed.

Just then, at the limit of my vision – perhaps fifty feet away – I noticed another very large pile of copper ingots and round bars. I was looking at a minimum of £1,000 worth of copper. I swam over to it, but in the excitement of the find I lost my bearings. As I looked around, I realised just how strong the tide had become. As sweat clouded the inside of my mask, I saw plankton, bits of weeds and debris hurtling past me. There was a thud as a thick piece of kelp stem banged into my mask and whirled away on the tide. I knew that if I let go of the ingot I was holding I would be swept away.

I glanced at my contents gauge. I had very little air left. I couldn't go straight to the surface, for I would have been whipped away like a cork in the surf, my cries drowned by the thundering roar of the tide surging through the narrows of the Firth. I came close to panic. All my landmarks had now disappeared, yet I had to find my original start or perish. I searched blindly, groping through the murky water tearing at me.

You do not use a compass when working on a wreck – it would not last long working among the tangles of jagged metal – but divers soon develop an awareness of where they are underwater and how far they have swum in any direction. You also use clues offered by the sea-bed. The angle of the sun's rays, the strata of the rock, the ripples in the sand, the direction of the tide – all may help you to navigate on the bottom and find your way back to your starting point.

I raked the sea-bed with my eyes, but could see nothing obvious. I knew that the tide swirled around the area of the wreck, so the tide direction didn't really help. I was on a rocky, broadly level area. The strata of the rock were similar to slate. I'd noticed the same strata on the island, running in a north-south direction, leaning towards the west. It was the only clue I could find. I set off to work my way across the line of the strata, following the direction that it was leaning. I pulled myself along, hand over hand, never releasing one handhold until I had secured another, my fingers scrabbling for grip on the slimy rock as the tide built towards the flood. If I lost my hold, I knew I would be swept away.

I fought down another wave of panic and crawled on, like a mountaineer dragging himself up a sheer rock face. After an eternity, the sea-bed started to slope upwards. Away to my left I caught a brief flash of something glittering in the murk. A long strand of thick copper wire, its end burnished by the action of the tide, was fluttering in the tidal rip like a cotton thread in a gale. I seized it and began to follow it upwards, still hauling myself hand over hand.

I dragged myself over a ridge and saw the bow section just below me. Almost sobbing with relief, I slid down the rock wall, feeling the strength of the tide easing as I dropped into the shelter of the reef. I climbed the rope to the boat and collapsed on the deck.

CHAPTER EIGHT

THE COPPER KINGS

The copper wire that had saved me on one occasion almost killed me on another. The wire in the holds was in huge tangled bundles of around two or three tons as a result of the breaking up of the vessel and we worked with large wire-clippers to cut away manageable sections.

I was cutting away one day, up inside a bundle when, unbeknown to me, my harness and I became entangled in the wire. I was held fast between the bundle being hauled to the surface and the mass of wire still on the bottom, in the middle of an agonising and terrifying tug-of-war. Somehow I kept my wits and managed to cut myself free before I or my equipment was torn apart.

There was an even worse experience to come, this time caused by sheer blind panic – not mine, because I knew that panic underwater had only one conclusion, death. It came without warning, from someone else. I won't name him, because by now he's probably a good and respected diver. By mid-season we'd increased our team to eight divers, paying them on tonnage recovered. I'd hired this man because of the reluctance of the regular diving team to go deep with me. This man said he would. I pointed out the depth we would be diving to – 120 feet – more than once and asked him if he had done it before.

'Of course, no problem,' was the confident reply.

'Good. Stick with me and we'll be fine.'

We had only been searching on the bottom for five minutes when it happened. He suddenly leaped on my back. His arms tightened round my neck and his legs wound around my waist. I twisted round and one look in his eyes told me everything. He was paralysed with terror.

I fought to free myself but there was no way of breaking his grip. Somehow I had to get us both to the surface. I began swimming slowly towards the downline and then painfully pulling myself upwards, battling against the dead weight of the panic-stricken diver, whose arms were cutting off my air supply.

Every time I looked upwards, the faint grey glow from the surface seemed as far away as ever. My lungs were bursting and my strength ebbing rapidly. Finning desperately up through the water, with the diver still clinging to my back like a limpet, I no longer dared to look up, but concentrated grimly on placing one hand above the other, the muscles in my arms screaming at the effort. Finally I felt the slap of a wave against my head. I spat out my mouthpiece and had just enough energy left to scream, 'Get this bloody monkey off my back.'

Even without attacks from panic-stricken divers, it was a miracle that I never suffered from the bends whilst diving that wreck. Even though I knew the risks, I often went too deep in search of copper. I was lucky, but I had enough sense not to push my luck too far. I was alert for the onset of any symptoms and made sure I always had enough air left to make a decompression stop if necessary. In the event I never needed to, probably because I'd also developed a measure of resistance from the long hours I'd spent underwater. I was more fish than man in those days.

There were rich compensations for the dangers. In 1969,

the first year we spent on the *Johanna Thorden*, we pulled up ninety tons of metal. With scrap copper at a price in excess of £500 per ton, we earned over £45,000 from our year's work. Just as important, from my point of view, I was demonstrating to the Salvage Association and the insurance underwriters that I could deliver the goods and earn them a return on cargoes long given up as lost.

One of our main problems with the copper we were landing was where to store the stuff. It had to be put straight into bond, but there was no customs enclosure on the island. Luckily, there were three old sheds standing empty on the end of Scapa Pier. We hired them from the Pier Master. The excise men took a more than passing interest in the sheds. They checked them regularly and put their own locks on the door.

We soon filled the sheds so full that we were forced to stop diving until we'd sold the copper. It was a jumbled mess of barnacle-encrusted ingots, bars, billets and wire, but it gleamed like gold to us. I called the Salvage Association in London. 'No problem,' Mr Smith said. 'Just inform Customs that you're going to ship the copper to the smelters in the Midlands.' I also had to sign a document allowing the customs officers to actually see the wire going into the furnaces, just to reassure themselves that we weren't pulling a scam and selling it as new copper.

All unwrought copper – bars, billets and ingots – comes into the country duty free. Duty is payable on wrought copper such as the copper wire which made up the majority of the *Johanna Thorden*'s cargo, unless it's classified as scrap. There had been no doubt in our own minds or those of the customs officers that our tangled mess of wire could only be scrap metal.

I strolled into the customs office in Kirkwall one day to finalise the details. The duty officer greeted me with a sardonic grin. 'Good morning, Mr Jessop, we have some good news for you. You owe us twenty-two thousand pounds. The copper incurs import duty of eleven thousand pounds and an import levy of another eleven thousand pounds. The wire is being classified as new rather than scrap.'

This was the year of Our Lord Harold Wilson. His government had decreed that all imports were to have an extra levy placed on them to deter people from buying goods from abroad and since the *Johanna Thorden*'s cargo of copper had been bound for Sweden when it sank, an import levy was now required.

'You're classifying it as new copper?'

'That's right.'

'Then get the price for new copper and I'll gladly pay you your duty.'

There was no response. I was speechless, but not for long. I raged around the office, threatening to throw all the copper back in the sea, though that wouldn't have pleased our bank manager, who had advanced us £10,000 against it.

I eventually stormed out of the office and phoned Mr Smith again. 'Calm down,' he said. 'Go and have a cup of coffee. I'll sort it out and call you back within fifteen minutes.'

He was as good as his word. After speaking to him again I went back to Customs with my wife Mildred as a witness, filled in a form and made a declaration that the copper was leaving bond only to be shipped abroad. With the help of the Salvage Association we then sold the copper to West Germany and received £14 per ton more than we'd been offered by the British scrap merchants. The Germans promptly melted it down and sold it back to Britain, placing a small extra strain on our balance of payments deficit. Before the following diving season, I received a letter from a senior government official asking us to dispose of the rest of the copper in Britain, where there was an urgent need for it. Of course there would be no duty or import levy to pay. Strange are the ways of governments.

Our first pay-out from the sale of the copper brought a few changes to my life. My promise to Mildred that one day my salvage efforts would pay off had now come true. For the first time in our married life we'd money in the bank and no debts. The first thing we did was to buy the council house we lived in, for cash, and then we spent almost as much again renovating the place. I also bought an almost new car, once again paid for in cash.

Although the *Johanna Thorden* was giving me a good living and occupying most of my attention, I wasn't averse to earning a few quid on the side when the opportunity presented itself. Towards the end of that first season in the Orkneys, I was introduced to Giles Neels, a BBC producer. He was making a programme about the scuttling of the German fleet in Scapa Flow at the end of the First World War and asked if I could shoot some film of one of the German vessels on the sea-bed. The fee was more than generous.

We had our own underwater camera, but Giles insisted that I use the BBC's top-quality equipment. 'We can't afford any mistakes, Keith.'

The next day dawned clear and calm, perfect for the job in hand. Frank and I got ourselves ready, dropped over the side and Giles passed me the camera. 'Be careful with it.'

'Of course.' As soon as I disappeared below the surface, I noticed a thin stream of air bubbles coming from the supposedly waterproof outer case of the camera. I peered at the lens. It was already a quarter full of sea water. I returned to the surface. 'Sorry Giles, but I think you'll find your camera is knackered.'

Giles returned to London without his underwater sequence, but I promised to do what I could with my own camera. A couple of days later, on our way back from the *Johanna Thorden*, we passed the wreck of the *Royal Oak*. The massive 35,000-ton battleship lay upside down on the bottom, its keel so close to the surface you could see it from the aircraft as you came in over Scapa Flow to land at Orkney Airport. I decided that one sunken wreck was as good as another and told the lads to drop me off and come back in ten minutes. If they'd stayed on site, someone would have been straight out to investigate what we were up to.

Looking up at the *Royal Oak* from the sea-bed was an awe-inspiring sight. She was resting on her director tower, her forward, aft and waist guns sticking out like so many fingers. I didn't let my awe blind me to more prosaic matters but sadly the ship's propellers were already missing, taken by the Navy for scrap.

Giles was delighted with my film and a few days later I saw my handiwork on the BBC, the unmistakable outline of the *Royal Oak* movingly described as a sunken German battleship. Sorry Giles.

Through the BBC I'd met Arthur Nundy, who owned the wrecks of the German fleet in Scapa Flow and the giant British naval bases on Hoy and Flotta. We made a trip over to Arthur's place on Hoy one day to borrow some detonators and had a good laugh over the filming incident. He always had a smile on his lips, but his dark eyes held the brooding look of a man who had seen many things in his life. He also had a damaged arm, the result of a bad bend while diving.

The fact that we were not just divers but salvage men made us an instant hit with Arthur, and he took us on a tour of his kingdom. For thousands of servicemen, the last sight of Britain had been this grim and lonely place. Some of the buildings had been pulled down, but many were still standing, including the mess halls and the camp cinema. They were eerie places, the sea-mist filling them with ghosts. There was also a ruined building with a domed roof like the London Planetarium, where gunners had once practised shooting at silhouettes of aircraft projected on to the dome.

Arthur's salvage vessel, the *Barholm*, was an ex-naval bar boat, stripped of every superfluous item; even the floor boards had been removed. The only inessential was the growth of weed on the bottom, which must have been at least a yard long.

The scrapyard at the pier was loaded with metal from the German fleet. There were stacks of massive pieces of armour-plating, and we saw a couple of his lads stripping a giant generator. Arthur was also sitting on a coal mine. The fleets of two world wars had coaled their vessels at the piers. Any time he needed some coal, all he had to do was put a grab on the derrick and drop it over the side of the pier.

As we were walking around the base, Arthur spotted a piece of thickish electric cable sticking up from the ground. 'Just wait here lads,' he said. He disappeared, only to return on his tractor. He tied the cable to the back of the tractor and started to pull it backwards and forwards. Somehow he managed to overturn the tractor in the process. He jumped clear but broke his arm.

With thousands of tons of scrap metal at his disposal, it seemed crazy to be dragging at a few pounds' worth with a tractor, but that was Arthur. He was a true scrap man at heart. Nothing that might have a value was ever thrown away. If he'd seen a sixpence superglued to a path he'd have used dynamite to get it off. He was still trying to do deals as we helped him on to the boat to take him to a doctor. 'Do you want some caustic soda for washing down?' he asked, pointing to a shed full of mouldering containers. He had tons of it, left by the Navy decades before. It was in a real state.

Arthur was nearing retirement and later offered to sell me his whole business – the naval base, the piers, his boat and the remains of the German fleet resting on the bottom. The asking price was £90,000. It was a huge amount of money in those days and reluctantly I turned it down. Had I bought it, I'd have made my first million without breaking sweat. The giant oil company Occidental later built their North Sea base there and paid a fortune for the site.

At the end of our first season on the *Johanna Thorden*, we went back to Islay for the winter period. By then we were one partner short however, for Snowy had done a bunk. One morning when the weather was too rough to dive, Frank and I had gone down to Kirkwall. By the time we got back, Snowy had disappeared, leaving no word of explanation. It saddened me. We'd been through a lot of tough times together and I liked and respected Snowy. I could think of no incident in the previous few days that would have driven him to leave.

Ever since Frank had joined us on a fairly full-time basis, there had been three of us, and when three work together, it always tends to be two against one. It changed around – it wasn't always the same two – but it created friction. Back in Keighley, we spent very little time in each other's company. We were three entirely different people, each with our own strengths and weaknesses, and had virtually nothing in common other than salvage, but until Snowy's disappearing act we'd always managed to set aside our personal differences.

We worked very well as a team on the wrecks and that was the bond – the only one – that held us together. The only reason I could come up with for Snowy's sudden exit was that up to that time we'd always worked as three equal partners and he might have felt that he was getting left out of the work in the Orkneys. That was certainly not my intention. There was no one more disappointed than me when I found he'd gone. If the three of us could have got along better, I really believe we could have gone on to build a very successful salvage business, outstripping any other in the British Isles at the time, but it just didn't work out, which was a great pity.

A short time later Snowy was back on Islay, but not to work with us. He'd joined forces with Peter Sellars and Big John to salvage the wreck of the *Rothesay Castle* off Nave Island, on the north-west tip. A little later he tried his hand in the North Sea, then gave up diving and bought himself a big lorry. Over the years he's done very well; he deserves to, he's worked hard for it, but I never did find out why he'd left us in Orkney.

We'd assembled a good team of divers during the summer and wanted to keep them together ready for the next season on Orkney. We hired an MFV, a 65-footer called the *Golden West*, out of Tarbert on Loch Fyne to help us work the *Otranto*. After a couple of good lifts from the wreck, we bought the boat outright for £4,000. Once again we were sailors, but this time the craft was a far cry from the oily old tub we had sailed out of Fleetwood a few years before.

After what had happened to Willy Burke's launch, we knew we couldn't berth the *Golden West* on the west coast of Islay overnight. We needed a safe harbour. There were only two choices: Port Ellen on the south-east corner of the island, or Port Askaig up the Sound of Islay. In the wrong conditions the approach to either of them could turn your hair white. We chose Port Ellen.

To reach the *Otranto* we had to pass first the Mull of Oa and then the Rhinns of Islay at the south-west tip of the island. The winds and tides there could be terrifying. If you caught it at the wrong time, a tremendous tidal race against the wind made it a passage for the brave only. Willy convinced us that he knew the passage between the main island and the small island, on which the lighthouse stood, like the back of his hand. The channel was narrow and shallow and we touched once or twice, but it was better than taking a battering from the wind and tide on the outside.

There were some tense moments at the top end of the passage, however. You had to line up a set of markers on the starboard side, then go hard a-port until the passage opened up between the island and Frenchman's Rocks, a vicious group of jagged rocks. Once through the gap, you were on the west coast. On the north-going tide the passage could be like a millpond, but when the tide was running south it was another story. Many times I steered the *Golden West* through the white water, with everything fastened down and the rest of the crew hanging on for grim death. Big as she was, the boat would go on her beam ends but somehow we always made it.

After one hard day's work, I was approaching the passage in a roughish sea, when I saw the power of the tide was making the water look calm. I looked to the south of the passage. If you could see white water there, you knew you were in for a rough one. The sea was boiling with foam. It was now 'make your mind up' time. I had to decide immediately, because once caught by the current, there was no chance of turning around, you just had to go for it. I turned the boat around and made the long journey all the way back round the island to Port Askaig. It was a long, rough journey, for by now a full south-west gale was blowing and a giant swell was building. It took us the best part of five hours. All that rather than face the 200 yards of wild water leading to the passage between the islands. Anyone who wants to dispute my choice is welcome to try it for themselves. Their boat could easily end up as an underwater salvage man's next job.

The only place that approached it for danger was off the north end of Jura. We'd often sail up the west coast, a magnificent journey on a good day. There were wild deer and goats feeding near the shoreline and golden eagles soaring over the rocky cliffs, an unforgettable sight. You had to be sure that the tide was right before entering the Gulf of Corryvreckan, however. There was a huge whirlpool there created by the tide and an awful battering awaited you if you got it wrong.

The *Golden West* changed our work routine in many ways. We could keep a better eye on the rest of the diving team now that they slept on board and we no longer needed the ferries to run our hard-earned scrap to the mainland. But using our own ship did bring its own problems. We put one load of scrap aboard the *Golden West* and sailed round the Mull of Kintyre and across the Firth of Clyde. Our lorry arrived at the docks early the next morning and we were just about to start loading it when down the jetty came a chap from the dockers' union with two of his henchmen.

'What do you think you're doing?' he said in his near-incomprehensible accent. 'What the fucking hell do you think you're doing?'

'Loading our scrap on our lorry.'

'You can't do that. This is a union-controlled dock.' He glanced around him. 'We need to have a chat.'

We stopped work and had a chat around a table over a mug of tea. It soon became obvious that union rights came a distant second to the chance of a back-hander. By luck one of the lads was taking a bottle of Islay whisky back home. This was put on the table, but it was made clear that would only do for starters. A cash donation would also be needed.

'Listen,' I said. 'The money for the sale of the scrap is being brought to the dock by car. We'll make sure a few quid finds its way into your pockets.'

By now he was convinced we were not a bad set of blokes, though he could also see that there were half a dozen of us, all very fit lads.

All good friends now, we asked, 'No problem loading the wagon whilst we wait for the money?'

'Go ahead,' he said, 'But don't leave the dock.' We took our time loading the wagon, skylarking to put the dockers at ease. Lunchtime approached and like all good union men on the docks, once it was time to stop doing nothing they all disappeared to the pub. We glanced around the deserted dock and were away like a shot from a gun. We had weighed in our scrap, collected our cash and were back at sea before the dockers even knew we were gone.

On our way back up to Islay one night the following week, we chose to go up in one of our divers' cars. His liking for all things American was reflected in his choice of vehicle, a large black American hearse. It was a handy car for the job, with lots of room for us and the 200 pounds of explosives we were taking up to the island. It was rather cramped in the front so I decided to get in the back and have a sleep. As we went down Western Avenue in Glasgow, I was awakened by a siren and the blue flashing lights of a police car. Oh hell, I thought, we're going to have to explain about the explosives.

The police thought they had caught us doing a runner with a corpse, as someone had reported seeing a body in the back. Then I came to life and reared up in the back. 'What the hell's going on?' They went white for a second, then burst out laughing. They waved us on our way, luckily without noticing the explosives. I didn't know much about the laws governing the transport of high explosive, but I was pretty sure that carrying it in the back of a hearse was not an approved method.

Early the next spring we sailed the *Golden West* all the way back from Islay to the Orkneys, stopping to follow up any rumours of wrecks along the way. We revelled in the challenges that presented themselves on those wild coasts, constantly breaking all the rules of diving and getting away with it. They were real roustabout days, full of adventure, incident and danger. Working the *Johanna Thorden* had earned us the local nickname the Copper Kings, and it was one of the most prosperous periods of my early career as a salvage diver. Looking back now, I turn cold at some of the risks I took, but I was in my prime then, supremely fit and confident to the point of arrogance in my ability.

When we arrived back in Orkney, we found another salvage vessel, a green trawler, tied up alongside the pier at St Margaret Hope. It belonged to a team from the south of England who had bought the rights to a sunken German U-boat, the U–116, for just seven shillings and sixpence. It had struck a mine and gone down in Panhope Bay during the First World War, while trying to get through Hoxa Sound into the fleet anchorage in Scapa Flow. We exchanged guarded greetings with the crew, not exactly thrilled to see another salvage boat on what we regarded as our turf. A few days later we were working on the *Johanna Thorden* when we heard a huge explosion. It sounded like a massive charge going off in a quarry. That evening the big green trawler limped back into harbour. Gone was the usual dash to tie-up, just to show us how quick they could do it.

No one wanted to talk but it doesn't take long for a story to get out in a close-knit community like Orkney. The team had set a number of charges on the U-boat to crack open the hull, but unknown to them there were live torpedoes in the forward tubes. They stood off the normal safe distance to blow the charges, but got rather a nasty shock. The charge went off all right, but so did the torpedoes. One of the crew, Plug Jenkins, was standing on the hatch ready to take a photo of the water splash, when the explosion sent him and the hatch covers straight up in the air. When they came down again they all disappeared into the hold together. Plug survived but the damage to the vessel was considerable. The engine bed was cracked and not a toilet bowl or basin was left in one piece.

After they'd repaired the ship, we saw them bring in the bulkhead plate with the torpedo tubes. They were quite a sight. They looked like exploding cigars, all plastered back against the bulkhead.

It was a good story around the islands for quite some time, and naturally no one enjoyed telling it more than us. They were the opposition after all, and even worse, they were southerners.

CHAPTER NINE

THE GOLDEN WEST

About halfway through 1970 the *Johanna Thorden*'s cargo was almost exhausted. The divers, employed on a 'no cure, no pay' system, were getting restless. I was spending every spare minute doing wreck research, in the hope of finding another *Johanna Thorden* or *Otranto*. As well as leading us to workable wrecks, my researches also began to turn up the things that governments often prefer to see buried in the ocean depths for all time.

I called in at a particular office in London to check some of my findings against the records available. The person in charge was called away for a few minutes, and whether intentionally or not, he left a cargo manifest on the desk alongside me. The position in which it had been placed made it impossible for me not to see it. Much to my surprise, I discovered that it was the cargo manifest of the *Lusitania*.

The sinking of this ship by a German U-boat was the event that brought the Americans into the First World War. The British government claimed at the time – and continues to claim to this day – that the *Lusitania* was carrying no war materials, only passengers. They accused the Germans of committing a war crime by sinking a vessel full of innocent civilians. The manifest told a different story. It was plain to see that the *Lusitania* had a huge cargo of armaments on board.

When the official returned to the office, he picked up the file, returned it to a cabinet and continued our conversation as if nothing had happened. He never referred to it again and taking my lead from him, I also kept silent.

I was unsure if I was being leaked a story the official wished to see published or being tested on my ability to keep a secret. I did know that if I was identified as the source of a leak, I could wave goodbye to any hopes of winning salvage contracts for any government-owned wrecks in the future. I've kept my silence until now.

I found the first traces of another government cover-up whilst looking for a shipwreck on the wild west coast of Orkney, near the memorial to Lord Kitchener at Marwick Head. He was killed when his ship, the *Hampshire*, allegedly struck a German mine during the First World War. He had been on his way to Archangel on a top-secret mission to bolster the Tsar and provide whatever inducements were necessary to prevent the Russians from agreeing a separate armistice with Germany.

The German Naval Command had intercepted a communication from a British minesweeper claiming to have cleared a path west of the Orkneys. They became suspicious when the message was repeated three times inside an hour and believing that an important shipment was about to be made through Scapa Flow, a U-boat was instructed to lay fresh mines off Marwick Head. The *Hampshire* and its two escort destroyers, HMS *Unity* and HMS *Victor*, left just before 5 p.m. on 5 June. Despite its heavy armament, the *Hampshire* was one of the Navy's fastest ships and it maintained sixteen knots despite storm-force headwinds and mountainous seas. The escorts could not match its speed and the *Hampshire*'s captain eventually signalled them to return to Scapa Flow. Not long afterwards there was a huge explosion towards the bows of the ship.

The *Hampshire* sank within minutes, bow first, driven down into the depths by the still-turning propellers. No lifeboats could be launched and though a few men managed to cling to floats thrown into the towering seas, most drowned or died of exposure before they reached shore. Only a dozen men of the 650 on board survived.

We met a very old farmer at Marwick Head and got into conversation with him. Unprompted, he started to tell us about the terrible night when the *Hampshire* had sunk. Because of the activity of Army and Navy units they knew something was afoot offshore and went down to the beach to have a look. Bodies and survivors were coming ashore but the locals' attempts to help were blocked by the military units guarding the beach. They were told that no one was to be touched and the survivors were left to die on the beach.

I can still remember the hurt in the old man's voice as he told us the tale, but at the time we took it with a pinch of salt; we were more interested in the wrecks close inshore. Some time later, a Scottish author, Alisdair Alpin MacGregor, suggested the British had sunk the *Hampshire* to get rid of Kitchener, who was becoming far too powerful a figure for the government's liking. Once more I dismissed it as a wild fantasy, but while doing research in the Public Record Office I withdrew the *Hampshire* file, for there was supposedly a large amount of gold on board at the time of the sinking. It made very interesting reading. According to the file, a lead-lined coffin was rumoured to be already waiting for Kitchener in Stromness before his ship had even left port.

As I searched for further information, I discovered that a salvage attempt had already been made. A team of divers recruited by the notorious arms dealer and conspirator, Sir Basil Zaharoff, found the wreck in 1932 and returned the

scrubby trees bent almost flat by the force of the prevailing wind. There was a scattering of single-storey cottages, a few farm buildings and one more substantial house, the Manse, at the southern end of the island. We decided to make that our starting-point. As we got closer we could see a small cannon on either side of the front door. It brought a smile to our faces; cannons equalled wrecks.

No one answered our knock, but we wandered down to the beach to have a look for ourselves. There was a cairn on a small hillock overlooking the sea. Perched on the top was a ship's bell, another very encouraging sign. At the edge of the beach, we came to a dry-stone wall which ran right the way around the island. It was built not to keep the sheep – of which there were plenty – in, but to make sure they stayed on the beach and foreshore. They fed on the abundant seaweed that showed itself between tides, leaving the sparse grazing on the island itself for a few bony cows.

Before leaving North Ronaldsay we made contact with an old man, the local historian, who knew everything there was to know about wrecks off the rocky coasts of the island. He confirmed the position of the *Bella Vista* and also told us about a Swedish sailing vessel that had wrecked long ago on a reef off the south-east tip of the island, carrying a huge cargo of 800,000 silver coins. We decided there and then to bring up the *Golden West*.

During our conversation he also talked about the Morton Papers, which had just been released by the family to the Record Office in Edinburgh. The Earl of Morton had controlled all the islands in the mid-seventeenth century and made himself a steady additional income from the cargoes of shipwrecks. I made haste to study them and discovered that the Earl had been a hard, stone-hearted character. He sent men out to dive for a handful of coins or whatever cargo they could find. They were diving in the wild, cold waters without safety gear, protective clothing or breathing apparatus. Many died and while Earl Morton prospered, the survivors' reward was almost nothing at all. I read a series of their pitiful letters amongst the papers, begging for some relief for their starving wives and children. There was no sign that Earl Morton paid any attention to their pleas.

The papers also referred to the Swedish sailing ship, the *Svicia*. To my immense disappointment I discovered that the cargo of silver coins had been carried on the outbound journey to the Indies. Her cargo on the return, paid for with the silver, was of silks, spices and timber. As I unrolled one letter, a silk handkerchief fluttered out, part of the *Svicia*'s cargo that had washed ashore on Reef Dyke on North Ronaldsay.

The Morton Papers also told of the *Kennermerland*, a Dutch merchantman wrecked on Out Skerries, in the Shetlands, in 1664. The vessel had been carrying six chests of gold and silver coins, but when Morton came to hand over the Crown's share of the recovery, he claimed only to have found three. It cost him dearly, for Charles II promptly stripped him of his earldom.

There was a strong possibility that Morton had been framed by Charles's agents, however. If he had been telling the truth, then three chests of gold and silver were still lying on the bottom waiting to be found. The odds weren't good, but in the absence of any better prospects, it seemed worth a gamble.

The papers describing the incident were in such archaic English that I'd had them translated at the University of Leeds. As we were about to set sail for the Shetlands, someone drew my attention to a story in the morning paper. A 'university diving team' were in the Shetlands hoping to find a cargo of gold coins. I didn't need to be a rocket scientist to work out which university the students were from. The last laugh was on them, however, for no trace of the gold coins remained on the wreck. Later research by students from Birmingham and Manchester appeared to establish that the three missing chests had been transferred to another Dutch ship and carried to the East Indies. It appeared that Earl Morton had been wronged, but I wasn't going to shed any tears on his behalf, after the way he'd treated his divers.

Although the *Kennermerland* and the *Svicia* had been write-offs, there appeared to be enough non-ferrous metal on the *Bella Vista* to make it worth salvage. We bought the rights and sailed the *Golden West* up to North Ronaldsay, but when we got in the water we found that someone had already stripped the wreck. The only remaining non-ferrous metal was a small condenser. It was a pathetically small load to take back with us.

When we got back to Orkney two of our divers had found a decent-sized propeller on the east side of the islands and applied for the rights to salve. We blew it into four sections, got it aboard and arrived in Kirkwall harbour after midnight. We were too late for a drink, so we decided to get the blades into the back of the Transit, out of harm's way. This time the weight in the back of the van must have been around three tons. Naturally we had to put a little extra air into the tyres the next morning. The garage owner took one look at the van and beat a hasty retreat before I'd even taken the dustcaps off.

By the end of the 1970 season we seemed to have reached the end of the line. We'd formally closed down the *Johanna Thorden* operation and informed the Salvage Association that we'd recovered all we could of the cargo. The stern section was still out there somewhere but it was beyond our reach.

I sailed away from the Tarf's Tail for the last time with a mixture of feelings. I was glad not to have to risk my life in

155

those turbulent waters and terrible tides again, but the *Johanna Thorden* had earned me a substantial sum of money and made my name with the Salvage Association. Every other salvor offered the chance of the *Johanna Thorden* had taken one look at the wreck-site and the sea conditions and turned it down flat. I now had the beginnings of a reputation as a man who could win a return from the least promising wrecks. I also had vital experience of working in the most difficult sea conditions and in sea temperatures that chilled men to the bone.

As I watched the coast of Swona receding into the mist, I began to think of other, richer cargoes lying waiting in the blackness of the ocean depths. One in particular, HMS *Edinburgh*, in the freezing waters of the Arctic, kept coming back into my mind. It was still well beyond my reach, but it no longer seemed an impossible dream. I could see a day coming when some diver would salvage the *Edinburgh*'s gold. The thought kept coming back to me, why not me?

I had other, more pressing concerns, however. Like the *Johanna Thorden*, the other wrecks around the Orkneys were now pretty well worked out. We laid up the *Golden West* in Crinan for the winter and in desperation I decided to try a ships' graveyard nearer to my home: Flamborough Head on the Yorkshire coast. Most of the wrecks there were below the 100-foot mark and the tides, sands and poor visibility all caused problems, but by then the choice was to dive there or pack it in altogether.

I made friends with Alwin Emmerson, who worked the lobsters with his cobble from North Landing and knew the waters around the Head like the back of his hand. He also knew the positions of a number of wrecks, having lost many lobster pots on them. He called me one afternoon. 'One of my pots is well fast in a wreck. Come on out.' After the long drive out to Flamborough, I got into the water just before dusk. Sea conditions were not bad but visibility was very marginal, with a haze of sediment hanging in the water like fog.

I was diving on my own, for Frank was back at his coal business. Down the pot line I went. By the time I'd reached the bottom, I was in total darkness. By feeling around I discovered that I was on the keel of a sunken vessel, which was lying on its side. Visibility was so bad that I couldn't even tell whether it was on its port or starboard side.

I then made a very foolish decision. I thought that if I just cleared the pot line and went back to the surface, Alwin would think that all his effort had been a waste of time. Next time he found a wreck he might not even bother to phone me. Instead of going back up the line, I began to feel my way along the keel, hoping to find the stern and, with luck, a nice bronze propeller. I groped my way right to the end but found nothing. I turned round and began to inch back along the keel, but after a few minutes I decided to abandon the search and come back when visibility was better. I was about to let go of the keel and swim to the surface when something stopped me. Some sixth sense, or perhaps the memory of the cave in the Dales all those years before, caused me to stop and feel my way back to the line instead. It saved my life.

Back on the surface, I could see the disappointment in Alwin's eyes, but I explained the conditions on the wreck, and told him to tie a white pint pot to a line and drop it over the side in future. He could then tell me the underwater visibility from the depth the pot disappeared from sight.

A couple of days later I was back on the wreck, this time in very clear water. I could see the ship before I got down to it. I also saw something else that made my blood run cold. A very big fishing net was draped right over the wreck, like a shroud. As I'd crawled along the keel in the darkness I'd been directly below it. Any attempt by me to swim to the surface would have left me hopelessly entangled in the net. My chances of getting clear before my air ran out would have been zero. That near miss persuaded me never to dive on my own again in those conditions.

In any event, there was virtually nowhere worth diving – around Britain at least. All the shallow-water wrecks – even off the Western Isles, Orkneys and Shetlands – had already been worked by ourselves or other salvors. There was nothing left except off-limits ships like the *Hampshire* and the *Royal Oak*, or wrecks that were already owned by our rivals. Frank had a secure wage from his coal business, but I was seeing my capital drain away in increasingly futile searches for new wrecks. I still had money in the bank, a car and a house, but my only other assets were the wreck of the *Otranto* and my research files.

My researches told me that there was a future in salvage, but not if we carried on the way we were. We could have gone back to the *Otranto* again, for there was still plenty of non-ferrous metal to be lifted from it, but that seemed to be merely postponing the inevitable, to no useful purpose. I made it clear to Frank that I was not prepared to do that. If the partnership was to continue we would have to find new wrecks together. I couldn't continue doing individual dives while Frank ran his coal round and turned up only when a wreck had finally been found.

It was high time to take stock of my situation. As I relaxed with my family, my thoughts began to crystallise. I decided the only thing to do was close down the diving operations in Scotland, sell the *Golden West* and break from my old partners. There had never been much love lost between us, so that part of the decision was easy to make.

I had sufficient capital to live in reasonable comfort for a year. I would spend that time planning my future, researching prospective wrecks and getting to know my children better. I'd missed much of their childhood. Whenever the weather was set fair, I had to be in the water salvaging metal, even if that meant missing Christmas or their birthdays. I'd come home from a trip to find that one of the children had taken their first steps or spoken their first words. It takes an awful lot of money to compensate for missing something like that.

I loved my homecomings; the only problem was that I'd sometimes be greeted by Mildred with a list of the children's misdemeanours in my absence and a demand that I discipline them – usually Graham or Carol. It was the last thing I wanted to do, but instead of scooping them up in my arms I'd try to look stern and take them upstairs to read them the Riot Act.

Each time I came home, I noticed a change in them. I like to think that Graham is a chip off the old block. He was – and still is to some extent – a lad straight out of the pages of *Tom Sawyer*. He was a stocky little character at birth and soon grew into a strapping young lad. We sent him to school smart, clean and spotless every morning but he invariably came home in the evenings looking as if he had been fighting most of the day. Out of school, he was the leader of his own version of the Jay Street Gang. They went everywhere together, with Sam, his Jack Russell terrier, tagging along behind. I shudder to think of some of the things they got up to, out of sight of their parents.

It was obvious from the start that Graham was going to follow me into the salvage-diving business. When I was working on the Scottish islands, the whole family used to come up for a long summer holiday. I can still remember Graham and his gang of mates all lined up in their swimming costumes, waiting for our boat to come in. If any scrap fell into the water as we were unloading it, they used to dive for it and then Graham would negotiate a price with us for its return.

Our second child, Carol, was the answer to a dad's prayer, a bonny baby with blonde hair and blue eyes. She soon learned how to get around her father. She had large, almond-shaped eyes just like her mother's, in which, it appeared, tears could flow at will whenever anything she wanted was refused. Unlike Graham, she was always neat and tidy and enjoyed housework. She played with her dolls and did all the things little girls do, but despite that, one of her biggest disappointments in life was that she was born a girl and wasn't allowed to do the same things as the boys. She hated to miss out and even now she still regrets that she had to stay at home when Graham and Ian went diving with me.

Ian was quite different from Graham and Carol. Never one for getting himself dirty, he preferred to stay around the house to play, rather than disappearing for hours on end like his brother. From an early age he was good with his hands and liked to make models, something which neither Graham nor I had the time, the patience or the know-how to do. Unlike his siblings, he was very shy and reluctant to speak to anyone he didn't know. That quiet, shy exterior concealed a sharp character in the making, however. I later learned that he often played truant from school. Mildred would leave him at the school gates but once she'd gone, he'd do a disappearing act down to town, returning just in time to meet his mother back at the gates after school.

I often wondered what it must have been like for the children at school, compared to my own schooldays. They missed me badly when I was away, but I also knew that I'd have given my right arm to have had a father who was leading such a life and getting stories written about him in the papers. I never had the privilege; I never had a father.

My local fame had its downside, however. I found out years afterwards that many of the fights Graham had in his schooldays were caused by some of the other boys' resentment of the press stories about my exploits.

Graham, Ian and Carol had grown up with only a part-time father, home for odd weekends, away the rest of the time. Shaken by that guilty realisation, I took the whole family away on holiday for the first time in years. As we lay on the beach, I watched Graham splashing around in the sea. He had grown into a strapping fifteen-year-old and thought of nothing else but becoming a diver like his dad. That suited me, I saw him as a future partner. The *Otranto*'s non-ferrous metal would keep for now, money in the bank for the future. When Graham was old enough to learn his father's trade, we would work it together.

When we returned from holiday I began intensive research, scouring every available source for details of valuable wrecks. One giant obstacle kept appearing however, the Southampton-based salvage company, Risdon Beazley. They specialised in 'blast and grab', lowering explosives down to wrecks using an observation bell and then blowing them apart. The cargo and other objects of value were then hauled to the surface using a giant mechanical grab. It was like one of those penny machines in an amusement arcade which snatches up sweets and plastic novelties, but though it was crude, it had worked well enough for Risdon Beazley to dominate the industry for many years. The company was so successful that in practical terms they had slammed the door shut in the face of every other would-be salvor.

I grew weary of following up leads on potentially lucrative wrecks, questioning survivors and witnesses and travelling to London to search official documents, only to find that Risdon Beazley had travelled the same path years before and already owned the salvage rights. There was virtually nothing left except the scraps from Risdon Beazley's groaning table.

In the course of my researches I'd developed strong contacts with the Salvage Association. Their officials were efficient and friendly and I received a good deal of advice from the manager, Mr Smith. It was clear that they felt a growing impatience with Risdon Beazley, which had been sitting on numerous valuable contracts for years. The Association had already begun moves to reclaim several of them.

A successful salvage operation on one of those contracts would yield enough profit to finance work on even more valuable and inaccessible wrecks. I knew of a score of immensely valuable deep-water wrecks scattered around the world. The most fabulous of all Spanish galleons, the *San José*, lay around thirty miles off the Colombian harbour of Cartagena, at a depth of around 750 feet. The sixty-gun flagship was leading a treasure fleet carrying twenty-two million pesos of gold and silver back to Spain from the New World in 1708.

Two fleets normally returned from the New World in Spain every year. The Tierra Firma Armada collected the gold and silver from the South American mainland, while the Nueva Espana Armada transported the treasure of Mexico. The yearly shipments had been interrupted by war in Europe however and no precious metal had been shipped for six years. As a result the Tierra Firma Armada led by the *San José* was bulging with silver and gold when it set sail.

On 8 June the treasure fleet was spotted by Charles Wagner, the captain of a seventy-gun British warship, HMS *Expedition*. With two other warships and a small fireship, Wagner's mission was to patrol the coasts of Colombia and Venezuela, destroying any Spanish shipping that crossed his path. At 5 p.m. *Expedition* fired the first broadside of the engagement. A fierce battle raged for two hours, with both ships sustaining damage from the close-range cannon fire. Then there was a massive explosion as the *San José*'s powder magazine erupted. The ship sank almost at once, as blazing spars and rigging showered down on the *Expedition*. Less than a dozen of the *San José*'s crew of more than 600 survived.

In addition to the official cargo of perhaps five million gold pesos and seven million silver pesos, the *San José* also carried the very considerable private wealth and jewellery of its noble passengers. The modern value of the ship's contents might reach £2 billion.

If the *San José* was the most fabulous wreck of all, there was no shortage of other valuable cargoes scattered around the oceans of the world. The *Central America*, a wooden side-wheel paddle steamer, sank in the Caribbean in 1857, on its way from the goldfields of San Francisco to New York. The cargo of gold bars and coins, then worth $2 million, would today fetch around £1 billion. The *Prins Frederik*, a Dutch steamer bound for Java, sank in the Bay of Biscay in June 1890 after colliding with a British steamship, the *Marpessa*, in thick fog. Its cargo included 400,000 silver rijksdaalders, payment for the Dutch army in Batavia. The coins were stowed in wooden casks and stored in a bullion room lined with quarter-inch iron plate.

The *City of Cairo*, a British-built passenger liner of 8,000 tons had been torpedoed by a German U-boat in the South Atlantic in November 1942. The ship had a crew of about 150 and about the same number of passengers, nearly a third of whom were women and children. A cargo of cotton and manganese ore had been supplemented at the last moment by 2,000 boxes of silver coins, weighing a total of three million ounces. The captain of the U-boat waited twenty minutes for the crew and passengers to abandon ship before firing a second torpedo, which sank the ship. The survivors, crammed into six tiny lifeboats, were over 1,000 miles from the African coast and twice as far from South America. The tiny island of St Helena, 500 miles to the north, was the nearest land.

The boats lost contact with each other almost at once and all the survivors of the sinking endured terrible hardships. The occupants of four of the boats were rescued after drifting for a fortnight, during which a score of people died. The occupants of the other two boats were less fortunate.

The fastest lifeboat, commanded by Chief Officer Sidney Britt, had fifty-four people on board. They attempted to reach St Helena, but missed the island and as they drifted on, the survivors began to fight over the dwindling water ration. Britt died on 20 November. Several others died of thirst or simply abandoned the struggle and threw themselves overboard, according to the three survivors still alive when the boat was finally spotted by a German blockade-runner, the *Rhakotis*, on 12 December, some 500 miles north-west of St Helena. One of the three men died just after the rescue. The remaining two were again shipwrecked when the *Rhakotis* itself was sunk. Both survived, although one of them became a prisoner-of-war.

The seventeen people in the last lifeboat endured an even more extraordinary voyage. After two and a half weeks adrift, having seen no trace of St Helena, they decided to set sail for the coast of South America, a further 1,500 miles away. After fifty-one days adrift they were spotted by the Brazilian ship *Caravellas* just eighty miles from the South American coast. Only two out of the seventeen remained alive.

There were countless other wartime wrecks including scores of German U-boats and Japanese cargo submarines such as the I-52, sunk by depth charges off the Azores in June 1944, with a cargo of wolfram, molybdenum, tin, rubber, quinine and several tons of gold ingots.

A great mystery surrounded the loss of the US liberty ship, *John Barry*, off Oman in August of the same year, carrying $26 million in silver bullion and three million silver Saudi riyals.

Any one of these wrecks or a score of others would make me rich beyond my imagination, but my thoughts remained focused on that other vessel, the British cruiser lying at the bottom of the Barents Sea. There would be time to think about the others in the future, but for the moment, the one wreck I wanted above all others was HMS *Edinburgh* and its cargo of ten tons of gold.

To salvage it would take capital I did not have and diving expertise that for all my experience, I did not yet possess, however. I had already gone as deep, and sometimes deeper, than it was safe to dive using conventional methods, but the more research I did, the more I realised that the most promising wrecks lay below those depths. Up to this time they had been the sole province of the blast-and-grab merchants like Risdon Beazley, but I knew even then that cargoes like diamonds and gold could only be recovered by divers. Before I could begin laying serious plans to claim the *Edinburgh*'s gold, I first had to learn the techniques being used in the one place in the world where the rules of diving technology were being torn up and rewritten daily – the North Sea oilfields. The advent of North Sea oil answered one of my prayers. When the chance came, late in 1971, I took it with both hands.

CHAPTER TEN

ULTIMA THULE

———◆———

My early days in salvage had taught me to look after myself, simply because we dived as individuals; we could pull up more scrap that way. In the offshore oil business it was different. You were very well paid but instead of relying on yourself, you had to put your faith and your life in the hands of the dive supervisors on the surface.

I entered a different world altogether. It was the first time I had gone down to the sea-bed in a diving bell. After years of swimming down to wrecks or travelling out to them in leaky boats, the bell was a luxury, like going to work in a taxi. There were no long swims, less exposure to the elements and if anything went wrong, the distance to safety was greatly reduced.

I went out to Norway with a friend, who had worked with me in Orkney, to join a US diving company. When we gathered for our first meeting with the operations manager, there were six of us off-the-peg guys and a couple of regulars who would run the dives. We were told the rate for the job. Divers were a scarce commodity in those days and paid accordingly, in dollars. It was well above anything we could have earned in the UK at the time, though still much less than the American divers were earning for the same job. Many of them already had years of oilfield diving experience and the commercial diving schools in the United States also turned out fine divers, but it was a source of some friction.

We were put up in a very smart hotel and our final instructions were, 'Don't get into trouble at the hotel and keep off the drink.' Despite the warning, I soon had my first taste of Norwegian beer. The price – £1.60 a pint – was a severe shock. Back in the UK, it would have bought you a gallon. The Norwegians had their own answer to the problem; they brewed their own beer and could certainly sink plenty of it.

Our first job was to blow up five well-heads in the Atlantic and the North Sea. Over the next few days we helped to load all the gear on to a supply vessel with a diving system mounted on the work-deck. Money appeared to be no object. All the equipment was new and the ropes were the best nylon. It was a far cry from the days when I used to scrounge ropes from fishermen or pick up the ones that had fallen off lorries on the road to Scotland.

The first well-head had a buoy attached to it and our instructions were very straightforward: 'Get hold of the buoy, slide the explosives down the cable and Bang! Job done.'

It didn't prove quite that easy. The weather and sea conditions were what you would expect near a location the Romans had christened *Ultima Thule* – the end of the earth. A long, lazy Atlantic swell caused the stern of our vessel to rise and fall twelve feet. As conditions deteriorated, the job became very dangerous. Getting the buoy on board was only the first of our problems. Fixing a bundle of explosives around the downline and then lowering it to the sea-bed was even worse. We lost about 600 feet of nylon line and seventy pounds of explosives in the process and I would take a fair bet that the well-head is still there.

When a storm blew up we took shelter, anchoring in a

secluded bay, well away from any habitation. This was by design rather than accident; the company's instructions to the captain had been quite explicit: 'Keep the divers away from drink.'

After three days at anchor, there was a near mutiny. Unlike the *Bounty*, we let the captain stay on board the ship and we set off for the shore in one of the lifeboats. We beached it and then started to walk to the nearest alehouse. It was a bloody long walk. After many miles we managed to find one, but we only had a couple of pints, because the thought of the long hike back to the vessel afterwards put us off. We arrived back on board completely exhausted.

Our next well-heads were all in the North Sea, but this time we had to find them first. We had an expert on board with a proton magnetometer, which registered the variations in the Earth's magnetic field caused by the faint magnetic fields generated by ferrous metal objects on the sea-bed. Developed for use by the Navy during the war, the magnetometer could in theory detect a substantial metal object like the steel hull of a submarine at a distance of up to a quarter of a mile. Any iron or steel object – a well-head, a cannonball from a shipwreck, or even a lump of ore-bearing rock – would cause a variation. However, and as soon became apparent, it took considerable skill and experience to evaluate the information collected.

The magnetometer was highly sensitive, giving readings in units of one millionth of a gamma, and was a grand-looking machine, but either it or its operator were in need of some adjustment. We searched and searched, but by the end of the second week not one well-head had been found. A crisis meeting was called. We all had hopes of some steady work in the North Sea for the next few years and none of us wanted to return and report such a cock-up. After a free and frank discussion, a solution was proposed.

We began to create a complete set of records showing that we'd found all the well-heads and destroyed them. One problem remained however. We still had about half a ton of explosives on board. If the story was true, they would all have been used. We decided to place them on the sea-bed and blow the lot.

The fateful day dawned beautiful and calm. The ship's boat was lowered and the explosives were loaded, accompanied by a few of the divers. They got well away from the mother ship before lowering the explosives to the sea-bed. Then they stood off a similar distance and fired the charges.

There was one more problem. We'd stood off to the north, while the lifeboat went away to the south. But unknown to anyone on board, as the lifeboat paid out its firing cable both boats were drifting south. I couldn't swear we were right over the explosives when they went off, but we must have been pretty close. I was standing on deck with my camera, ready to film the eruption of any waterspout, when, just like Plug Jenkins on his salvage boat, my feet left the deck by several inches. Every fuse on board blew and the crew came out of the engine room like bullets. It was pure luck that there was no major damage to the ship.

When we got back, the oil company and the diving company were both so delighted with our performance that they wanted to turn the ship around and send us straight out again to blow another five well-heads. They sat there baffled as an ever-lengthening list of divers all offered excuses for having to go home instead. Never have so many grandmothers' funerals occurred on one weekend; mine was being buried for the second time, thirty years after the first.

I soon discovered that it wasn't wise to say no to any job in the North Sea. Employment lasted only as long as the particular job you were doing. You were constantly changing jobs and companies, but once your name was known, you were put on the list, and if a job came up you got the call. It could come at any time of day or night and I lost a few jobs because there was no one at home to answer the phone. On receiving the call you had to be ready to go immediately. To turn down a job, whatever the reason, meant you went to the bottom of the list, only to be called if they were desperate for divers.

On the exploration rigs, which provided regular work, divers worked a simple routine of two weeks on and two weeks off. On the construction barges, all the underwater work for setting up the oilfield was generally done 'on, stop, on'. That was usually six weeks on and six weeks off, although I met divers who had been on barges for months on end. Most of the work was saturation diving. It gave us the chance to earn big money, but it was money hard earned.

Saturation diving had revolutionised offshore oil exploration. In almost any deep dive, the amount of time actually needed for the task is far exceeded by the time required in decompression afterwards. A diver working for an hour at 200 feet needs to spend a further three hours and twenty minutes in decompression and the time required for decompression increases at an exponential rate. The deeper the dive and the longer its duration, the worse the ratio between work time and non-productive decompression time. That holds true until a diver reaches the point where his body can absorb no more gas – depending on the gas, that takes between eight and twenty-four hours. His blood and body tissue are now saturated with the gas and provided he goes no deeper, his decompression time remains the same, no matter how much longer he remains at that depth.

Once accurate decompression tables for different depths and durations of dives had been compiled – a dangerous process of trial and error with little theoretical underpinning

– the only restrictions on a diver were those imposed by his equipment and by his physical and psychological limitations.

Lengthy periods of decompression in the water were a practical impossibility for a free-swimming diver. He could not carry enough gas to sustain him over the course of hours or even days at depth and was vulnerable to everything from hypothermia to the effects of sudden surface storms. The introduction of deep-diving systems – a diving bell pressurised independently of the surrounding ocean and a chamber on deck in which divers could undergo decompression in dryness and relative comfort – was the essential accompaniment to the development of saturation diving techniques.

Diving bells were far from a new invention; they had been in use for centuries. The name came from the shape of the original ones, which were open at the bottom and shaped like a church bell. The air trapped inside a bell as it was lowered into the depths enabled a diver to breathe, but his freedom of operation was very limited, and being reliant on his shipmates to haul him up before his air was exhausted, his life expectancy was not very great. Modern enclosed diving bells offered greater comfort, safety and work efficiency for divers – once the theories of saturation diving and decompression had been put to the test.

The theory of saturation diving – such as it was – was largely proved by the pioneering efforts of three men: Jacques Cousteau, Edwin Link and George Bond. In September 1962, Cousteau sent two divers down to thirty-three feet in the pressure-balanced, gas-filled, Conshelf I – Continental Shelf Station Number One – off Marseilles. They remained there for a week, making daily dives down to eighty-five feet. At almost the same time, Edwin Link, the American inventor of a flight simulator used to train air crew, devised a diving system in which his chief diver,

Robert Stenuit, remained at 243 feet for twenty-six hours before returning safely to the surface.

Cousteau pushed back the frontiers a little further the next summer, when six of his divers spent one month in Conshelf II at 36 feet and made daily dives to 100 feet for up to five hours, without decompression. Two of them were lowered to 90 feet in another chamber and made dives from there to a depth of 363 feet. The following year, 1964, Link again leap-frogged Cousteau's experiments by sending two divers, Robert Stenuit and Jon Lindbergh, down to 432 feet for forty-eight hours.

The US armed forces were showing considerable interest in the military applications of saturation diving and US Navy Captain George Bond pioneered the next leap forward in the same year. The Sealab experiment saw four divers operate at 192 feet for nine days. The Sealab was then raised to 81 feet and the divers transferred to a chamber. It was craned aboard a support ship, allowing them to complete their decompression on deck. Sealab II, launched in 1965, sent three groups of ten divers down to 205 feet. They all remained there for fifteen days and one man – astronaut Scott Carpenter – actually spent a month at that depth.

The experiments had significance for both Navy divers and NASA astronauts, but the implications for the offshore oil industry were enormous. Saturation diving and deck decompression allowed divers to work for sustained periods at previously unheard-of depths, but also dramatically reduced the overall duration of such diving operations. A task at a depth of 200 feet that would take forty days of bounce diving to accomplish could be completed in seven days by a diver remaining in saturation – five days at work, two days in decompression afterwards.

Men operating from diving bells, whether bounce diving or in saturation, could be returned under bottom pressure to the deck of an oil rig or exploration vessel and transferred to a chamber. There they could be maintained at pressure or decompressed in relative comfort and safety, while the bell returned to the depths with another pair of divers. Work could continue round the clock and as the depth at which divers could operate was steadily increased, the cost in dive time and the necessary support staff and equipment was massively reduced.

The offshore exploration rigs ran all year but the construction barges could not operate in the North Sea storms and shut down during the winter. Divers then had to look for work abroad. The phone would ring. 'Are you available for a job?', and it could be anywhere in the world. After asking the rate and giving a tentative yes, I'd ask, 'When do I go?' The answer was usually, 'You're booked on the next flight to Heathrow.' You then transferred to a flight to Muscat, Bombay, Rio or Manila – wherever there was offshore oil to be found.

After what could be a thirty-hour journey by plane, helicopter and boat, it was not unusual to step on board and find that a dive had been called. There were no prizes for guessing who was making the dive.

One job was on a drill ship off Oman in the Arabian Sea, drilling a single hole for exploration purposes. After a night in Muscat, we took an early-morning flight down to an airstrip in the south of Oman, a line of oil drums in the desert.

We stepped out of the aircraft into an oven. Our nice new lightweight blue overalls were soaked with sweat in seconds. There was nothing but shimmering sand and rock as far as the eye could see, apart from a tall individual in rather tatty Arab clothing making his way across the sand towards us, from a drab huddle of tents in the distance. Across his shoulder was the oldest-looking rifle that I had ever seen. As he approached, we noticed what appeared to be a black cloud around him. It turned out to be a million flies. They all left our new Arab friend and descended on us. I ran off into the desert trying to get rid of them. When I looked back, the rest of the team were doing the same thing.

We were taken out by helicopter to the drill ship, *Glomar Conception*. One of the first things we noticed was the size of the sharks swimming around the rig and my mate John was less than thrilled when he was given the job of swimming a line from the moon-pool out to the side of the ship. I've never seen a diver move as fast. He jumped into the moon-pool and by the time we turned around to help him up the outside, he was already waiting for us.

After that burst of excitement, time started to drag. We had very little to do, apart from maintenance of the diving equipment and a few practice dives to help us cool off. It was hot as hell, any metal you touched could burn you. To pass the time we decided to do a little fishing. We started by trying to catch the colourful fish that swam around the rig but before long we'd graduated to shark fishing. We used a plastic drum as a float and made our first shark hook out of a half-inch diameter steel bar. It was fastened to a ten-foot chain, which in turn was fastened to a large float, then attached to the steel cable of the tugger winch. True sportsmen, we were taking no chances. There was now only one minor problem: we had no bait. We solved that by going down to the galley and scrounging a joint of prime beef.

Nothing happened the first night, although we saw quite a number of sharks swimming around. On the second evening, we'd barely got the hook into the water before there was a tremendous commotion. We gave the signal to pull in on the winch, which was capable of hauling a few tons, and a monster shark bounced across the waves to the ship's side. It was so big that the winch couldn't lift it clear of the water. We decided to hook up another tugger winch and this time I drew the short straw. I had to go over the side, drop down on to the steel fenders and fix the extra cable around the shark.

The monster hung there half in and half out of the water, with its mouth fully open, showing some very large and very sharp teeth. The nearer I got to it, the bigger it looked. I felt that if I slipped I'd disappear down its mouth without even touching the sides. I took my time getting down there because the shark was thrashing about wildly, turning the water to foam as it crashed against the side of the ship. Much to my relief, it broke free and went back to the depths before I reached it. I picked up the hook. The half-inch steel bar had completely straightened out. Undeterred, we made a stronger hook and tried again. A couple of days later we landed a thirteen-foot tiger shark. The poor thing had no chance. No sooner had it landed on deck than its teeth had been removed. I still have one mounted on a gold chain.

Over the next few years I worked in the Middle East, India and the Far East, but whenever possible I preferred the exploration rigs in the North Sea. The money was good and two weeks off in every four also gave me time to continue my research and keep my hand in at salvage.

One of my first permanent jobs in the North Sea was on board the *Drillmaster*, a giant semi-submersible drilling rig. I drove or flew up to Aberdeen on the Friday, ready for the crew change on Saturday morning. I met the rest of the diving team to down a few last drinks in one of the hotels that were springing up around the airport. The rigs themselves were as dry as the deserts of Saudi Arabia.

The following morning, hung over, we flew out to the rig. In those days, anyone wanting a job offshore just had to turn up at the heliport. Any crews short at departure time would hire you on the spot. It was very different from all the rules and regulations that have been brought in since then, but we don't need the oil quite as badly now.

Flight time to the rig was about three and a half hours and it was always a good idea to have a leak before boarding the helicopter; there were no toilets on it. In winter, to make life more exciting, the rotors were continually icing up. We only discovered this when lumps of ice broke off them and crashed into the side of the helicopter.

Despite the occasional dangers of air travel, the slow, uncomfortable workboats were never a popular alternative, particularly when the weather was rough. On one trip out to a construction barge in the North Sea, the sea conditions were so bad it was touch and go whether we could be transferred from the workboat to the barge. The transfer basket looked like a cage. A rubber tyre contained a round base four feet across and the nets enclosing the whole thing were attached to the hook on the crane by a fifteen-foot nylon lifting line. Just above the hook was the 'headache ball' – a huge steel ball. The crane driver swung the basket across to the workboat, and lowered it until it was standing upright on the deck. Four or five divers threw their luggage into the centre of the basket and stood on the outside, holding on to the netting. The crane driver then lifted the basket and swung it across to the barge.

That was the theory anyway. It was simple in good weather but we were attempting a transfer when the deck of the workboat was rising and falling well over fifteen feet and yawing all over the place. The barge also had a bit of a swing on it. Over came the basket and out we rushed to attempt the transfer. Keeping hold of my Samsonite briefcase in one hand, I threw my bag into the centre and made to grab the netting for support. Just then the deck of the workboat pitched upwards. The 'headache ball' missed us by inches and hit the deck with a crash. Had it hit us, it would have killed us.

Two of the lads slipped and rolled away across the deck, but it was my lucky day. The workboat dropped back into a trough and the basket was snatched from the deck with two of us still hanging on grimly. My knees buckled with the sharpness of the lift, as the crane driver tried to raise the 'headache ball' out of our way. We were dropped safely on the deck of the barge, but after that near miss he didn't try another lift. The workboat pulled away and stood by until the storm abated. I was glad to be on board the barge and not with my workmates as they pitched and tossed on the workboat for the next twenty-four hours.

Once safely on the barge, we settled into the hard routine of being on call twenty-four hours a day, with constant work dives being called.

On the rigs life was easier and boredom was always a problem. Divers always find something to do, however. There was the maintenance of the gear, practice dives, the keep-fit routine and lots of use of the 'hairy stick' – the paint brush. Some also tried to sleep the clock round for the Golden Pillow award. One dive supervisor used to sleep so long that he even had to hand-wind his automatic watch. His slumbers were apt to be rudely interrupted at any time however. The huge operating costs of the exploration rigs ensured that there was always a sense of frantic urgency. The well had to be drilled and tested now, whatever the problems and obstacles. When something went wrong on the bottom – a fractured hydraulic pipe on the blow-out preventer (BOP) or any one of a myriad other problems – the rig stopped working and the Diving Supervisor was told, 'A dive is required.'

Getting ready for a bell dive always reminded me of a space shot. Instead of blasting off into outer space we were descending into inner space, as Cousteau termed life beneath the surface of the ocean.

We worked in pairs on a rota. While the rest of the team began checking the equipment to be used, my mate and I were briefed on the task to be completed, then we sorted out the dive masks, suits, hoods, fins, gloves and weight-belts each of us would be using. Having checked our personal gear thoroughly, we began the exhaustive checks on the bell. Working from a prepared list we ensured that the gas cylinders fixed to the diving bell for emergency use were full of the correct diving mixtures – a bottom mix of 93 per cent helium/7 per cent oxygen, an intermediate mix of 84 per cent helium/16 per cent oxygen, plus one cylinder of oxygen and one of air.

The drop weight controls also had to be checked just in case we had to bring the bell to the surface ourselves. We made sure that all outside and inside valves and connections were effective, and, most important of all, that O-seals (circular rubber seals) were in place on both the inner and outer doors. Inside the bell we connected our dive masks to the divers' umbilicals, checked that the CO_2 scrubbers were working and had new sodasorb canisters fitted. We made sure that the first-aid kit was on board, and the emergency decompression tables and stop watches in case we had to do our own stage decompression. We also checked the tool box on the outside of the bell as the tools had a habit of disappearing.

Checks complete, we ordered the meal we wanted on our return to the surface and placed a set of clean clothes in the decompression chamber. We then changed into our diving suits. We were using 'hot water suits', warmed by hot water pumped down through the umbilical from the surface. The diver adjusted temperature by controlling the flow rate of the water using a valve on the side of the suit. The water circulated around the suit, then flowed back into the sea through the wrist, ankle and neck openings. Diving in suits like these was certainly far more comfortable than the old dry type, like being in a bath of hot water. We now climbed up through the bell trunking – a circular tube with a steel door at each end – into the bell. As usual it was cold and damp, with a strong smell of rubber and the sea. The bottom door clanged shut behind us. As the diver on this job, I sat to one side while my mate, the bellman, began to talk to the diving supervisor over the radio, running through even more bell checks. In case of accidents, all communications were taped.

'Bottom door closed, ready to go,' reported the bellman.'

I heard the grinding noise as the winch took up the strain and felt the bell lurch as it came free of the deck, rocking gently as it was swung out over the trapdoors cut in the deck. Then the bell was lowered, slowly at first, but accelerating to ensure a good seal was acquired on the bottom door as the bell plunged below the surface. It would be held shut by the outside water pressure only. We checked for signs of water leaking in, then the bellman reported, 'We have a seal.'

Usually, you can tell by the slight pressure change on your eardrums that a seal has been achieved on the bottom door. However, on one previous dive, each of us thought that the other had checked the O-seals were in place. It was surprising how quickly the bell flooded before we got a message through to the surface. Much to our embarrassment we found that on that occasion there were no O-seals on the door.

We were lowered to thirty feet and then paused while we tested the acoustic communications – a back-up if our main communications failed. Then we began the descent, passing rapidly from the light of the surface into the blackness of the depths. The bellman called out our depth from our outside depth gauge at fifty-foot intervals, until we reached the bottom at 450 feet.

I began putting on the rest of my equipment. The swim fins came first followed by a diving knife strapped to my leg. I could then lower my legs into the trunking, giving the bellman more room to help me on with the rest of my gear. Next I strapped on my weight-belt. Then followed the diving harness with the 'bail-out bottle' – filled with enough bottom gas to get me back to the bell if the supply from the surface failed. I next connected my hot water hose, after first making sure that I had hot water coming through, so as not to get a suit full of very cold water at the start.

My bellman now reported to the surface, 'Diver ready, ready for blow-down.' The supervisor on the surface set his clocks and stop watches running, and gave the command to go. The dive had officially begun. Its duration would dictate the amount of time we spent in decompression afterwards.

The bellman threw the lever and there was a high-pitched whine as high-pressure gas began flooding the bell. We both tried to clear our ears as the inside pressure mounted. Finally the noise wound down. A quick look at the interior depth gauge told me that we were almost at our depth. Suddenly, the whine of the incoming gas stopped as the bottom door came free of its seal. The inside bell pressure exactly matched that of the water outside.

The bellman now helped me on with my diving mask, held in place by a rubber spider, a six-legged, rubber fitting that sits on the back of the head and each leg in turn is locked on to lugs around the mask. A protective helmet is also clamped over the top for safety. I slipped on my gloves. The bellman made a final check of my gear, gave me the usual tap on the helmet, then reported once again to the surface: 'Diver leaving the bell.'

I took a few experimental breaths and then checked my communications equipment with a few words to the surface. With the bottom door now open I dropped through the trunking into the bright pool of light flooding the work area around the massive Blow Out Preventor on the sea-bed, being careful not to snag any of my equipment.

Ahead was a job that might take five minutes or stretch into hours. I took a few moments to look around and get my bearings. I scanned the bell for leaks and flushed my mask to clear the condensation that had formed on the glass. There was no point in hanging around any longer than was necessary. The quicker I completed the job, the less time I would have to spend in decompression afterwards.

The BOP's function was to prevent a blowout of the well. It was clamped to a steel base-plate, fixed securely to the casing – the steel tubing lining the well that is concreted into the sea-bed. Any dangerous build-up of pressure in the well could be controlled from the surface by closing down a series of huge valves on the BOP. A massive steel tube, the Riser, sat on top of the BOP and connected it with the surface. The drill pipe is lowered down inside the Riser to drill down to the oil-bearing strata deep below the ocean floor. If something went wrong with the BOP, the Toolpusher – the man in charge – had to decide whether to send down a diver to fix it or 'pull the stack', raising the BOP to the surface on guide-wires connecting the rig to the base-plate. It took a brave – or desperate – man to do it, for it burned up the rig operators' dollars at a frightening rate.

This time the problem was not serious. One of the four guide-wires joined to the base plate had snagged on the Riser, preventing the TV camera from being lowered to do visual checks on the BOP.

I decided to swim across to look at the wire. It was caught on one of the clamp bolts. I gave it a couple of tugs. It was jammed but not that tightly, and rather than go back to the bell for a crowbar, I decided to give it one good pull in an attempt to free it.

I got myself into a horizontal position, my feet against the Riser and then hurled myself backwards, giving the wire an almighty tug. It came free. I smiled to myself; if only all the jobs were this easy. I now checked to see that no damage had been done and then reported to the surface, asking them to take up the slack in the wire.

Then I reported, 'Diver returning to the bell, job complete.' Moving back to the bell was easy. My bellman was pulling in on my umbilical giving me a free ride back. He had allowed the trunking to flood by lowering the pressure inside the bell a little. Up inside the trunking I pulled off my mask but stayed there until the bellman had finished stowing the umbilical. Then he helped me off with my bail-out bottle, weight-belt and fins and stacked them away. Once I was back in the bell and all the housekeeping had been done, bottom and top doors on the trunking closed, the bellman reported to the surface, 'Dive complete, ready to go for a seal.'

Each company I worked for in the oil industry had their own set of bounce dive decompression tables which varied considerably from company to company. From the time the bell started its journey from the sea-bed to the surface you were operating under the instructions of the dive supervisor. Depending on which company you worked for, you were sometimes brought straight back to the surface in the bell, and then transferred into the deck decompression chambers to have all your decompression done on the surface. Other companies started decompression in the bell whilst on the way back to the surface.

All different systems gradually brought you back to surface pressure, changing breathing gas from bottom mix, to first an intermediate mix that increased the oxygen content, and finally to oxygen from masks on the final ascent to the surface.

On this particular dive, the bell was brought up to fifty feet and then held whilst we commenced our stage decompression from inside the diving bell, working on instructions from the surface. Once having reached a depth decided by the supervisor, we changed our breathing gas from bottom mix to an intermediate, this bringing up the oxygen content. Once this had been completed, the bell was lifted out of the water and mated up with the deck decompression chamber, which was also at the same pressure as the inside of the diving bell. We could hear the clamps that locked bell and chamber together being tightened, then the whine as more gas was pumped into the trunking to equalise the pressure; this allowed both doors on the chamber and the bell to open. We could now crawl down into the chamber – our temporary home for the next few hours. The bell and trunking were then bled down completing the seal on the chamber.

As we struggled out of our diving suits and took a shower, the rest of the team were already at work cleaning and preparing the bell for its next dive. Some of the deckhands took the chance to have a whiff of the helium diving mixture just for the laugh of hearing their voices in Minnie Mouse mode.

Inside the chamber, we ate our meal and then settled down to listen to tapes, read or sleep away the time until decompression was complete. The moment was easily recognizable. The chamber door, now free of the internal pressure cracked open, and we were free to leave the chamber. Total decompression time for a bottom dive of say eleven minutes was somewhere in the region of four hours.

Chapter Eleven

Pushing at the Frontiers

———— • ————

I was now nearing forty – pensionable age for a diver – but I found that the younger divers valued my experience and I graduated to Diving Supervisor, controlling the dives and monitoring the safety of the younger men taking my place. I attempted to learn everything there was to know about deep-diving and a fair bit about crisis management, for the North Sea oilfields in those early days had a lot of the Wild West about them. The North Sea was a new environment even for the oil companies. A lot of learning was going on and lives were being lost. There was no government department then to deal with diver safety and the rules tended to be made up as you went along. Exploration rigs and construction barges cost tens of thousands of dollars a day to keep running and any suggestions that diving operations be suspended because conditions were too dangerous were apt to be treated with contempt. Divers' lives took a distant second place to the almighty dollar.

'When I holler for a diver,' one Texan oilman told me, 'the only answer I ever want to hear is "Splash".'

I saw several examples of the dangerous consequences of this attitude while working as the supervisor on the dive ship *Northern Protector*. It was a DP – dynamic positioning – vessel, able to maintain its position precisely by the use of its propellers and bow thrusters, controlled by an on-board computer. When the ship was on station, a sonar beacon was lowered to the sea-bed. Its signal was picked up by four hydrophones. The computer continually compared the ship's actual and required positions relative to the beacon and made the necessary constant minute changes by the use of the ship's propellers and side thrusters to keep it precisely positioned.

We were doing non-destructive testing, checking the underwater condition of the giant Claymore oil-production platform. We stationed ourselves alongside the platform, which towered above us like a skyscraper. There was a constant barrage of noise from the giant generators on the platform, counterpointed by the din from our own engines as they strained to keep us on station, battling the heavy swell of the North Sea.

At night, everything was a blaze of light. Torrents of sparks cascaded from the torches of welders working on the structure, but they were mere pinpricks beside the flame belching from the giant flare stack as it burned off the excess gas. The heat from it would scorch your head, just walking out on deck. I was in charge of the night shift and worked from midnight until noon. It was a hard twelve hours and there were constant incidents caused by the oilmen's indifference to diver safety.

Many times we had to launch the diving bell even though the surge and swell of the sea were far above the safety limit. On one particularly wild night, I expected the captain of the ship to tell the dive superintendent that he wouldn't be able to hold his ship steady enough, but he said nothing. We looked at each other in the growing silence. Downtime was logged against the company who called it. Too much downtime against your name and you would be making a one-way trip back to Aberdeen. The captain of the ship, the

185

diving superintendent and the diving supervisor all knew the safety limit for holding and launching the diving bell, but each wanted one of the others to make the decision. In the meantime, until somebody acted, the bell had to be launched.

On this occasion, I blew my top and told the superintendent exactly what I thought of him. He just stared back at me. 'Why don't we let the divers decide?'

It was an apparently reasonable compromise, but every one of us knew that the divers' supposed free choice was really no choice at all. Anyone refusing to dive would have been shipped out immediately and blacklisted throughout the oil industry. Given the choice between diving in unsafe conditions or never working as a diver again, all the men made the inevitable decision.

The shrieking wind and salt spray were lashing at the rig as I made my way to the control van. I took up my usual position, monitoring the equipment and talking to the divers on the radio link as the diving bell was lowered 350 feet below the vessel. One diver stayed in the bell while the other worked seventy feet up inside the platform, photographing the welds around one of the joints. Suddenly the alarm bells in the control van began clanging and red lights flashed insistently. I knew immediately what had happened. The DP had failed and the ship was drifting off position fast. The diver inside the bell was safe because the stout steel cable for lifting and lowering it would not fail, but the diver working up inside the rig was only attached to the bell by his umbilical. He was seconds from death.

I had to pray that he hadn't tied himself off for stability. The wave action and the ocean currents pulled and pushed at you as you tried to work and though it was strictly forbidden on safety grounds, many divers tied themselves to the steel structure. If he had done so, or if his umbilical was wrapped around a couple of the horizontals or verticals of the structure, he would die. Once the weight of the drifting vessel took up the slack, the umbilical would snap like rotten thread and the diver couldn't swim to the surface because he'd die from the bends.

I had only those few seconds in which to save his life.

'Diver. Drop what you're doing and return to the diving bell.' I kept my voice even and neutral. I couldn't allow any trace of the tension I was feeling to communicate itself, for panic underwater will kill you quicker than anything.

'What?' he replied. 'Something wrong topside?'

This wasn't the time for an explanation. 'No, just make your way back to the bell now.'

'What about the camera?'

He was holding a £10,000 piece of equipment in his hands.

'Just drop it.'

'Surface? Should—'

I cut him off short. 'Just get back to the bell now.'

'Returning to bell.'

There was nothing further I could do. The seconds dragged by as I watched the ship drifting steadily further from the rig. There was a sick feeling in the pit of my stomach as I waited, fearing that at any moment my headset would crackle and fall silent. It would be the only sign that a man's life had ended.

Finally the line did crackle, but instead of silence there was the diver's voice. 'Clear of the structure. Shall I go back for the camera now?'

I almost cried with relief. 'Not bloody likely.'

On that occasion we were lucky, but there were other times – too many – when men died. One particularly bad accident happened aboard the *Drillmaster*. Two divers were on the bottom, one inside the diving bell, the other working outside it. The heavy drop-weight that took the bell down to the sea-bed was on a cable connected to a winch. There were two safety devices, a disc brake which was always locked on and a sprocket that was dogged firmly in place. The same safety system was used by the US Navy, but on this dive, both systems suddenly failed for some unknown reason.

Free of its brake and dog, the winch started to pay out and the bell began to rise, accelerating faster and faster as the gas escaping from inside acted like a propellant. The bell rocketed to the surface like a cork and both the divers died horrible deaths from embolisms and massive attacks of the bends. The bell drop-weight system was changed after that, but it was too late for the two divers.

On one job, working as a diver, we'd fallen well behind schedule on one pipe-laying job, but conditions were atrocious and my view was that we should have stopped diving. The dive superintendent, who I thought had been drinking, overruled the divers and the job continued in sea conditions so bad that I believe even a lifeboatman would have hesitated to launch his craft. When a diver became trapped at depth, another diver had to jump into that boiling sea to free him. It was almost a suicide mission, but more by luck than anything else, we managed to get them both safely back on board.

Another incident also affected me deeply, the more tragic because it was the result of such a simple and easily preventable error. Two divers were undergoing decompression in the chamber on board the rig when the dive supervisor in the control van noticed that the pressure was falling very fast in the chamber. He began pumping in gas to compensate for it, but the gauge continued to fall and he pumped in more and more in a desperate attempt to save the divers' lives.

A large leak had developed, but only in the small transfer chamber used to link the decompression chamber itself to the diving bell. The connecting door had closed and the pressure in the main chamber remained normal. The pressure gauges for each chamber had been interlinked, however, and all of them recorded the same rapid drop in pressure. By the time the error was realised the men were dead from hypothermia.

Once more modifications were made to prevent such an accident ever happening again, but once more it was too late for two divers.

Another tragedy, even more terrible because the men involved had much longer to contemplate their fate, killed a friend of mine. He was in the Far East doing saturation work in an oilfield construction barge. He was in the decompression chamber with the rest of his dive team when a hurricane developed and the barge began to founder. There are lifeboat chambers on barges and dive ships today, which can be launched over the side in such an emergency. The divers remain afloat in their chamber, controlling their own environment until a rescue comes. But there was no such system on that construction barge. The decompression chamber was fixed to the deck. There was no way of removing it and if the divers trapped inside had tried to leave it, they would have suffered an agonising death from the bends.

Instead they were given time to write a last letter home, which they passed out through the hatch before the barge was abandoned. As the lifeboats moved away, the barge broke up and sank. The divers inside the decompression chamber went down with it to the bottom of the ocean.

Black humour was often the only response to such tragedies. We would just look at each other, shrug and say, 'No problem. Just open another box of English divers.'

The offshore oil industry brought tremendous advances in deep-diving techniques, but it also brought greatly increased danger. Mechanical and human failure, and the risks taken under financial pressure, led to many lost lives. I was one of the lucky ones. I have friends who are in wheel-chairs for life and others who are dead – the price they paid for working at the limits of diving technology and human endurance to bring oil into the UK.

In return for the risks, we were very well paid, in dollars and with no deductions for tax. The Inland Revenue knew all about our tax-free money but chose to ignore it. The Arabs had us over a barrel at the time and the government priority was to get the North Sea oil onshore quick. Once the oil started to flow, a deal was done with the Inland Revenue and we all became regular taxpayers and decent citizens again.

The young divers spent their money on women and booze, BMWs and Porsches and Samsonite briefcases, which usually contained nothing but a few magazines and a calculator to convert dollars into pounds.

Like sportsmen, divers have a very limited working life and it upset me to see the way many of the younger ones blew their money – and there were always plenty of people ready to help them spend it. My days in salvage had taught me to look after my hard-earned cash and though I earned remarkably good money in the North Sea, I never lost sight of my long-term goal. Much of my income was ploughed back, building comprehensive research files on wrecks and lost cargoes and paying for a number of expeditions that were to pave the way to the greatest prize of all.

The money I earned and the knowledge and experience I gained laid the foundations of the next stage of my sal-vage career. But one event in particular confirmed my belief that the door to the deepest wrecks was now ajar. I was working for Ocean Systems on one of the giant drilling rigs. We were contracted to work on a drilling rig that was exploring for oil way out in the North Atlantic, well to the west of the Shetland Islands. We were operating at the limits of diving technology, deeper than any oil-field diver had been before.

During my two weeks off, a number of deep depressions swept across the North Atlantic. I could well imagine the conditions on the rig, for my previous spell on it had also been a rough one, with giant waves battering against it. At times I could not bring myself to look at the sea while struggling around the rig, battling the gales. I just prayed that whoever had designed and built it knew what he was doing.

Crew-change day came and I flew up to Aberdeen, then took the old DC3 up to Sumburgh in the Shetlands before the usual helicopter ride out to the rig. As soon as I landed, I saw a dozen lengths of badly bent drill-string – the immensely strong toughened steel shaft that drove the drill-bit through the bedrock below the ocean floor. I hurried to swap stories with my opposite number in the crew going ashore.

It turned out that the company representative had kept the rig drilling during a particularly bad spell of weather instead of pulling off and riding out the storm. By the time he finally agreed to pull the drill-string out of the hole and detach the BOP from the sea-bed, the drill-string was bent like a banana.

We got to work, checking the diving equipment and paperwork to ensure that we were ready to go should a dive be called. Conditions were not bad for a rig of its size: a fresh westerly was blowing and a very long Atlantic swell was running from the west.

We hadn't been on board long before a dive was called. They couldn't get a seal on the BOP, and without one they couldn't drill because of the risk of a blow-out. Full control of the well was an absolute priority at all times. The BOP was well illuminated by sub-sea lighting, including the TV lights for our remote camera. An observation dive was called, with a diver inspecting the BOP from the safety of the bell and reporting his findings to the surface. No one got wet and no decompression was needed.

The diver was on his way down to the sea-bed when the rep came into the dive shack. It was obvious from his temper that he'd been getting a fair amount of flak from head office for the downtime and was looking to shift the blame.

The diver's voice came over the intercom. 'Bell to surface.'

'Go ahead diver.'

'The BOP is not upright. It's got one hell of a lean on it.'

At this the rep lost control. 'Who the hell have you got down there, some sort of idiot?'

The supervisor ignored him. 'Diver, how can you tell the BOP isn't straight?'

'Surface, I'm looking out of the porthole straight at the BOP. I assume the bell is hanging straight up and down. The central line of the BOP is running across the porthole from seven o'clock to one o'clock, so I think it's safe to assume the BOP is leaning.'

The rep had lost his appetite for any more argument. He turned on his heel and stormed out of the dive shack.

Worse was to follow. We all watched the pictures from the sea-bed camera as the drilling crew began to pull the BOP from its base-plate on the sea-bed. As it started to lift, a five-foot length of the casing lining the well came out of the hole with it. We now knew why they couldn't get a seal on the well. By staying drilling too long in atrocious conditions, the rep had caused the impossible to happen; part of the casing had broken inside the well.

A special tool, designed to be lowered into the well to cut out and remove the damaged sections of casing, had to be flown out from the United States. A section of sleeving with new casing attached would then be lowered on to the down-well section. When all had been pressure-tested, the BOP and riser could be lowered back into place, and drilling could resume.

Then another disaster struck. Just as the cutting tool was being pulled out of the well, it snapped in two as cleanly as if it had been cut and part of it fell back into the hole, blocking the well. It could have been worse, for it could easily have slipped right down inside the well, which would have meant abandoning it altogether.

The broken tool had a small circular hole in the centre, no more than two inches across. The call went out for another specially made tool, like a spear with a roughened surface. If they could get the spear into the hole, it would grip it enough to enable the tool to be pulled out of the well – that was the theory anyway. But we had to wait a few days for the tool to be flown in, which was expensive.

The scale of the problem was immense. The sea state was not good and the fifteen-foot swell was causing a little movement on the rig. The driller in charge on the platform had to watch his TV monitor and at just the right moment drop the spear on the end of an 800-foot drill-string into a hole just two inches wide. Threading a needle blindfold in a fast-moving car while someone jogged your arms would have been easy by comparison.

We watched the operation from the dive shack for over two days as a succession of drillers endlessly tried and endlessly failed to drop the spear in the hole. The tension was bad enough in the dive shack, I cannot begin to imagine what it must have been like on the drill floor itself. It was a good time to keep well out of the rep's way. He ran the full gamut of human emotions, from fury to despair. It caused us just a little amusement, for he wasn't the most popular man on the rig.

I happened to be watching the monitor when I saw the spear at last enter the hole in the cutting tool. Even that was only half the job done. There was a long pause and then the lift started – very, very slowly. The damaged tool was lifted from the hole, but when it was only five feet above it, it dropped off the spear and bounced down on to the well-head. It rolled around the lip for a moment, then dropped off the side and came to rest in the mud.

There was a great collective sigh of relief, which must have been echoed back at the company's headquarters, after one of the longest and most expensive spells of downtime in its history.

The fitting of the new length of casing was completed in a remarkably short time, considering what had to be achieved. Then the BOP and the other equipment was lowered back to the sea-bed and pressure checks on the well were carried out. A final dive was now called, to recover the broken tool. It was lying at a depth of 720 feet, a record for a bounce dive at this time. Two divers duly retrieved the tool and got certificates commemorating the record, but their dive had a far greater significance for me.

All the time I'd been working in the offshore oil industry, the depth at which divers were operating had been gradually increasing. The deeper waters of the North Sea and the North Atlantic were the testing grounds for a revolution in diving technology. It was a risky business for the pioneers pushing at the frontiers, but the knowledge gained by the divers breathing mixed gases enabled diving companies to compile decompression tables. They set the safe limits of diving operations, the correct mixture of gases and the length and frequency of decompression stops on the way back up from the depths. The tables were guarded like state secrets, for they were priceless commercial information.

We already knew that the only theoretical limits to the depths to which we could dive were imposed by the length of time needed for decompression afterwards. As divers were being pushed deeper, the ratio between work time and decompression time grew ever bigger, and bounce dives became less and less economic. Having got a diver down to a depth of several hundred feet it made financial sense to keep him there. The technique of saturation diving was developed in response to that need. Divers would stay at great depths for long periods – a week or even a month – both in the ocean and under the artificial pressure of a steel chamber on the rig. They would then decompress only once, at the end of the operation or their tour of duty.

That was the theory, but it was one thing to know that something was theoretically possible and quite another to be the first one to prove it. Enough test pilots are lying dead to prove that what works in theory doesn't always hold up in practice. Divers were often operating as underwater test pilots.

Now two divers had pushed past the 700-foot barrier, opening up the possible salvage of a whole range of rich and previously unattainable wrecks on the sea-bed. There were valuable, even priceless cargoes well beyond the range of the ordinary scuba diver, from Japan to South America, and from the desolate reaches of the Arctic to the depths of the southern oceans. There were wrecks of antiquity in the Americas and the Indian Ocean, galleons laden with treasure. And I knew of countless modern wrecks: merchantmen and warships, German U-boats and Japanese submarines, sunk with cargoes of tin and copper, opium and quinine, mercury and industrial diamonds, gold and precious stones.

The pioneering work at the frontiers of diving technology in the oilfields had now brought those wrecks and their cargoes within my reach. I still had one particular wreck in mind, however, with a cargo of stupendous value, which to my mind could only be salvaged by divers, not mechanical grabs. The *Edinburgh* was getting closer. All I needed was my first really big recovery, the one that would give me the capital to turn my dreams into reality.

Developing a thirst for thrills and spills with the Keighley cycle club.

Killing time before joining the Marines: 'Beneath the veneer of Yorkshire machismo, I was quite a shy person.'

Not for claustrophobics: cave diving: 'Never have I been more glad to break surface.'

The recovery vessel—not the most sophisticated equipment: 'If someone dropped just one piece of scrap too many into the basket, it sank.'

Salvaging the *Otranto*'s riches. This blade weighed 3 tons.

'Yellow Submarine': not such a hit for Jessop and Co who leave court £50 a man poorer.

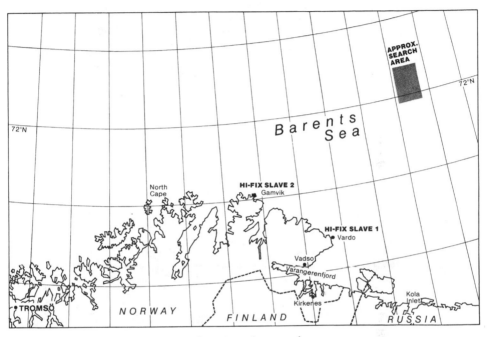

Map showing the search area.

H.M.S. *Edinburgh* in its prime and crippled by torpedoes.

202

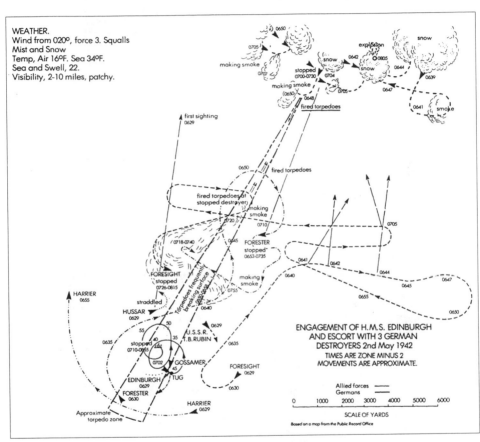

H.M.S. *Edinburgh*'s final battle.

'Keith's wreath': in remembrance of the 57 men who went down with the *Edinburgh*.

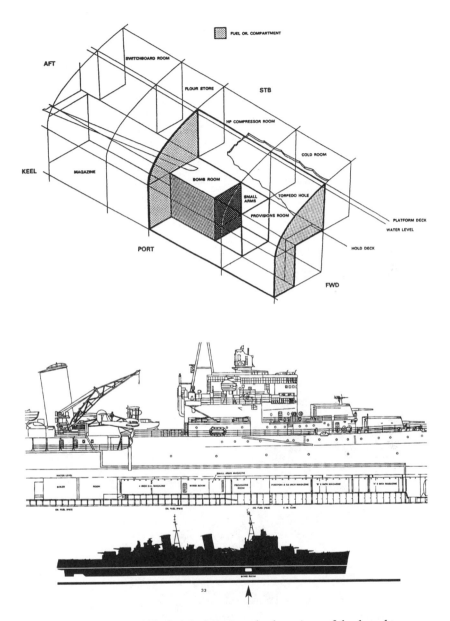

Cross section of the *Edinburgh* showing the location of the bomb room.

MV Stependium on location. Divers down.   The First bar.

KPO 620, the first ingot to be recovered: 'That one bar's value was around the £100,000 mark but it was worth far more than that to me . . .'

£1,000,000 in a bucket! Covered in solidified oil.

Getting back to work: I land the task of cleaning up.

£6,000,000's worth of cleaned-up gold.

Celebration time.

With Harold Wilson at the *Edinburgh* exhibition on board her sister ship H.M.S. *Belfast*.

Ads 5 North Sea diving bell: 'After years of swimming down to wrecks it was like going to work in a taxi.'

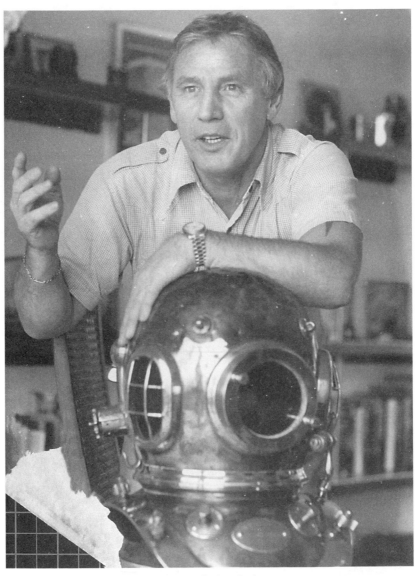

Deep-sea diving helmet.

DEPARTMENT OF TRADE

1 Victoria Street, London SW1H 0ET
Press Office: 01-215 5061
Out of hours: 01-215 7877

Ref 497   **Press notice**   October 16 1981

<u>HMS EDINBURGH - MINISTER PAYS</u>

<u>TRIBUTE TO BRITISH ENTERPRISE</u>

The successful salvage of gold from HMS Edinburgh is a tribute
to British initiative and the meticulous planning of the British
salvor Jessop Marine Recoveries Limited, Iain Sproat, Parliamentary
Under Secretary of State for Trade, said today.

Commenting on the arrival at Peterhead today of the salvage
vessel Stephaniturm, Mr Sproat said:

"This is the culmination of the most successful salvage operation
in history, resulting in the recovery of over 90 per cent of the gold
bullion which has lain for nearly 40 years in the wreck of HMS
"EDINBURGH" nearly 800 feet down in the Barents Sea.

"The success is a tribute to the iniative and meticulous planning
of the British salvor, Jessop Marine Recoveries Limited and to the
expertise of its associate members of a consortium formed to bring
the most advanced technology available to the operation.

"The consortium comprises Wharton Williams Ltd who have been
responsible for the most daring free swimming diving operation ever
undertaken, The Offshore Supply Association owners of the
"STEPHANITURM" which embodies the most modern salvage facilities
currently available and Decca Survey Ltd whose equipment successfully
located the wreck.

"Above all the success of the operation is attributable to the
courage, tenacity and endurance of the team of divers who have operated
on the bed of the Barents Sea in extremely arduous conditions and at
the limit of free swimming diver technology."

CHAPTER TWELVE

SPITZBERGEN

———— • ————

Throughout my time in the North Sea oilfields, I kept in close touch with the Salvage Association and the War Risks Insurance Office, and I was continually pestering them for a crack at another lost cargo.

Risdon Beazley, the giant of the salvage world, already held most of the type of contracts that I was chasing. But they had been sitting on some of them for several years without making any attempt to salvage them, and the Salvage Association, along with the Department of Trade, finally forced them to return a number of them. One day in April 1975, they called me to say that they were now to be put out to tender.

Before I looked at the details of those wrecks, I drew up a list of my own requirements. As a ragged-arsed salvage diver from Keighley with no capital to my name, I could not afford to chase deep-water wrecks at this stage. First I needed a wreck in shallow water – not more than 100 feet down – with a good cargo, but in a position where it was unlikely that any other salvor had already cleared it. With the profits from that, I could finance deep-water salvage work.

When I looked at the list of wrecks, my hopes weren't high. There would be no gifts. The returned contracts would inevitably be ones that Risdon Beazley couldn't find, or were too deep or in a dangerous position or condition. The list contained wrecks in all the world's oceans. I rejected many immediately and still more fell by the wayside as I did the preliminary research. One close to the West African coast looked promising, but turned out to lie in water several thousand feet deep. There were a handful of others that I had to rule out because of their difficulty or because their location made it likely that they'd already been stripped.

Much to my surprise however, I found one wreck that appeared to fulfil all my requirements. The SS *Chulmleigh*, built for the Atlantic Shipping and Trading Company in the year before the outbreak of war, had sunk in shallow water in the Arctic Ocean on 5 November 1942. The 5,500-ton steamship was carrying a cargo of tin ingots now worth around £1.5 million. The wreck was jointly owned by the British and Soviet governments. The stated position was on the South Cape, the southernmost tip of the Arctic island of Svalbard, better known to us as Spitzbergen. It was only 850 miles from the North Pole and ice-bound for at least six months of the year.

The mere mention of the Arctic provoked visions of ferocious gales, frozen seas and howling blizzards, but my research had shown that during the summer months, it is a far more benevolent place than the Western Isles of Scotland. The area becomes a high-pressure zone with twenty-four hours of daylight and very light winds. What more could a salvage man ask?

I couldn't be categorically sure that the wreck had not already been plundered of its cargo, but that is always one of the gambles you have to take. And it seemed unlikely that the *Chulmleigh*'s cargo of tin would have been taken when so many other prizes in warmer and less treacherous waters had yet to be claimed. Just the same, the Arctic was not a place to venture in a fourth-hand Scottish fishing boat. With my limited capital, even getting there would prove difficult, but I felt that given the chance, I'd find a way to do it.

I now had a new partner in salvage, even though he didn't bring much capital with him. After a fair amount of effort, I'd managed to get Graham his first job as a diving tender in the North Sea. He then began going to the diving schools and graduated as a diver, eventually reaching the stage where he could actively help me on expeditions.

Salvage, and the money it generates, creates problems. One of the adages in the salvage world is: If you can't trust your own, who can you trust? It was a big help to have someone I knew I could rely on absolutely. Graham also took a great deal of interest in my research on sunken wrecks and lost cargoes, and became very good at research himself. I discussed the *Chulmleigh* at length with him and we decided that it could be the perfect venture with which to launch Jessop & Sons. A successful recovery would produce the capital to enter big-time salvage.

My initial research showed that the ship was far from the only wreck in those treacherous waters, one of the favourite hunting grounds for German U-boats during the war. Convoys from Britain and the United States, laden with war supplies, stayed as far to the north as possible, at the limit of range for German aircraft based in northern Norway. But the U-boat commanders knew that the convoys bound for the Soviet ports of Archangel and Murmansk had to turn to the east to pass between Svalbard and Bear Island, or south of Bear Island. There they lay in wait and exacted a terrible toll.

Few of those sunken ships had ever been salvaged. In the end I decided to tender for two wrecks, the *Chulmleigh* and the *Waziristan*, which had been sunk just south of Bear Island with a cargo of 1,000 tons of copper ingots. The

5,000-ton *Waziristan*, built for the Hindustan Steamship Sailing Company in 1924, sailed from Rekjavik on Boxing Day 1941, bound for Murmansk. It was last seen by the Panamanian steamship *Cold Harbor* on New Year's Day 1942, 300 miles north-west of Jan Mayen Island.

Nothing more was heard of the ship or its forty-seven-man crew and it was at first thought to have been crushed in thick ice, driven by fierce easterly gales. Only after the war did it emerge that it had been sunk by a German U-boat. The skipper of the U-boat that torpedoed it had even been kind enough to do a drawing in his log book, showing the position of the sinking in relation to Bear Island. I was confident it would take no finding at all.

If my bids were successful, my plan was to recover the *Chulmleigh*'s tin and then drop down to Bear Island for the copper ingots from the *Waziristan*. After completing those two, I'd then approach both the Russian and British governments via the Salvage Association for permission to attempt the recovery of another cargo sunk deep in Arctic waters — the gold of HMS *Edinburgh*.

While awaiting the outcome of my bids, I did further research on the *Chulmleigh* and began piecing together the story of its last voyage and the fate that awaited its crew. Every shipwreck is a tragedy, but the sinking of the *Chulmleigh* was one of the most awful I had ever encountered.

Allied convoys carried five million tons of war material on 'the road to hell' across the Arctic during the war, but almost a quarter of the 720 ships which made the journey were sunk. Six months after the catastrophic convoy PQ 17 — the last to sail during the summer months — when twenty-three of the thirty-four ships were sunk, the Allies tried a new tactic. Ten fast merchantmen, five British and five American, were ordered to make solo voyages to penetrate the ring of U-boats blockading Murmansk. It was not a success. Only seven of the ships survived the journey and two of them were badly damaged by bombing attacks.

Amongst the merchantmen was the *Chulmleigh*, which sailed from Hvalfjord in Iceland on 31 October 1942. It was fully laden with 5,000 tons of supplies for Stalin's armament factories, including 3,942 ingots of tin, 50 casks of nickel pellets, 24 casks of silver steel and 12 cases of hard metal. The thirty-six-year-old Captain Williams had command of fifty-eight men – forty sailors and eighteen gunners. For four days he steered a north-easterly course, steaming through heavy snow storms under a leaden sky. The ship was thirty miles from Svalbard when the first distress signals were heard over the radio. German bombers had attacked another ship to the south of them. During the following morning, 4 November, another four ships were attacked.

The Admiralty in London sent a signal at midnight, ordering the *Chulmleigh* north at full speed. But the heavy overcast had prevented Captain Williams from fixing the ship's position for the previous forty-eight hours. Uncertain of his exact position in those perilous waters, he delayed turning northwards for another five hours. During the brief winter daylight, a German reconnaissance plane circled the ship, but no attack came before night fell. Captain Williams altered course twice more, heading first south and then due east. He was trying to round the southern point of Svalbard under cover of darkness and then follow the edge of the pack ice eastwards, before making the final turn south towards Murmansk.

A blizzard was blowing, hampering visibility and a heavy sea was running. Half an hour after turning east, at 2330 hours on 5 November 1942, the *Chumleigh* struck a reef at a speed of seven knots. Captain Williams had steered straight into the tiny island of Sørkapp Oya at the South Cape, a treacherous maze of shallows and rocks. The ship was aground, held fast amidships.

Captain Williams put out an SOS and, fearing that the seas would break the ship's back, he gave the order to lower the lifeboats. Three boats were safely launched but the fourth was swamped and two crewmen were thrown into the water. Their crewmates had already fallen into a frozen, sullen torpor and ignored pleas from Captain Williams to help them. Eventually the captain, the bosun and an apprentice succeeded in dragging one of the men back into the boat but the other drowned within sight of them.

An hour later, the captain called the boats back alongside the *Chulmleigh* and asked for volunteers to help refloat the ship on the rising tide. Soaked to the skin and already suffering in the vicious cold, the crew refused to go back on board, but eventually two firemen agreed to help the captain, the chief officer and the second engineer. Steam was raised, but even with the engines full astern, the ship remained impaled on the rocks. At four o'clock the radio officer was persuaded to come on board and send the signal that they were abandoning ship. They joined the bedraggled, half-frozen crew in the lifeboats. They began to pull away from the vessel but found themselves trapped in a horseshoe lagoon, with heavy seas and breakers all around them. Unable to find a gap in the reefs in the darkness, they were forced to sit out the rest of the night alongside their stricken ship.

The dawn brought only a faint greying of the southern sky. In the depths of the Arctic winter, the only other light was the faint, faraway red glow from the burning coal stores at Longyearbyen, where fires had raged unchecked for over a year. In the twilight, they spotted a break in the encircling reef and broke through into clear water. One of the three lifeboats was barely navigable, however, and after a short while it was abandoned and the men transferred to the other two. They began to head even further into the icy darkness, towards the Norwegian garrison at Barentsburg, 130 nautical miles to the north.

As they did so, they heard aircraft engines approaching from the south. Four Ju-88s and a Heinkel flew in at mast-top height to attack the doomed ship. A column of dense, oily smoke spiralled upwards as two bombs struck the *Chulmleigh*, but it was still lying on the rocks, its stern jutting high above the water, as the lifeboats disappeared over the horizon.

Alerted by the *Chulmleigh*'s SOS, a British submarine, HMS *Tuna*, had sailed to the South Cape, arriving just before dawn. The captain, Commander Raikes, glimpsed the reefs surrounding the Cape through the squalls of snow. He recorded in his war diary: 'I saw two objects in front of me. The southerly one was almost certainly the *Chulmleigh* in a capsized condition. I extricated myself from this position in heavy snow showers and moved into deeper water to await day-break.' The snow cleared just after 8.30 and the *Tuna* began to search the west coast for the *Chulmleigh*'s lifeboats. Commander Raikes reported hearing explosions, but saw no trace of any boats. He concluded that the *Chulmleigh* had been sunk with all hands and as darkness fell, he abandoned the search and set course away from Svalbard.

The *Tuna* was not the only submarine off the South Cape that day, however. The U-boat U-625 was patrolling between Svalbard and Bear Island when it received a radio message: 'British steamer aground, South Cape Svalbard.' The captain, Oberleutnant Hans Benker, immediately altered course. At two o'clock that afternoon, over six hours after Commander Raikes reported seeing the *Chulmleigh* 'in a capsized condition', Benker was studying the ship through his periscope. He reported: 'Have mast-heads in sight.

Diving to have a look at the steamer from underwater. The vessel makes a normal impression. No damage can be seen, the stern is about one metre down. Apparently there is life on it, smoking out of the chimney, two guns can be seen, the small boats are not in sight, I estimate about four thousand tons.

'It is getting dark soon. Surfaced to give vessel above water a warning shot. It is not so badly damaged that it could not be taken in tow. The vessel is upright and lies in a circle of steep rocks [he later described it as a *klippencrantz*, a garland of rocks] which it could have entered from the south. The entrance however is closed by floating ice.

'I am shooting between two rocks. Shot from tube three . . . Hit after one hundred and sixteen seconds running time. Shot from tube one . . . Misfire. I suppose the torpedo was damaged on the rocks that abound in this area. No explosion followed, rocks were everywhere. The steamer sank after hit by the bows, then turned on to its starboard side. The stern seems to be held fast. I have another twenty incendiary shells fired into it, it is a very good exercise for the gun crew, but in spite of several hits, it does not burn.'

Before he could fire again, he spotted another merchantman on her way eastwards and gave chase. 'Sixteen-thirty. We are running back to our attack position.' Not long afterwards, the ammunition ship *Empire Sky* erupted in a ball of flame and sank.

Benker then returned to the South Cape to apply the *coup de grace* to the *Chulmleigh*, but in the place it had lain, there were now only empty rocks, washed by the sea.

The two open lifeboats sailed slowly north along the coast. They took in water and the salt spray, snow showers and numbing cold steadily drained the fifty-eight survivors of their strength. The sails and the men's clothes were stiff with frost and the boats were covered in a thick layer of ice. At first they were driven north by a moderate southerly wind, but the wind soon died, leaving them becalmed, battling the tide and the drifting pack ice. During the night, the two boats drifted apart and by morning Captain Williams could see no sign of the other one.

The next day the wind rose again, to gale force. In the mountainous seas, the boat shipped a lot of water and they were forced to rig a sea anchor and ride out the storm, baling constantly to keep the boat from being swamped.

The following morning, 9 November, they found they had drifted out of sight of land. They started the engine and after running back in towards the coast for a couple of hours, they caught sight of the other lifeboat, which had no engine. They took it in tow but after a couple of hours of painfully slow progress, Captain Williams took note of his dwindling fuel stocks and gave the order to cut the second boat loose, allowing him to make faster time towards Barentsburg in search of help.

As he steered his ice-encrusted craft northwards, First Mate Finn and twenty-eight men were left behind in the other boat. Its grey sail disappeared astern, hidden by snow flurries. It was never seen again. The men in Captain Williams's boat huddled together for warmth, but the savage cold, fuelled by the keen northerly wind, began to take its toll. The steward became delirious and died during the night of 10 November. His frozen body was manhandled over the side and consigned to the deep.

The next afternoon they glimpsed the headland guarding Isfjord, the approach to Barentsburg. They were only a couple of hours from rescue when the engine failed. So near they could see the entrance to the fjord, they watched helplessly as the wind and tide began to carry them away.

Captain Williams now suffered a breakdown and the

third mate, D.F. Clark, had to take command. The crew were all exhausted and suffering from frostbite and exposure. Only a few of them could eat. The rest just drank a little water.

After another night adrift on the open sea, during which another man died, Clark realised that they had to find shelter or freeze to death. He set course for the shore near Cape Linne, but there were huge breakers and he could see no way through the reefs guarding the coast before nightfall. He dropped sail and decided to row in, trying to find a way through the rocks. In the darkness, with snow falling, it was a near-impossible task. There was a grinding crash as they hit a reef. The seas were breaking over the boat and the men had given themselves up for lost when a giant wave dragged the lifeboat over the reef to the shore.

Two men already lay dead in the boat, another died on the beach, but the rest – twenty-three men, more dead than alive – eased their thirst with mouthfuls of snow and then managed to crawl to three dilapidated wooden huts no more than twenty yards away. By sheer luck they had beached at one of the few places on the entire, barren coast where there was any shelter. They collapsed inside and slept where they fell.

The next morning, in what seemed an even greater miracle, they discovered that one of the huts had a little stove and plenty of wood and coal. The men lit a fire, fetched the remaining rations from the lifeboat and made hot coffee and Horlicks with melted snow.

After six days in an open boat in the depths of the Arctic winter, however, the food and shelter came too late for half the men. Over the next four days, another thirteen bodies were piled outside the hut, buried in clefts in the rock and covered with snow. The survivors found a sack of flour and some tins of corned beef and cocoa in one of the other huts, but soon the stocks of food were shrinking. They were down to a single tin of seal blubber preserved in oil. They ate the blubber a tiny portion at a time and drank the oil.

The three strongest men, D.F. Clark, the third officer and an army gunner, Lance-Sergeant Peyer, made two attempts to reach Barentsburg. Each time, the thick snow, the terrible cold and the rock-strewn terrain, pierced by steep ravines, combined to defeat them. Captain Williams had recovered a little and resumed command from Clark who was now suffering badly from gangrene. Just before Christmas, Williams, Peyer and another gunner, Whiteside, made a final attempt to reach Barentsburg. Once more they failed and collapsed on their return to the hut.

The men's Christmas dinner was a few scraps of rancid, foul-smelling blubber. As they began the New Year, more of them continued to die – of exposure, frostbite, gangrene and starvation. Only the survivors can know to what desperate lengths they were driven to remain alive. Most gave up and lay down to await the end.

On 2 January 1943, two Norwegian soldiers were checking their fox traps in a desolate area near Cape Linne. They were part of a 180-man Norwegian force which had occupied Svalbard since the spring of 1942, despite constant German attacks. They had been skiing over the wastes for three hours when they came across tracks in the snow leading to a ramshackle hut. They were sure they could only have been made by a raiding party of German troops and prepared to storm the hut.

They crouched low and wormed their way forward through the snowdrifts, then stopped and listened. There was the faint sound of voices. One soldier kicked open the ice-encrusted door and shouted, 'Hands up! There are ten men outside with loaded machine guns. Come out with your hands—'

His words died on his lips as he looked around, gagging on the stench of rotting seal blubber and gangrenous flesh. There were nine men in the hut, the only survivors of the wreck of the *Chulmleigh* fifty-seven days before. Only two could walk. The other seven lay half-frozen, their limbs covered with suppurating sores. Outside, buried under a snowdrift, was a stack of frozen corpses, laid out in the snow as they died one by one.

The soldiers hurried back to their base and over the next two days a large party of men with dog-sleds brought the survivors, including Captain Williams and his third mate, D.F. Clark, to Barentsburg. Though none of them knew it, they had been just fifteen kilometres from safety throughout their ordeal.

Patrols were sent further down the coast to search for survivors from the other lifeboat, but no trace of them was ever found. Their boat had either been swamped by the waves, crushed by the ice or splintered on the rocks somewhere on that frozen coast.

Chapter Thirteen

The South Cape

A s well as revealing the horrors of the story, the differing accounts of the principals had thrown up some puzzling contradictions. I'd acquired copies of the logs of the *Tuna* and the U-625. Both gave a very clear report of the happenings on that November morning at the South Cape. Unfortunately one of them had to be wrong.

Commander Raikes claimed to have seen the *Chulmleigh* capsized at a time when both Captain Williams and Oberleutnant Benker insisted it was still upright, impaled on the rocks. And each man gave a different position for the sinking. The Luftwaffe records covering the bombing of the *Chulmleigh* by the Ju-88s might have clarified the situation, but when I tried to get hold of them I received a very short reply: 'All official records of the Luftwaffe are lost. The archives were destroyed at the end of the war.'

My next task was to trace any surviving members of the crews of the *Chulmleigh*, *Tuna* or U-625, particularly the captains. Oberleutnant Benker had been lost overboard on 2 January 1944, but with the help of the Admiralty I traced Commander Raikes. To my amazement he told me that he knew the exact position of the wreck. With the help of his personal war diary and charts, he talked me through the happenings of that long ago morning, plotting the positions as he went along. He had no doubt in his mind that he'd seen the *Chulmleigh* 'in an almost certainly capsized condition', just to the south of Sørkapp Oya, off the South Cape.

You rarely get first-hand reports such as that in the salvage business, but I was still sceptical. Commander Raikes's position still did not fit with the one from which Benker claimed to have torpedoed and shelled the *Chulmleigh*. That lay another mile and a half to the north-west, approximately one-third of the way up the west side of the island.

I now knew the approximate location of the wreck, within a few miles either way, but I couldn't just search the coastline around the South Cape until I found it. That would have taken time and resources that I simply couldn't afford. I needed more accurate information. A letter to the former owners of the *Chulmleigh* produced one name, the only living member of the crew, as far as they were aware. Their information was several years out of date, but if he was still alive, it was an enormous stroke of luck, for the sole survivor was Captain Williams.

I discovered from the report on the sinking in the Public Record Office that Captain Williams had then lived in Cardigan. I took a chance and looked him up in the telephone directory. By unbelievable good luck he was not only still alive but still living at the same address. I rang the number and spoke to him. He was far from keen to revive those long-buried memories but in the end he agreed to talk under certain conditions. He would discuss the sinking of the *Chulmleigh* itself, but there were to be no questions about the subsequent events in the lifeboats and at the huts.

Once more, however, his answers to my questions created as much confusion as clarification. There seemed little doubt from the other two men's reports that the ship had gone aground somewhere on Sørkapp Oya, yet Captain Williams insisted, 'If I could have seen land, I would have gone to it to await rescue.' The island is very low-lying and might have been difficult to see when covered with snow in conditions of bad visibility. Yet if the *Chulmleigh* had hit the rocks around Sørkapp Oya, it was difficult to believe that Captain Williams could see no land, when the German aircraft had had no trouble in finding the ship.

Despite the first-hand accounts of the two British captains involved, I still faced the same contradiction. Captain Williams claimed to have been on board the *Chulmleigh* just before the Luftwaffe appeared and started to bomb the ship; Commander Raikes said he saw the ship in a capsized condition several hours earlier. Both were unshakeable in their conviction. I did not resolve that dilemma until I actually sailed to Svalbard.

I could do no more for the moment to pinpoint the location of the wreck, but there was still research to do on tidal conditions and sea-water temperatures around the South Cape. I wrote to the Norsk Polar Institute in Oslo asking for information and a chart of the area. The reply was prompt, but a little depressing.

We should first mention that Sørkapp Oya is a bird sanctuary, and is also included in the South Svalbard National Park. One of the rules for bird sanctuaries is all traffic 'shall be prohibited during the period from May 15 to August 15'.

The Governor may grant dispensation in respect of:

1. Scientific investigations which do not conflict with the purpose of the bird sanctuaries.
2. Other acts for special reasons which do not conflict with the purpose of the bird sanctuaries.

You will need especially good reasons to obtain permission from the Governor of Svalbard to land on Sørkapp Oya. You must also ask him about possible restrictive security rules for diving in Svalbard waters.

The Sørkapp current is a cold one and you cannot expect summer temperatures higher than in the range of minus four to plus three Celsius.

The letter also mentioned that members of the Institute had witnessed another wreck on Sørkapp Oya during one of their summer trips to the South Cape. The *Red Gauntlet*, a trawler out of Grimsby, had grounded at the head of a long lead on the island, sailing straight up between two long rows of rocks 'in a miraculous manner, with the assistance of a sleeping helmsman'. The crew just abandoned ship and rowed across to another British trawler, *Northern Spray*, and sailed away into the distance.

The news of the other wreck was helpful – unlike the rest of the letter. Unless I could get round the bird sanctuary rules, I'd be diving at the start of the Arctic winter. It would be hellish cold, but I wasn't going to let that put me off. I'd been under the ice before and I'd come too far to let a few problems throw me off course now. If salvaging the *Chulmleigh* had been easy, others would have done it years before.

By the next post I received a letter from the Governor of Svalbard. Having reminded me again that Sørkapp Oya was a bird sanctuary, he went on, 'No permission has so far been granted to you to enter the area. An exemption from this provision of the regulations should not be taken for granted, or counted upon. Thus you will appreciate that a visit to Sørkapp Oya and stay there cannot be realised during the summer months.'

I sent a grovelling reply, pointing out that the first expedition would be for the purpose of finding the wreck and ensuring that the cargo was still on board. Recovery work would only start after a successful outcome of the survey, and with the full permission of the Norwegian government. If necessary it could take place at the end of the exemption period, the onset of the northern winter. The Salvage Association sent a copy of the letter to the Minister of the Environment in Olso, which seemed to do the trick. He replied that he could see no reason why the Governor of Svalbard should not grant me a dispensation to look for the wreck at any time and to salvage the cargo from 1 August onwards.

The dispensation duly arrived a few days later, giving me permission for both the search and the salvage. The only small cloud on the horizon came from Captain Williams. He called to say that a Norwegian called Hovding had come to see him some years before, also asking questions about the *Chulmleigh*. I passed the information on to the Salvage Association but, like me, they didn't take it too seriously. No attempt to find the wreck, let alone a successful salvage operation, could take place without the knowledge of the Governor of Svalbard. Had one already taken place, I reasoned, he would have let me know just to keep me out of the area of the bird sanctuary.

The final hurdle I had to clear was the award of the tender. On 27 May 1976 I received a letter from the Salvage Association. My offer of £100 plus a percentage of the proceeds from the sale of the tin had been successful. I had also bought the rights to the *Waziristan* for the same amount. I had five years to complete the salvage before the contracts lapsed. I had done the easy part. All I had to do now was find the wrecks and lift their cargoes.

Almost as soon as I'd signed the contract, the price of tin started a downward spiral to below £4,000 per ton. That confirmed the plan I'd already formed in my mind. The year was now well advanced and I was worried that if I located the *Chulmleigh* without having time to lift the cargo before winter, the position of the wreck might become known to others before I could get back to it. Apart from the mysterious Norwegian who'd visited Captain Williams, there were a number of keen divers in Tromsø, from where I'd be chartering a boat for the search. Frustrating though it was, I decided to leave the *Chulmleigh* for the year, and go for a good start next spring. I went back to work in the oil-fields for what I hoped would be the last time.

By early January 1977 the price of tin had gone back to over £5,000 per ton. I hoped it was a good omen for the year. I made my first trip to Tromsø that month and put on charter what looked like the perfect vessel for the voyage to the South Cape, a former Norwegian lifeboat, the *Caroline Mathilda*, which had been converted from sail to diesel power. It had a good ice crew, very experienced in Arctic conditions. I arranged with the skipper that as soon as the South Cape was clear of pack ice, he would give me the call. My dive team had been picked for some time: Ron Pritchard, one of my old diving team from Orkney and Islay days, my son Graham, who by now was very good in the water, and myself. I'd ordered special diving suits to help us combat the icy water. I also obtained satellite pictures of the South Cape at regular intervals. They covered the whole area from as far east as Novaya Zemlya across to the North Cape, Bear Island and Svalbard, and showed the exact position of the ice pack.

While I waited for the ice to clear I reviewed all my research material on the *Chulmleigh*. I had two positions where it could or should be. My number one position was that given by Oberleutnant Benker of the U–625. Captain Williams's reports seemed to point in roughly the same direction. I couldn't ignore Commander Raikes's position however, and though it was second in order of likelihood, I decided to look at it first since it could be searched and cleared in a relatively short time. Sørkapp Oya was in an exposed position at the very tip of a large land mass. There were bound to be strong tides, but both areas could be searched within a matter of days, given the correct sea conditions. If the wreck was there to be found, we would find it.

I had one final preparation to make. I'd done a fair bit of reading about life on Svalbard and it was clear that there were polar bears on the island. Past expeditions had had trouble with them, including a couple of deaths. Divers in the water look very much like seals to polar bears. It was not a reassuring thought; seal meat is one of the bears' favourite foods. I was sufficiently worried to present myself at the Keighley police station.

'How do I go about getting a fireams licence?'

The sergeant gave me a suspicious look. 'And what do you want a firearms certificate for, lad?'

'To shoot polar bears, Sergeant.'

From the look on his face, he wasn't sure if I was a local nutcase or just jerking his string. 'So where is this going to happen?'

'On the island of Svalbard.'

'And why do you want to shoot polar bears there, lad?'

'To stop my divers being killed by them.'

A smile came over his face, 'You're the diver who's going to work in the Arctic, aren't you?' The story had been in the local paper.

I was soon the proud owner of a fully licensed ex-service .303 rifle, plus enough ammunition to shoot any bears that tried to mishandle my divers. Thankfully I never had to use it.

There was little else I could do. All the plans for the trip had been finalised. I just had to sit back and wait for the call. It was a long time coming. The ice appeared to be taking forever to clear that year. A hurry-up call to Tromsø supplied the reason; it was the coldest winter in the Arctic for forty years, even worse than the one in which the *Chulmleigh* had sunk.

At last the long-awaited message came through: 'The South Cape is clear of ice.' It sent shivers down my spine. After all the years of waiting, I was finally going to get my chance. In a matter of weeks I could be a rich man. I harboured no doubts. I'd worked hard for the chance. Now it was here, I intended to grab it with both hands.

We crossed to Gothenburg on the ferry from Newcastle on 25 June, then made the long drive north, pausing for team photographs as we crossed the Arctic Circle. We finally arrived in Tromsø at 1.30 the following afternoon, tired out and sick of the endless miles of fir trees. We'd stopped to sleep on the way but because of the intense cold, we soon gave up; at least while driving we could run the heater.

We had a couple of days in Tromsø before sailing. The first thing I did was to check the ice conditions at the Cape. The most recent pictures at the satellite station showed ice fields around Bear Island and loose, drifting pack ice between Bear Island and the Cape. But the Cape itself looked clear. I asked the station director a straightforward question, 'Bearing in mind what we hope to accomplish, would you sail to the Cape in these conditions?' The answer was an unequivocal 'Yes.'

I also visited the local graveyard, where I'd been told some of the dead from the *Chulmleigh* had been brought for burial. I laid some flowers and stood in silence for a few moments in tribute to the brave men of the crew. One

232

headstone was for a young apprentice, just sixteen years old. I couldn't get that stone out of my mind for weeks afterwards.

We set sail for the South Cape on 27 June. We were bathed in the near-permanent daylight of high summer in the Arctic, but the journey was one of the worst I'd ever made in my life. The seas were only moderate in a Force 5 wind from the north-east, but the vessel was another story. Once we'd cleared the long sail down from Tromsø Fjord and reached the open sea, it started. I'd spent a number of years on trawlers and other small vessels, and had my share of rough seas, but nothing had prepared me for this.

Although the *Caroline Mathilda* had been converted to engine power from sail, we now discovered that it still had its heavyweight keel in place. When a wave pushed the ship on to its beam, the response as it swung back through ninety degrees was so quick that it flipped you off your feet.

I wedged myself in the wheelhouse between a radar box and the depth sounder, but one second I was looking down into the sea on one side and the next I was gazing down on the opposite side. It wasn't a journey for anyone who suffered from seasickness. We could only move about the vessel by lurching from handhold to handhold and even lying down on our bunks was impossible. I was flipped on to the deck more times than I care to remember and I spent more time floating in space than any astronaut. Wedging yourself into the bunk worked up to a point, but if you relaxed enough to fall asleep you found yourself straight back on the floor again. Graham's cabin was just aft of the chain locker. It had looked a good berth in harbour, but was a nightmare at sea. Not only was he in space most of the time, but so was the anchor chain. The noise of it hitting the deck made the whole vessel shudder.

There was a well-equipped galley, but hot food was

233

impossible. We were lucky to get a warm drink and attempting to swallow it without spilling it all over the place was a work of art. Only the lure of the *Chulmleigh*'s million-pound cargo stopped me from turning the vessel around and heading back to port.

On a subsequent trip I had a North Sea diving friend with me, who'd spent a number of years in the Royal Navy. I started to tell him about the *Caroline Mathilda*, but he interrupted me. 'I spent a lot of my time in minesweepers, Keith,' he said. 'Nothing can be worse than them.'

'Whatever you say, John.'

Sailing down the fjord, I took up a prone position in the day cabin to read a book. John disappeared below, but within ten minutes he shot out of the hatch.

'All okay John?' I asked innocently.

'Yeah. All okay,' he said, disappearing towards the stern. If the sounds I heard were correct, he definitely wasn't fishing.

He went back down below with the words, 'That's it Keith. No more sickness now, just getting used to the boat.'

'Whatever you say, John.'

It happened at least four more times.

Sailing north through the Arctic, we passed a massive fishing fleet. Vessels flying the flags of a score of different nations stretched from one horizon to the other. I'd never seen such a fleet before. The scale of it made me realise for the first time how fish stocks in the world's oceans are being plundered to the point of extinction.

We passed Bear Island the following night and skirted the first couple of pack-ice fields. I hoped they would be the last. There was one advantage of being in the ice, however. The sea became quite calm and I fell asleep at last.

The next morning, our calculations showed that Svalbard was dead ahead, just over the horizon. We were about four hours from the Cape and what we hoped were the last of the ice fields were well to the south. By eleven o'clock we were less than thirty miles from the Cape. Ahead I could see light drift ice speckling the sea like snowflakes on a lawn, but the nearer we got to the Cape, the thicker the ice became. Small floes banged into the sides of the boat, grinding their way slowly along the wooden hull with a noise as unsettling as chalk screeching on a school blackboard. It grew even more dense, the floes bumping and jostling around the boat like pickets round a factory gate. We were forced to steer to the west, away from the direction of the Cape, in the hope that a way round the ice pack could be found.

The South Cape showed on the horizon at last. For the first time I could see the place I had been dreaming about. It was not a pleasant sight. I could just make out the mountains and glaciers through the thin mist clinging to the ice, but between the boat and that distant shore was nothing but a solid expanse of ice drifting slowly away to the north. I thought about Captain Williams and his crew in conditions far worse than these.

Our radar showed us to be about ten miles from the Cape; it might as well have been ten thousand. There was not a hope of getting through to the island. The skipper said that it could take weeks to clear. After taking some photos, all I could do was instruct him to turn around and head back to Tromsø. It was one of the biggest disappointments of my life.

The journey back was miserable, even worse than the outward one. We had nothing to look forward to but returning home to say we failed. Back in Tromsø I made arrangements to return to the Cape once conditions cleared. It would have to be on the *Caroline Mathilda*, for all the other suitable boats were already chartered. Then I went back to the North Sea to earn some money.

We arrived back at the South Cape late on 17 August, after another gut-wrenching voyage. We had time for only one dive before darkness. It produced nothing but we did discover that on that particular tide we had a current running from the east at about four knots. It swirled between the rocks, making it difficult to hold position near the diver.

I called a stop while there was still light enough to put a party ashore on Sørkapp Oya. I wanted a recce done to look for clues of a shipwreck on the west side of the island. Past experience told me that a wreck the size of the *Chulmleigh* would have left signs on the beach. Sure enough, almost opposite my number one position we found ship's hatch covers and American-manufactured tyres and battery boxes, which had been listed on the manifest of the *Chulmleigh*. Captain Williams had also told me that he took on a part-cargo of tyres in New York.

The find caused great excitement amongst the team. It was certainly looking good for the morning. Back on board we got ourselves ready for the following day – cylinders fully charged, all diving gear prepared – then discussed our plan of action. We decided to make one more dive at Commander Raikes's position. If we found nothing, we'd move the 1,500 metres to Benker's position, which was now backed by all the findings on the beach.

I made it clear during the talk that should we find the wreck and its cargo, we must play it very quiet, just reporting to the surface that we'd found signs of a wreck and nothing else. I wanted no ingot-waving to alert the ship's crew. It could well be the next year before we could return to the site and I didn't want anyone helping themselves in the meantime.

We awoke the following morning to find the whole area covered in a thick mist. It was a common occurrence in these latitudes and could last for minutes or days. I got the skipper to move the vessel a lot closer to the dive-site; I didn't fancy losing sight of it and drifting away in these conditions.

A comedy of errors then began, though it felt more like a tragedy to us. One of the Norwegian seamen had left the big outboard motor on the inflatable when he'd tied it up alongside the previous night. No safety line had been fixed to the engine. During the move closer to the site, the outboard had come loose and disappeared into the depths. Not knowing at what point it had fallen into the sea made it impossible to even consider a dive search for it.

We attempted to row the Zodiac across to the site but without an outboard it doesn't take much tide or breeze to make a Zodiac unmanageable, and we had plenty of both. The tide was taking us further and further away and we were also starting to lose sight of our mother ship, the last thing I wanted in these conditions. I had to admit defeat and call in the mother ship to pick us up. There was no way we could have rowed back against the tide. In desperation, we pressed the ship's big wooden lifeboat into service. It must have weighed tons; it certainly felt like it as we rowed the monster in our super-thick diving suits.

In the end, more by luck than management I managed to get a diver down in the area I wanted to search. He found a mess of ship's plates and condenser piping almost immediately, certainly enough to show that there was a wreck of considerable size in the area, but was it our wreck or the *Red Gauntlet*?

As I was pondering this, I got my second shock. The Norwegian skipper informed me it was time for us to return to Tromsø. A furious argument erupted, for I'd requested a week on the site. It soon became obvious that a mistake had been made in translation. They'd thought that I wanted the vessel for a week in total, rather than a week on site, not including sailing time. I was told the boat was back on charter in four days' time. As if to rub salt in the wound, the mist began to lift. After another free and frank exchange of views I managed to persuade the captain to stay on site for a few more hours. During the argument we had drifted close to the point from which Commander Raikes had made his sighting of the capsized *Chulmleigh*.

Stretching away from the South Cape were two parallel lines of reefs, black rocks ground and worn smooth by the winter ice which sweeps over and round them, borne on the fierce tides. As I gazed at the reefs, my attention was caught by the southernmost rock of all. It had been ground by the sea ice into the shape of an upturned ship's hull. I now had little doubt that what Commander Raikes had seen through the snow flurries that morning over thirty years before had been the rock, not the *Chulmleigh*. At the time he turned away and sailed south, believing the ship lost with all hands, the *Chulmleigh* was still afloat no more than 1,500 metres away, its crew fighting desperately to save their lives.

After another ferocious argument, I persuaded the captain to take the ship close to Benker's position before turning for home. As we sailed up the coast, we came to a line of jagged rocks stretching the length of the island some 200 metres from the shore. The tide had forced the sea ice into the gaps between them, forming a circle of blue ice, the black rocks studding it like jewels in a necklace. I remembered the report that the U-boat captain had sent to his base. He said the ship was surrounded by a *klippencrantz* – a garland of rocks. It was not hard to imagine the dying *Chulmleigh* caught at the heart of this wreath of rock and ice.

I ached for the chance of just one dive to confirm that the *Chulmleigh* and its cargo lay there, but the captain would brook no further delays. There was nothing for it but to leave.

CHAPTER FOURTEEN

BEAR ISLAND

———— • ————

Once again we were on our way south but despite another crushing disappointment, we were in better heart. We'd found wreckage in the position given by Commander Raikes and on the shore by my number one position. We'd also located Benker's *klippencrantz*. The more we talked about it, the more I got to like it. Pinpointing the wreck on our return would take little time. It was far too late to attempt to put a salvage package together for this season anyway and had we found the ingots we would all have been very depressed at having to leave them there. Once again I went back to the oilfields to earn some more money, certain that the first stage of my dream would at last be realised the next diving season.

I should have known better. The next March I applied as usual to the Governor of Svalbard for the renewal of my permission to enter the area of the South Cape to complete my survey. It was refused. I spent weeks trying to obtain a reason for this abrupt reversal but no explanation was ever offered. The reason was only to become apparent much later.

The letter from the Governor also noted that Ulrich Harms, a big West German salvage company operating out of Hamburg, had expressed interest in the *Chulmleigh*. This was not good news at all. If they'd done their research Ulrich Harms would certainly know that I'd been granted the rights to salve the cargo. I began to get an uneasy feeling. The Germans had been associated with Risdon Beazley in the past, and they had no desire to see a new competitor breach their British monopoly.

Months slipped past as the Salvage Association tried to warn off the German firm and the British Embassy did their best to persuade the Norwegians to grant me access to the site, but once more the diving season was all but over when I was finally allowed access.

To heighten my frustration, the weather and ice conditions at the South Cape had been as good that year as they'd been bad the year before. They were still good now, but the uncertainty about a departure date meant that I'd been unable to confirm the charter of a boat. I now found that every available ocean-going boat from Tromsø to as far up as Hammerfest was fully booked for the remainder of the season. We spent a month in northern Norway searching for any boat willing to take us across, but with winter fast approaching, we were once again forced to abandon the search for another year, this time without even reaching the site. Three years of my five-year contract had already elapsed and I had still to confirm the finding of the wreck-site, let alone lift its cargo.

Back in the North Sea for yet another winter, I was starting to get some funny looks whenever I mentioned the *Chulmleigh*. To most divers salvage was pie in the sky. Only oil money was for real. If anything went wrong in the oil-fields they just threw money at it until it came right. When I explained that the roots of my problem were a few nesting birds and the Governor of some far-off northern land that most of them had never heard of, it caused more than a little mirth.

I didn't share the amusement. By now I was getting desperate. After a meeting with the Salvage Association and the Department of Trade and Industry to discuss my problems in gaining access to the South Cape, John Jackson of the Salvage Association and I flew to Oslo for a meeting with the Norwegian Minister of the Environment.

After a formal introduction, I outlined my proposed methods and the area I was planning to search, and expressed my willingness to carry a Norwegian observer to ensure that I stuck to any conditions imposed. Within half an hour I had full authority to start work at the Cape as soon as the ice had cleared. After months of frustration, thirty minutes with the Minister had cleared all the obstacles.

As I was making preparations for the trip to the South Cape, I received a phone call from Chris 'Plug' Jenkins. The last time I'd seen him he'd been falling through a hatch after his salvage team had blown up the live torpedoes in the U-boat off the Orkneys. He now worked for Seaway, a multi-million pound Norwegian company with interests in many fields, including diving. There had been a big turn-down in the North Sea and Seaway now had surplus capacity in diving vessels and divers. They wanted to diversify into marine salvage in a big way and were interested in working with me.

Chris had actually walked into the offices of the Salvage Association and asked for some cargo-recovery contracts, but John Jackson told him, 'It doesn't work that way. You have to initiate a research programme of your own and find wrecks with cargoes, then come back to the Salvage Association to see if the contract is available. The alternative is to find someone who's already done the research work for you.' Knowing that I had bulging research files but a chronic shortage of capital, John mentioned my name to Chris.

I met him at the offices of Seaway Diving in London. He

was little changed. He had hands that made a ball-point pen look like a matchstick, hair so blond it was almost white and a pink complexion that flushed red when he was arguing. I was to see a lot of that over the coming weeks and months.

That first meeting lasted over seven hours. He told me that Seaway wanted to use salvage to keep their vessels and divers in employment and were willing to form a new company with me.

It was a flattering offer from such a large and well-established company and it seemed a natural marriage; they had the equipment, I had the knowledge. I needed to be sure that it was in my best interests, however. When the meeting finally broke up, I promised to give them my terms for a partnership between us in the next couple of days.

I did a great deal of soul-searching over those few days. After all the years of frustration I felt that the cargoes of the *Chulmleigh* and the *Waziristan* were at last almost within my grasp. I was reluctant to share them with a latecomer on the scene, but I was not so slow that I couldn't see the long-term advantages to me of a partnership with Seaway. Their resources and diving assets could turn the *Edinburgh* project from a dream into a reality. After a great deal of thought I offered Seaway five per cent of the *Chulmleigh* cargo and forty-five per cent of that of the *Waziristan*. In return, they would have to produce or hire a small trawler to find both wrecks. We would then jointly charter a suitable vessel to lift the cargo from the *Waziristan* and I would go back to the *Chulmleigh* site and complete the recovery of that cargo before returning to London to form the new salvage company with Seaway.

Chris made a counter-offer. Seaway would pay me my expenses for all the research done over the past five years and give me fifty per cent of the net value of both cargoes, after expenses. I would be made a director of the new company,

Seaway–Jessop. It seemed a reasonable offer on the face of it, but the 'after expenses' clause put me off. Seaway naturally wanted to use their own big diving vessels, but from the figures I'd seen, there would be very little left after expenses.

The offers and counteroffers continued for several more days and to help me keep track of all the offers flying about, I began making diary notes. I kept up the habit of making a daily record of events for the rest of my diving career. It proved to be one of the wisest moves I ever made.

Seaway's own potential contribution to the partnership was obvious; they had ships, hardware, experienced divers and capital. They naturally wanted to see what I was bringing to the party in return, but I faced an insuperable problem. If I showed them my research, I would have given away the crown jewels and have nothing left to sell. We had only proceeded so far by hints, nods, winks and nudges, however. In the end I either had to pull out of the negotiations altogether or put my trust in their good faith and let them see some of my research. I took a deep breath and agreed to let them see my material on the *Chulmleigh* and the *Waziristan*.

Foolishly I also mentioned the *Edinburgh*. They'd never even heard of it before but they weren't stupid; they didn't need to have the value of ten tons of gold explained to them. They asked for proof of what I said and believing in their enthusiasm for a partnership with me, I gave them a full verbal briefing, while still keeping my research papers in reserve.

Negotiations did not progress as smoothly after that and more than once I wondered if my naïvety in the world of big business was going to cost me everything I'd worked for. On two occasions I considered that we had verbally agreed a deal only for Seaway to come back a couple of days later and make a new and worse offer.

I was not only losing patience with Seaway, I was irate at the waste of valuable preparation time for the *Chulmleigh* salvage. Having gone this far and given them so much, however, I clung to the hope that we could yet strike a deal. I also didn't want the Salvage Association to think that I was being the awkward party in the negotiations.

I prepared one final offer. I would pass the *Waziristan* contract to them in its entirety for the sum of £25,000. This offer was promptly accepted by Chris Jenkins. Later the same day he called back to say they would only pay the £25,000 on completion, not up front. I told him to stop wasting my time and go and find someone else to play with, then slammed the phone down. Half an hour later he called again, asking me to listen to a fresh proposal. I told him it was his last chance.

Graham and I went down to London the following day. We arrived at the Seaway offices at 10.30 and by the end of the afternoon we'd reached yet another agreement with Chris Jenkins and the £25,000 was back as an up-front payment. He had it typed by his secretary. He put a call through to Oslo, to confirm the heads of agreement between us, but the first cracks appeared immediately. The £25,000 was now to be paid 'at a later date'.

Chris then told me that Christian Selmer, the Chief Executive of Seaway, would send me a telex clarifying everything. I found this rather strange. We'd just spent several hours reaching a basic agreement, and now we were being told that a man we didn't know, who had taken no part in the negotiations, would need to clarify it. When the telex arrived, it contained a whole series of fresh proposals and conditions. It appeared negotiating control was in Oslo and that everything we thought that we'd agreed was once more being torn up.

As soon as we got home, I contacted my solicitor and

then sent a telex to Seaway pointing out that the proposed contract bore no relation to the heads of agreement. I saw no possibility of reconciling our differences and would be returning to the South Cape in the near future. Jacob Stolt-Neilsen, the owner of Seaway, then called me on the phone. He blamed the breakdown on a lack of communication within Seaway and asked me to come across to Oslo, all expenses paid, to sort it all out. I agreed to make one last effort to conclude a deal.

Graham and I flew across to Oslo on the morning of 10 July. Chris Jenkins made contact with the weather station that afternoon to check the conditions at the South Cape. It was now clear of ice, which appeared to be a good omen. At the meeting the next morning we were introduced to Christian Selmer and Jacob Stolt-Neilsen. Christian was immaculately groomed and his delicate, manicured hands looked as if they had never gripped anything more weighty than a gold pen. He spoke slowly, almost grudgingly, as if it was costing him money to utter every word. Jacob was older, with thick, wavy hair running to grey. He peered at me through his glasses with an irritating mixture of condescension and impatience.

I didn't exactly find myself warming to them, but I didn't have to; this was strictly business. During the discussion I raised the promised £25,000. Jacob interrupted me to say there was no need to discuss it; they were giving me the money in full. We were soon in full agreement and a draft contract was drawn up. A diving support vessel, the *Seaway Hawk*, was put on stand-by for a voyage to the South Cape to complete the search for the *Chulmleigh* and the *Waziristan*. Now I was finally dealing directly with the top men in Seaway, I felt that all would be well at last.

On the flight home both Graham and I were feeling pretty good about the day's work. I decided to look at the contract to see just how and when the £25,000 was to be paid. Once more there was no mention of it.

Apart from that little oversight, things now began to move fast. Within a fortnight, Ron Pritchard, Graham, my younger son Ian and I were on our way to the Seaway base at Haugesund in Norway to board the *Seaway Hawk*. Before we sailed, I put in a call to Christian Selmer to raise the missing £25,000. Once again, I was met with prevarications, but I had no appetite for another fall-out at this stage. Seaway's tactics rankled with me, but the immediate prospect of finding a £1.5 million cargo made the whereabouts of the £25,000 seem a minor problem. We finally agreed the contract by telex with Oslo, and it was signed just before our departure for the South Cape.

It was a relief when we finally put to sea. I'd neither the desire nor the patience for any more wrangling over the fine print of contracts, but I still had doubts about Seaway's ultimate intentions. I knew my job of wreck research and salvage inside out and was proud of the fact that I could do it anywhere in the world. But I felt that having come so far, I was now putting my family's future on the line with people I found it hard to trust.

My doubt did not extend to the search for the *Chulmleigh* and the *Waziristan*, however. I was full of confidence that we would find both ships. My research had been thoroughly checked by Seaway's own people, who agreed with my conclusions about the most likely positions of the two wrecks.

The *Waziristan* was in about 200 feet of water, some ten miles to the south-east of Bear Island. We were using a side-scan sonar to detect the wreck on the bottom. An electronic 'towfish' was towed behind the boat and a powerful electrical charge caused a crystal transducer in the towfish to vibrate, emitting an ultra-high-frequency sound wave. The returning echo from any object in its path was picked up by the crystal and the resulting vibrations were converted to electrical impulses. A set of styluses recorded the impulses on to chemically sensitised paper.

Unlike the sonar depth recorders that created a single line image of the contours of the ocean bottom, the side-scan, as the name suggests, scanned out to both sides, effectively drawing a three-dimensional image of objects on the sea-bed with sound. By a curious twist, the acoustical shadow of a wreck recorded by the side-scan often showed more detail than the image of the wreck itself.

The equipment was by no means as sophisticated as the side-scans available today, but it worked well enough in the hands of a skilled operator. In order to establish a comprehensive search pattern, however, it was essential that the ship had an accurate means of fixing its position. The *Seaway Hawk* would be using the ship's radar to position itself, taking a fix on Bull Head, the southern tip of Bear Island. I expressed some doubts about the accuracy of this method, but the skipper assured me there would be no problems with it. It was only when we were actually at sea that I discovered that the radar was on the blink.

The attitude of some of the crew matched the quality of the radar equipment. The dive team was as keen as mustard but I got the strong impression that the crew would have been far more happy tied up at the dock at Haugersund, where they'd spent most of the recent months.

We arrived at the South Cape late on the afternoon of Sunday, 29 July, to find a large amount of drift ice in what was supposed to have been an ice-free area. Mist hung over the water, reducing visibility to a few yards. We launched the Zodiac anyway, but were constantly losing sight of the *Hawk*, and in the end I decided to stand down for the night.

The next morning we dropped anchor a mile to the west of my number one position. The pack ice appeared to be thinning out but ice floes the size of small houses were still moving with the current at a speed of two or three knots, making it almost impossible to do a systematic search. During the day the wind had gone round to the north-east and fresh drift ice began coming round the point from the east. Despite the conditions, the diving team performed very well and a good search was made of the bottom section of the number one area.

At about 8 p.m., at the end of a long day's diving in very cold water, one of the most experienced divers in the team reported objects to his front and shapes that were out of keeping with the bottom pattern in the area. At that point he ran out of air and we were unable to verify what he'd seen that night, but I went to bed happy. I was up at 6.30 the next morning, eager to confirm the finding of the wreck.

It was dry and sunny, but we were surrounded by pack ice. It was impossible to dive in those conditions and we were in a position of some danger; if the wind had gone round to the east, we would have been completely trapped in the ice. After a meeting with the skipper, we decided to sail for Bear Island and begin the search for the *Waziristan*. It was a long time before we broke clear of the ice pack.

That night I went back to the logbook of U-143, the U-boat that had sunk the *Waziristan*, and dissected every word of Captain Rudolf von Schendel's report. Early in the morning of 2 January 1942, U-143 was patrolling south of Bear Island. It was still dark and heavy snow showers were falling, driven by a strong wind. Through the snows von Schendel caught sight of the *Waziristan* steaming eastwards at eleven knots, close to the edge of the ice pack.

Von Schendel was making his first voyage as a U-boat

skipper. A few days earlier, he had misidentified a German ship, the *Steinbek*, off the Finmark coast and torpedoed it. This was his first chance to make amends. He fired his first torpedo at 0622 hours from a distance of 600 metres. There was no hit, but he reported a detonation seven minutes later. He fired another torpedo at 0639 hours from a distance of 500 metres. Again it missed its intended target, but exploded seven minutes later. The torpedoes would only detonate on impact with a solid object. Apart from the *Waziristan*, the only other solid object in the area was Bear Island itself.

For the two torpedoes to have hit Bear Island after exactly the same running time, the *Waziristan* must have been holding a course parallel to the coast. The speed of German torpedoes – about 41 knots – put the U-boat four and a half miles from the island. The *Waziristan* had therefore been just over four miles from it.

The log of the U-143 gave the ship's speed as eleven knots, but having rechecked the specification of the *Waziristan*, I felt it was an unrealistically high estimate for a fully-laden steamer of its vintage. A speed of nearer eight knots seemed more realistic, which would explain von Schendel's failure to hit the ship with either of the first two torpedoes.

At 0648 hours U-143 fired a third torpedo from a distance of 400 metres and this one struck home after a running time of twenty-four seconds. Von Schendel recorded the result in his log: 'A short sharp flame, mast-high spout of water, then the steamer breaks in the middle and starts to sink. Two lifeboats are put out. At 7.20 the vessel has disappeared.' British cryptologists at Bletchley Park intercepted the weak, coded signal from von Schendel recording the sinking, but though he saw the lifeboats launched, no distress signals were sent. The fifty-man crew were posted missing, presumed lost.

Some twenty-six minutes had elapsed from the time of the first attack to the third torpedo strike, during which time the *Waziristan* would have covered no more than four and a half miles. After it was struck by the torpedo, I felt the maximum distance it could have travelled would be a further one and a half miles, plus any tidal assistance. Even with a generous margin for error, the area we would have to search was only sixty square miles.

Bear Island is pear-shaped and about eleven miles long by seven miles wide. It rises steadily from the flat northern end to the peak of the aptly-named Misery Mountain, then drops away sharply to the southern tip of the island, Bull Head. We arrived off it at 2 a.m. and started the side-scan search just two hours later. We hit immediate problems. We were trying to carry out a methodical search of a box of ocean six miles wide and ten miles long, but the ship's faulty radar made it next to impossible to fix our position with any certainty.

Even worse, it now transpired that Seaway had not hired the special winch that helped to raise and lower the fish of the side-scan, which had to be kept at a constant distance of fifteen metres from the sea-bed. Had I not been occupied with contract negotiations up to the moment of departure I would have spotted the omission before we left port. But I'd left it to Seaway to organise the equipment and now it was too late to repair the omission.

We did what we could, and in areas where the bottom was relatively flat we managed to control the height of the fish by varying the speed of the boat. But in the shallower areas there were steep peaks and troughs on the sea-bed and it was impossible to keep the fish the correct distance from the bottom.

We covered the area without finding a trace of the *Waziristan*, but given the two problems it was entirely possible that we had sailed either side of it or even straight over the top of it without detecting it.

We searched my second- and third-choice areas with similar lack of success and as we began the search of the fourth and final area, the towfish fouled the bottom, damaging the towing cable. The side-scan operator then told me it would take six days to repair. I managed to curb my desire to send him down to do a personal inspection of the sea-bed in a concrete swimsuit.

Rather than abandon the search altogether, I sent a party out in the Zodiac to scour the coast of the island for wreckage. On a rocky beach on the west coast they found a ship's boiler, similar in size to the one carried by the *Waziristan*. While it was an encouraging find, it was by no means certain to lead to the wreck. Ship's boilers were naturally buoyant and were usually one of the first things to pop out of a wreck. They could float on the tide for a considerable distance before being washed up on a beach.

We then went ashore to ask the Norwegians manning the radio station at the northern end of the island if they had any information about wrecks. Even landing a Zodiac on the island was a struggle. The whole coast has been undercut by the grinding action of the winter pack ice over thousands of years and the island sits on its base column of rock like a cap on a mushroom.

The people at the radio station gave us a friendly reception, perhaps glad of the diversion provided by any visitor during their lonely twelve-month tour of duty in one of the most desolate places on earth. They could give us little information however. They knew of no wrecks on that coast apart from a small British trawler lost in the 1930s, but pointed us to a small, unofficial graveyard nearby, where the bodies of a number of foreign sailors had been buried after being washed ashore from ships sunk during the war. As we walked across to it, we came face to face with an arctic fox. It sniffed the air, then turned its back and walked slowly away, showing no fear of us whatsoever.

When we reached the graveyard, we found British names engraved on some of the graves, but no clues to their ships, nor to the whereabouts of the *Waziristan*.

The Norwegians had also told us about an abandoned coal mine on the island and we visited that too, out of curiosity. It was an eerie sight. The mine had shut down in the early years of this century after the owners gave up the unequal struggle to win coal in such a bleak and terrible place. They had simply walked away, leaving everything as it was. In the intervening decades the cold, dry air had pre-served everything almost intact. The wooden miners' huts still stood, and pushing open a door was like entering a cabin on the *Marie Celeste*. Fading pictures hung on the walls, the chairs were pushed back from a table still laid with cups and plates, as if the occupants had finished breakfast seventy minutes, not seventy years before.

Even more astonishing, two steam engines still stood on the narrow-gauge lines leading to the cliff edge, from where the coal was loaded for shipment to Norway. In any popu-lated area, anywhere in the world, they would have been stripped of everything movable years ago. Here in this for-gotten frozen desert, they stood untouched. Even the few things that had rusted and dropped off down the years still lay on the ground where they had fallen.

I would have liked to spend longer exploring the island, but the priority was to find the *Waziristan* not abandoned coal mines. We returned to the boat and did a towed diver search of the inshore area alongside the beach where we had found the boiler. We searched out to a depth of some twenty-five metres but found nothing. There was now really nowhere left to search, and when the message came that the South Cape was once more free of ice, I bowed to the inevitable and returned there to confirm the finding of the *Chulmleigh*.

This time the information was accurate; the South Cape was ice-free. We wasted no time in getting divers in the water. The *Chulmleigh* was there all right, just where the diver had spotted it, but one hard look was enough to show that someone had been there before us. All the tell-tale signs were there. Pieces of old mooring rope were still tied on to various parts of the wreck and on a wreck of this age, at this shallow depth, the original ropes would long since have rotted away. We could also see that the wreck had been worked. Wreckage had been dragged to one side and scattered over the ocean floor to expose the cargo, which had then been removed. Bits of the hull were strewn around the bottom for a considerable distance but the cargo of tin had disappeared without trace. Not a single ingot remained.

The shouts of jubilation at finding the wreck were silenced within five minutes. When I heard, it was the blackest moment of my diving career. I could have cried with disappointment. Years of difficulties and delays, painstaking research, unrelenting effort and the expenditure of a huge amount of money I could ill afford had come to nothing. The cargo had been removed by a pirate salvor − in my view it was theft. I remembered Captain Williams's description of the Norwegian who had asked him about the *Chulmleigh*, and I began to wonder if concern for the welfare of the bird colonies on Sørkapp Oya had been the only reason for the difficulties I had experienced in getting access to the area over the previous few years.

Back in Norway I began to make enquiries. I made contact with an investigative reporter, Alf Jacobsen, and over the next few months he uncovered the story of the 'theft' of the *Chulmleigh*'s cargo. Possibly tipped off by the disgruntled Risdon Beazley, it looked like Einar Hovding, a Norwegian scrap dealer, shipowner and wreck hunter had searched the coastline until he found the wreck. More than likely he'd stripped it of its cargo and taken it to his shipbreaker's yard in Sandnessjöen.

Alf Jacobsen found one of the many witnesses who saw the cargo of tin ingots landed in two shipments, hidden under a layer of scrap metal.

> The scrap metal lay on top, while the ingots of tin were piled in the bottom of the ships. I remember well that the tin was brought ashore at Hovding's quay, grey-coloured ingots the size of loaves of bread.
>
> At the time it was said that they came from a wreck off Sørkapp, in shallow water just at the edge of the ice. The salvage crew had apparently been told to keep quiet, but said it had been a tough and demanding job.
>
> Einar Hovding has repeatedly refused to comment but his actions have been both self-contradictory and evasive. Recently he has also threatened anyone who mentions the case. It has become quite obvious, however, that Hovding's top secret operations have already created shock waves in Moscow, where the Russian government is unlikely to allow anyone to help themselves to valuables which can be converted into hard currency.

Jacobsen's scoop was confirmed by another reporter, Terje Halvorsen, in *VG* magazine. He traced the diver, Bruno Kuttner, who'd actually carried out the salvage work.

> The ingots lay in shallow water, ten to fifteen metres deep, but there was a lot of silt, making it difficult to see. The ingots lay relatively close together. I brought up the

first ones by hand, but the working conditions were too difficult.

They returned to the wreck site a few months later with a mechanical grab. 'It made powerful inroads into the heap of metal and I was able to load it all,' Kuttner said. 'Only three or four ingots were left behind.'

Kuttner also claimed that he'd since been approached by representatives of the Hovding company warning him not to reveal what had taken place off Svalbard. Hovding refused to confirm the story but did admit that he had sent expeditions to the South Cape and knew of the *Chulmleigh*'s position and the cargo it carried.

There was no way that I could afford to chase Hovding through the courts, but like Alf Jacobsen, I had every confidence that the Soviet and British governments, co-owners of the wreck, would pursue him for the value of the cargo. Not for the first time in my life, I was to be disappointed. Despite the evidence against Hovding, neither government has ever begun proceedings against him. I couldn't help reflecting on the time I'd been taken to court in Scotland for the theft of a couple of hundred pounds' worth of torpedo tubes from HMS *Graph*. I'd been convicted and fined for that; Hovding had got away scot-free with tin worth over £1.5 million pounds.

Although I'd lost a fortune on the *Chulmleigh*, I could cling to a couple of straws. The experience I'd gained of diving in Arctic waters would be invaluable if I could win the contract for the wreck that was still my main goal, carrying a prize infinitely more precious than base metal. And of one thing I was certain: no ships could operate in secret that close to the massive Soviet naval base at Murmansk. No one, not Einar Hovding, not Risdon Beazley, had touched HMS *Edinburgh* since it sank almost forty years before.

CHAPTER FIFTEEN

U-456

---•---

Launched at the Swan Hunter shipyard in March 1938 and commissioned the following year, just before the outbreak of war, the 10,000-ton *Edinburgh* was a formidable cruiser, packed with weaponry. She was armed with four triple turrets of 6-inch guns, twelve 4-inch guns and a score of smaller ones, and also had triple torpedo tubes on either side, firing 21-inch torpedoes, packed with 750 pounds of TNT. She was commanded by Captain Hugh Faulkner, but during her final, fateful voyage, Rear-Admiral Sir Stuart Bonham-Carter was on board. Outranking Faulkner, he had effective command of the ship.

In late April 1942, the *Edinburgh* lay at anchor in Vaenga Bay, a few miles down the Kola Inlet from Murmansk. It was the safest available anchorage, but was still dangerously close to the German front line, only twenty miles away, and there were daily raids on Murmansk by German bombers. Although winter had given way to the semi-permanent daylight of the Arctic summer, there were still ice floes on the dark waters of the inlet and the superstructure of the *Edinburgh* was covered in a thick layer of snow.

She had arrived in Murmansk a week earlier after escorting a convoy laden with vital war materials through the U-boat-infested waters between the coast of Norway and the polar ice pack to the north. Now she was about to make the return journey, escorting the surviving empty merchant ships back to Reykjavik before another suicide run to Murmansk.

In addition to her 550-man crew, she was carrying over 200 passengers. A few were Poles and Czechs interned by the Russians, but most were frost-bitten survivors of sinkings on earlier convoys. The stretchers of a never-ending stream of sick and injured seamen were laid in rows in the spare hangar for the *Edinburgh*'s Walrus aircraft and the ship's surgeons worked night and day to operate, or amputate where gangrene had set in.

The men had been holed up in Murmansk for months, their condition steadily deteriorating. The Russians had no food or medical supplies to spare; their own people were starving and their hospitals were crammed with casualties from the battles raging just to the west.

Just before midnight on 25 April 1942, the crew of the *Edinburgh* were woken by the sound of the bugler summoning both watches of duty hands. The men stumbled on deck to see a strange sight. Two barges were tied up alongside, their decks lined with heavily armed Red Army soldiers. The *Edinburgh*'s contingent of Royal Marines stood guard on her own decks. The tarpaulins covering the barges' holds were pulled back to reveal ammunition boxes, but the presence of so many guards made it clear that something far more valuable than ammunition was being loaded.

Sleet was falling steadily as the duty hands began transferring the heavy wooden boxes to the *Edinburgh*, hauling them up to the flight deck by their rope handles. Their weight was enough to convince the seamen that they were handling a very unusual cargo, and the attempted secrecy was rendered useless as one of the boxes slipped from the slings and crashed to the deck. As it split open, five gold bars spilled out of the sawdust lining it.

An officer held the crew at bay until a hastily summoned shipwright had repaired the box. It was raised to the flight deck, the last of ninety-three, and then lowered like the others down a shaft to the bomb room three decks below. The bomb room lay next to the magazine where ammunition for the ship's 4-inch guns was stored, and was formidably protected. The deck above it was of two and a half-inch armour-plate, the side wall was of six-inch armour.

Several sailors later claimed to have had premonitions of disaster as they loaded the gold. The boxes were stencilled with crimson letters and as the sleet settled on them, the ink began to dissolve and run, dripping on to the snow-covered deck. Superstitious seamen needed no other omen than that. As one said to an officer, 'This is Russian gold, dripping with blood.'

The journey the gold had already made was perilous enough; the 1,000-mile, single-track railway line linking Murmansk with Moscow ran less than fifty miles from the front line in places, putting it well within striking distance of the German armies. The next 1,000 miles was even more hazardous, through the most dangerous waters on earth, where ice floes, fog banks and violent storms were lesser dangers than the German aircraft, destroyers and above all, the predatory U-boats lying in wait.

The convoy sailed on the morning of Tuesday, 28 April, its departure clearly visible to the German forces manning a headland to the west. It was an impressive sight. The thirteen merchant ships were surrounded by a substantial escort. Apart from the *Edinburgh*, there were six British destroyers – *Amazon, Beagle, Beverley, Bulldog, Foresight* and *Forester* – four corvettes, an armed trawler and two Soviet destroyers. Four British minesweepers – *Gossamer, Harrier, Hussar* and *Niger* – also sailed with them to clear a path through any German minefields before returning to port to await the arrival of the next Murmansk-bound convoy.

None of the escorts was capable of matching the fire-power of the large Narvik-class German destroyers based at Kirkenes in northern Norway, but *Edinburgh* more than outgunned them. Her sole function was to guard the convoy against attack by such surface craft, for despite her heavy armament, she was not equipped to deal with U-boat attacks and needed a destroyer escort to protect her from them.

By three o'clock that afternoon convoy QP11 had formed up and begun its painfully slow, six-knot progress, heading due north. Only when the polar ice pack was in sight would it turn west, beyond the range of German bombers operating from Norway. But nothing was beyond the range of the U-boat pack. A stiff north-east wind whipped constant flurries of snow over the towering grey seas and the mist and spray coated every exposed surface in a skin of ice up to an inch thick. Deck hands were constantly at work, breaking off the encrusting ice, before the extra weight made the ships unstable. The empty merchant ships rode high in the water, pitching and tossing on the swell. The escort vessels also rolled heavily in the steep seas as they patrolled the flanks and ranged ahead of the slow-moving convoy. The *Edinburgh* remained astern, guarding the rear.

Although he knew their departure from the Kola Inlet would have been observed and word passed to the German naval headquarters, Rear-Admiral Bonham-Carter hoped that his convoy could disappear into the vastness of the Arctic and evade the searching German reconnaissance planes. It was a false hope. A Junkers Ju-88 found them at eight o'clock the next morning. It sat on the horizon, safely out of range of the *Edinburgh's* guns, reporting the convoy's speed and heading.

To be spotted so early in the journey was ominous. The

Germans had ample time to position their vessels for an ambush as the lumbering convoy turned west.

The German Navy was so short of fuel oil that its destroyers in Kirkenes were only unleashed on the high seas in exceptional circumstances, but the chance to destroy the *Edinburgh* and then embark on a turkey-shoot among the escorts and merchant ships of the convoy was too good to miss. Three Narvik-class destroyers, *Hermann Schoemann*, Z24 and Z25, were readied to put to sea and the bomber squadrons were put on alert as the U-boat pack took up position in the convoy's path.

Twenty-four hours after the first sighting, on the morning of 30 April, the escorts ranging ahead of the convoy began reporting frequent U-boat sightings. As the destroyers sped around the flanks of the convoy, dropping depth-charge patterns, the *Edinburgh* took evasive action. To be trailing the convoy at only six knots was to invite a U-boat attack against which the cruiser had no real defences.

The decision to raise steam and patrol twenty miles ahead of the convoy on a zigzag course was not illogical, but in an astonishing blunder that was effectively to seal the *Edinburgh*'s fate, no destroyer escort was detached to accompany her. She was free of the burden of tracking a slow-speed convoy, but remained vulnerable to any U-boat in her path. Captain Faulkner's reaction can only be guessed at; he had no choice but to acquiesce in the decision of his superior officer, Rear-Admiral Bonham-Carter. Apart from the risk to the *Edinburgh*, it also left the convoy in increased danger from surface attack. The *Edinburgh* would act as an effective picket in front of the convoy but if the Germans attacked from astern or from the south – the direction of their base at Kirkenes – *Edinburgh* would be twenty miles distant when the alarm was raised.

At four o'clock that afternoon, Lieutenant Max Teichert,

the captain of U-456, was lying in wait for the convoy when he saw an unexpected sight through his periscope, an unaccompanied heavy cruiser. The *Edinburgh* was steaming at only nineteen knots, barely half its maximum speed. Teichert should have been heading back to base to refuel and rearm, for he had only two torpedoes remaining after attacking an eastward-bound convoy, but he had held station hoping for one more kill and his patience had been rewarded.

He observed the *Edinburgh*'s zigzag course for a few minutes as it drew steadily nearer, timing the intervals between course changes. He held his nerve until the moment the cruiser swung on to a new leg of the zigzag, then gave the order to fire both torpedoes.

The *Edinburgh*'s young asdic operator had already picked up a contact but when he relayed the information to the bridge, Bonham-Carter brusquely ordered him to disregard it, claiming that if there were a submarine almost dead ahead at such close range it would have been seen from the bridge. False echoes were far from unknown in the Arctic, where the mingling of the warm waters of the Gulf Stream with the ice-cold flow from the polar regions produced abnormal changes in the ocean's thermal layers, but the contact was clear and sharp and this time the asdic operator had made no mistake.

The *Edinburgh* had almost completed its patrol and the order to fall out from action stations had just been sounded. No one, not even the look-outs on the bridge, saw the twin tracks of the torpedoes.

At 4.13, both struck home. The first struck amidships on the starboard side, blasting apart the fuel tank next to the bomb room and tearing its way through the heart of the ship towards the forward boiler rooms. The second ripped away the stern section, taking with it the rudder and two of the four propeller shafts. The whole of the quarter-deck was twisted upwards and back on itself by the blast, like a sheet of paper burned in a fire, while the bottom-plates were forced downwards, dragging on the ship like a sea anchor.

Had Teichert been able to fire even one more torpedo, he would have ended the *Edinburgh*'s days there and then. As it was he could only report the torpedo strikes to his Norwegian base and await the arrival of others to finish the job he had begun.

The cruiser wallowed to a halt as tons of sea water poured through the gaping holes and ruptured bulkheads. All water-tight doors and hatches were sealed at once, leaving some men trapped on the wrong side of them. Others scrambled up ladders and companionways to safety, smothered in black, stinking fuel oil. As he began to survey the damage, Captain Faulkner's only comment on the decisions that had led to the virtual destruction of his ship was 'the Admiral has accepted full responsibility'.

The ship was listing heavily to starboard. Captain Faulkner immediately ordered the torpedo tubes on that side to be fired, which partially corrected the list. A signal requesting assistance was sent to Commander Richmond on board *Bulldog*, but the convoy had problems of its own, with U-boats circling astern and ahead of it. He dispatched *Foresight*, *Forester* and the two Russian destroyers to help *Edinburgh*. They reached the cruiser at 5.30.

As the other three ships fanned out in a defensive screen *Forester* took her in tow, but the mountainous seas and the dead weight of the crippled cruiser were too much. Four times the steel tow-line snapped like cotton. Some of the mangled mass of metal dragging at the *Edinburgh*'s stern was then cut away with oxyacetylene torches but enough remained to make her almost unsteerable. Steam was raised to turn one of the remaining propellers, however, and with the *Forester* now taking up station astern to act as an improvised rudder for the *Edinburgh*, she began to limp back towards Murmansk at a paltry three knots.

All that night and through the early hours of the following morning, the cruiser moved slowly southwards. Then at six o'clock the two Russian destroyers signalled that they were running short of fuel. They sped away towards Murmansk, leaving the *Edinburgh* with only two escorts. The *Forester* had to cut her tow-line and join *Foresight* as a screen, and without her improvised rudder, *Edinburgh*'s course became even more erratic and her speed dropped to two knots.

Her position remained perilous. At her present rate of progress it would take four days to cover the remaining 200 miles back to Murmansk. Even without the shadowing U-boat, an oil-slick stretched back for miles behind the ship, a signpost to the *Edinburgh* that no German aircraft or surface ship could miss. Signals from Murmansk and the Admiralty increased the sense of doom on board the ship. Enemy submarines were reported to be massing between the *Edinburgh*'s current position and the Kola Inlet, while enemy destroyers had also put to sea from Kirkenes, heading in their direction.

Four minesweepers were on their way out from Murmansk to aid the *Edinburgh*, but they were each armed with only a single 4-inch gun. The crippled *Edinburgh* seemed unlikely to make any significant contribution to a fight and the combined firepower of the two destroyers and four minesweepers was no match for that of three Narvik-class German destroyers.

Throughout that long night, as the temperature dropped to ten degrees below freezing, they kept up their painful progress, while the look-outs scanned the horizon for the enemy ships. They were granted a brief respite, however, for the German commander had set course for the convoy, still making its slow way westwards. After he had destroyed the escorts, the merchant ships would be powerless to defend themselves. Only when they were all on their way to the bottom of the ocean would he turn his attention to the crippled cruiser.

At one o'clock that afternoon the German ships spotted the convoy and the attack began. Despite being outgunned, the defensive line of British escorts held and the German destroyers could not break through. They renewed the attack six times in the course of the next five hours, but each time by a mixture of guts, bluff and sheer good fortune, the British ships drove them off. One merchant ship was sunk and one destroyer crippled, but by six o'clock, having used up two-thirds of their ammunition to little avail, the frustrated German commander broke off the engagement. His ships headed away from the convoy, determined to restore their pride by seeking out and destroying the *Edinburgh*.

At about the same time, a Russian tug, the *Rubin*, had been sighted by *Edinburgh*. The four minesweepers arrived six hours later, in the brief greying that passed for midnight in the Arctic summer. Even under tow from the tug, however, *Edinburgh*'s speed was little improved. Warned of the imminent arrival of the German destroyers, Rear-Admiral Bonham-Carter signalled his own escorts to take 'every opportunity to defeat the enemy without taking undue risks to themselves in defending *Edinburgh*'.

Just after six o'clock the next morning, the three German ships spotted a long slick of black oil and fifteen minutes later they sighted the *Edinburgh*. The plan had been to launch a simultaneous barrage of torpedoes from long range, disappearing back into the haze and snow clouds before the *Edinburgh*'s guns could respond. In the event they emerged from a bank of cloud to find themselves almost on top of the British ships.

They took individual rather than co-ordinated action and once more, though heavily outgunned, the British escorts took the fight to them. While her escorts harried the Germans, *Edinburgh* cast off her tow, increased her speed to the maximum her battered engines would allow – eight knots – and opened up with her one workable 6-inch gun whenever her helpless circling brought it to bear.

The *Hermann Schoemann* was unlucky enough to appear out of the cover of a snow cloud just as the *Edinburgh*'s B-turret guns came to bear. The cruiser's sophisticated fire control systems had been destroyed in the torpedo strikes, but her gun-crew opened up using nothing more sophisticated than shouted commands and the human eye. The first salvo fell close to the German ship, the second blew her engine rooms apart, and she ground to a halt, crippled and helpless.

The gun-crew of the *Edinburgh* had only two minutes in which to celebrate their marksmanship. At 6.52 a salvo of torpedoes fired from one of the remaining German destroyers missed its intended targets, *Foresight* and *Forester*, but the *Edinburgh* was still steaming in circles behind her escort. One of the torpedoes was now heading straight for her. It was almost at the end of its run. It rose to the surface and skimmed through the waves like a pebble thrown from a beach. Another hundred yards and it might have sunk harmlessly into the depths, but it still had enough velocity to reach the hull of the *Edinburgh* and detonate. The impact was midships on the port side, almost exactly opposite the hole made by the first torpedo strike. It came close to cutting the ship in half.

The *Edinburgh* was as good as dead in the water and the British destroyers' situation looked equally bleak. *Forester* and *Foresight* had both suffered direct hits from the remaining German destroyers. *Forester* came to a dead stop and

Foresight was also badly damaged, with only one engine and one gun still firing.

The last line of defence, the minesweepers, now advanced on the German ships with their single guns blazing. It was a last throw of the dice, as glorious – and as futile – as the Charge of the Light Brigade.

Astonishingly the German ships did not press home their advantage. The sudden appearance of the minesweepers darting out of the mist, smoke and confusion of battle firing their small guns appeared to convince the Germans that a fresh escort of destroyers had arrived. They turned tail. They paused two miles away, long enough to transfer the remaining crew from the deck of the *Hermann Schoemann*, then it was sent to the bottom, scuttled by two depth charges. Without even pausing to pick up those survivors who had already cast off in lifeboats, Z24 and Z25 then ran for Kirkenes. A few minutes later they disappeared over the horizon, leaving the battered but still surviving British ships alone in the icy waters.

Although the immediate danger was past, U-boats remained an ever-present threat. The British ships were virtually defenceless and the *Edinburgh* was now even more of an albatross around their necks. It had once more come to a dead stop, riding low in the water and listing heavily. The Admiral believed it could break up at any moment and gave the order to abandon ship. *Harrier* and *Gossamer* came alongside to take off the crew and passengers. Among them were the luckless survivors of earlier convoys, some being rescued from a stricken ship for the second, third and even fourth time.

There was no possibility of the gold being rescued. The bomb room was flooded and out of reach beyond sealed hatches and watertight doors.

As the rescue continued, the decks of the minesweepers

became so densely packed with men that there was a risk of them capsizing. Attempts to persuade the men to go below were understandably resisted. Many of the soaked and shivering seamen huddling together for warmth had already come close to drowning in the flooded sections of the *Edinburgh*. Eventually the first lieutenant of the *Edinburgh* managed to persuade them to follow him below decks.

Captain Faulkner and Rear-Admiral Bonham-Carter were among the last to leave the *Edinburgh*. They transferred to the *Harrier* and the two minesweepers cast off and pulled clear. Everyone waited for the end but the ship still refused to go down. It was no longer settling deeper in the water and for a moment Bonham-Carter contemplated reboarding with a skeleton crew, but felt the risk of the German destroyers returning to capture the ship and its gold was too great. After waiting some minutes, he took steps to hasten her end.

An attempt to sink her by gunfire failed, twenty rounds at point-blank range from the *Harrier*'s gun producing no other effect than a couple of small fires. Two patterns of depth charges were then dropped close to the *Edinburgh*'s hull, a risky operation that still failed to produced the desired result. The only reaction came from the survivors packed below the minesweepers' decks. They had not been warned of the plan and came swarming back on deck in a panic, assuming that they were once more under attack.

When order had been restored, Bonham-Carter ordered *Foresight* to fire her one remaining torpedo into the *Edinburgh*. As the torpedo was launched he began counting down the running time and had just exclaimed, 'He's missed,' when there was a huge explosion. As he later reported, '*Edinburgh* had had all she could take. She rolled over to port, her back broke and the last seen of her was her bows rising vertically in the air and then disappearing.'

The *Edinburgh* sank below the surface at 8.55 on the morning of 2 May 1942. The minesweepers and the two badly damaged destroyers limped south towards Murmansk. As they disappeared from sight, U-456 surfaced and Lieutenant Max Teichert came up into the conning tower. He had tracked the *Edinburgh* ever since his first torpedo strike and had remained below the surface throughout the ensuing naval battle. He and his crew had heard the detonation of the last torpedo from the *Foresight* and the familiar sounds of a big ship sinking.

He glanced around him. The sea was empty of shipping, but a massive oil slick covered the surface, damping down the swell which lapped against the hull of the U-boat, leaving a filthy tidemark. A welter of oil-covered debris floated in the slick – chairs, tables, bottles, tins, uniform caps and even white tropical helmets – but the ten tons of Russian gold lay buried with fifty-seven men in the steel coffin of the *Edinburgh*, settling slowly into the mud of the ocean floor 800 feet below him.

CHAPTER SIXTEEN

SEAWAY HAWK

———•———

Seaway held a debriefing meeting in Haugesund on our return from the disastrous trip to the South Cape and Bear Island, but it soon became obvious that they were not too disturbed by the outcome of the search for the *Chulmleigh* and the *Waziristan*. Copper and tin were now well down their list of priorities, for gold fever had overwhelmed Seaway's higher management and I was told that it was 'all go for the *Edinburgh*'.

They were exciting times; all the secrecy involved, including the use of codes, made it feel like taking part in a spy thriller. We had even taken to talking in whispers. I began collecting all my research together while Chris Jenkins was dispatched to take a series of photographs of HMS *Belfast*, a Second World War cruiser pensioned off as a floating museum on the Thames. It was the identical twin of the *Edinburgh*, almost to the rivet, a great piece of good luck for us.

I also paid a call on Ken Knox in Hull. He was a former trawler skipper who had fished the Barents Sea for many years. He now ran a chart-making company, Kingfisher Charts, and his own knowledge was augmented by the notebooks and charts of many other retired skippers.

The locations of sunken warships – whether or not they

carry gold – are not conveniently marked on navigation charts. If marked at all, they are recorded only as underwater obstructions. The system keeps pleasure divers away from wrecks that may contain unexploded ordnance as well as the bodies of dead servicemen, but it also keeps treasure divers away from the cargoes that the ships may contain.

Part of his work was to plot on the fishing charts all the known fasteners – the places where trawler nets had become caught on undersea obstructions. It was valuable information. A net lost on a wreck could cost a trawler skipper many thousands of pounds in lost fishing time and replacement costs.

Trying not to give the game away, I began asking Ken about the particular area of the Barents Sea I was interested in. He glanced up at me. 'I know what you're looking for. It's the *Edinburgh*, isn't it?'

I took a deep breath. 'How do you know that, Ken?'

'Because my nets were once fast in the bloody thing for over eighteen hours.'

'But how do you know it was the *Edinburgh*?'

He began rummaging through his charts. 'Because when we finally got our net free, some wreckage – including some bulkhead lights and switches – came up with it. Half my crew were ex-RN and they recognised the switches as being Royal Navy ones.'

I kept my voice even. 'It could still have been another British wreck, though.'

He just smiled. He found the right chart and spread it on the table. I leaned forward as he tapped a mark on the chart. His finger was almost directly over the spot given by Rear-Admiral Bonham-Carter as the position where the *Edinburgh* sank. From my own researches I knew that no other British warships had been sunk in this part of the Barents Sea. I tried to mask my excitement, but Ken's quiet smile showed that he wasn't fooled.

'What happened to the switches you pulled up?' I said.

'I've kept them in the garage for years. Would you like a look?'

'I certainly would.'

His confident smile faded as he turned his garage upside down, trying to find them. Finally he called to his wife. 'Where are those switches I had on the shelf at the back of the garage?'

'Oh, I threw them out with some other rubbish ages ago.' She took one look at our faces and retreated into the house.

Ken produced a special chart for me, showing all the known fasteners in the area of the *Edinburgh*'s given sinking position, not least the point where Ken himself had been fast for over eighteen hours. The number of fasteners scattered around the area seemed very high but I let that pass, assuming them to be the wrecks of fishing boats. One other thing gave me pause, however. Ken had told me that the *Edinburgh* was in soft ground at a depth of 122 fathoms – 732 feet – yet the position he had marked on the chart showed a depth of 250 metres – well over 800 feet.

He checked the Decca navigation handbook for the area, then waved my doubts away. 'Just use the Decca clocks to go to that position, Keith. You'll find the wreck within three hundred metres of that, or maybe a little more; the Decca can be a bit off at this time of year.'

The other worrying point about the *Edinburgh*'s likely position was that it appeared from the charts to be very close to Soviet territorial waters. When Seaway contacted the Norwegian Embassy, they confirmed that the area was within the 'grey zone' where jurisdiction between the Soviet Union and Norway had not been agreed. That was not good news.

By mid-August Chris Jenkins and I were ready to present

the Salvage Association with our joint plan for a survey to find and photograph the *Edinburgh*. A fortnight later, on 31 August 1979, permission was granted, subject to strict limitations on what we could do on site:

a) Only the external features of the wreck are to be sighted or filmed.
b) No attempt is to be made to land on, or gain access to the inside of the vessel, or to disturb, touch or in any way interfere with the wreck.
c) You must comply fully with the requirements of the Norwegian authorities to whom full details of your proposed venture must be given and copied to this Association.
d) All results of your survey are to be made available to this Association.

Lastly, we are requested to remind you that the wreck HMS *Edinburgh* is still classed as a War Grave and must therefore be given due respect.

Autumn was now fast approaching, and with only a few weeks of the Arctic diving season remaining we began hurried preparations for the voyage. While Seaway were preparing the vessel and its equipment, Graham and I made a visit to the Public Record Office at Kew in London. We failed to find the manifest of the gold loaded on to the *Edinburgh*, but we managed to unearth the paperwork that confirmed that the gold had been stored in the bomb room. We also found a copy of a signal to the Admiralty confirming that the gold had not been removed at the time of the sinking: 'Your 1842B/7. No. Nothing saved except personnel. Gold was in compartment flooded by first torpedo.'

I was a little nervous about unearthing this document

because I'd always been wary of using places like the Public Record Office. The person who photocopied the documents could see their contents. He would be less than human if a mention of gold didn't catch his attention, and less than normal, considering his wages, if he didn't make an extra copy on the side, to sell on to willing buyers. It happens in archives around the world and there seemed no reason why Kew would be an exception. It was a risk we had to take, however; we needed that information.

Seaway's need was even greater than mine. I was asked to send all my research material on the *Edinburgh* to Oslo and they were so keen to get their hands on it that they sent a taxi from Norwich to Keighley – a 450-mile round trip – to collect it. I later found out that they'd used the material to persuade a Norwegian shipowner to invest a substantial sum in the project; no wonder they weren't bothered about the taxi fare.

The days dragged by, but at last we received the message we'd been waiting for. The *Seaway Hawk* would sail from Haugesund on 1 October 1979. We could count on no more than two or three weeks to find the *Edinburgh* before the onset of the winter storms drove us from the Arctic.

We made the flight down from Leeds/Bradford to London in thick cloud. I sat by the window and only saw the ground once between take-off and landing. Just as we were making our approach into Heathrow, we flew over a small hole in the cloud. Directly below me for an instant, ringed by cloud, I caught a glimpse of the *Edinburgh*'s sister ship, HMS *Belfast* at her anchorage on the Thames. It was a good omen, if ever I saw one.

The flight from Oslo to Haugesund was less encouraging, one of the worst flights I'd ever taken. I'd even have swapped my seat for a berth on the *Caroline Mathilda*. Storm-force winds threw the aircraft all over the sky and our approach through the mountains in dense cloud was so steep that we appeared to be dive-bombing the runway.

An ex-Royal Navy officer, James Ringrose, was waiting for us in Haugersund. I'd agreed with Seaway that we should employ a marine surveyor on the search for the *Edinburgh* to ensure that we didn't have the same problems we'd had searching for the *Waziristan*. Ringrose had been recommended to me by an ex-officer friend of his who was working as a diver for Seaway.

James McKenzie Ringrose was in his late twenties but had the look of an overgrown public schoolboy, complete with fair hair, pink cheeks and slightly braying laugh. His air of fresh-faced innocence was marred only by his eyes, which were deep-set and calculating. It transpired that he had been out of work for some time, but he told me that he was a fully qualified Royal Navy surveyor and had served as First Lieutenant on the minesweeper HMS *Bronington* with Prince Charles.

The way he walked and held himself carried the hint of a swagger and though he always feigned reticence on the subject of his friendship with Prince Charles, it was remarkable how many different and subtle ways he found to introduce the subject into a conversation. If only slightly pressed, he'd regale us with tales of the happy evenings he spent playing 'Flip the Kipper' with HRH in the Mess, and he let it be known that he still maintained contact with him. He claimed to know the back way into Buckingham Palace and had Charles's personal telephone number, where he could reach him at any time.

James and I weren't so much from opposite sides of the tracks as different ends of the planet. I'm sure he had met a few characters like me in the Navy, but they would have been stoking the boilers, not hobnobbing with Charles, as he called him, on the bridge. It was even stretching a point to say we shared a common language. I had a broad Yorkshire accent and tended to use words of one syllable, direct and to the point. His accent – to my untutored ear at least – was impeccably upper-crust and he would take the dictionary for a stroll, circling the point for some time before making any approach towards it.

His alleged royal connections were less interesting to me at the time than his abilities as a surveyor. On the basis of his Royal Navy experience, we agreed to take him on the expedition to find the *Edinburgh*. We put him to work immediately as we began testing the ship's search and navigation equipment. Although time was at a premium this late in the season, I was still surprised that Seaway had not allowed a couple of extra days for preparation, to ensure that the mistakes of our first expedition to the Arctic were not repeated. With so much at stake, we could not afford further cock-ups.

We sailed at ten o'clock on the evening of 1 October, accompanied by a representative from a big Norwegian company called Sig Bergesen, Seaway's new partner in this venture. During the four-day passage to the Barents Sea, taking on fuel in Bergen, I made my research papers available to James Ringrose and, like Seaway, he agreed that the only place to begin the search was the position given by Rear-Admiral Bonham-Carter and confirmed many years later by Ken Knox. After sheltering in Mageroy Sound – the passage between the Norwegian mainland and North Cape Island – for twelve hours to ride out a Force 8 gale, we arrived on location early in the morning of 5 October.

A Russian AIG 'trawler' – an advanced information gatherer bristling with antennae – was waiting for us. It was our shadow for the next three weeks, coming close alongside every time we lowered anything into the water or recovered anything from the bottom.

The wind had dropped to Force 5 and though a heavy swell was running, we began immediate preparations for the search. We lowered the side-scan sonar, which swept a large area of the sea-bed on both sides of the vessel, and began our first run through the search area. Half an hour later we got a huge 'hit' on the side-scan, showing that we had passed very close to a very large metal object. The return signal was so strong that it scorched the print-out paper. Jim Ringrose was certain that we'd found the *Edinburgh*.

It seemed too good to be true that we could have found the wreck so quickly, but we marked the same object again – though the contact was less strong – on two more passes with the side-scan, despite an attempt by the Russian ship to block our way.

The side-scan towfish had accidentally made contact with the bottom at a depth of 220 metres – 120 fathoms – and when we retrieved it, we found it covered in soft clay, the depth and ground that Ken Knox had described. Bad weather was again threatening, however, and with the seas rising and darkness closing in fast, I called a halt to the search. We dropped three buoys to mark the position, then stood off to ride out the storm.

All the next day we were pounded by heavy seas driven by the Force 9 gale and snow squalls reduced visibility to nil. All we could do was wait. By the next morning the seas had abated enough for us to resume the search. All that day and for many days to follow, we searched the area for some trace of the huge sonar contact or even the three buoys we had dropped. None was found.

The side-scan showed that we were in a heavily fished area; the print-out showed scratches from trawler otter-boards all over the sea-bed. Although the ship's equipment was showing the same position, we were obviously not in the right place.

The unreliability of the navigational equipment was not Seaway's fault. At those extreme latitudes, we were outside the limits of reliability for the Decca Main Chain navigation system. When we changed to the spare Decca receiver, it gave us a completely different position. Our recorded position varied wildly in different weather conditions and at night, producing errors of several nautical miles. The alternative system, Consol, a wartime development of an aerial bombing system, was even less accurate so far from land. I began to realise that the numerous different fasteners marked on the charts were often the same one. The Decca gave different readings to different trawler skippers at different times.

Surrounded by nothing but an endless expanse of grey ocean, there were no landmarks to help us. We could sail to the position shown on the Decca clock, but the depth of water and the sea-bed showed us that we were not where we should have been. We were effectively lost within a 100-square-mile search area. Without the means to fix our position, it was impossible to conduct a methodical search. We cobbled together a large buoy covered in radar reflectors and used that as a fixed reference point for the search grid, but it was often obscured by the mountainous seas, and even when visible it still could not tell us if we were even in the right area.

We were forced to steadily widen the search area to allow for the worst-case navigational error. Four days later we had completed – as far as we could tell – a search of the number one area without finding any trace of the original contact or the three buoys we had dropped. It was possible that the buoys had been lost in the storm or had even been lifted by the Russian AIG. With the difficulties in running a proper search pattern, it was also possible that we had passed close to the wreck-site without detecting it. What was definitely not possible was that a wreck on the bottom had simply disappeared. Despite James Ringrose's initial certainty, I was now convinced that what we had marked that first day could only have been a Russian submarine.

We returned to Hammerfest to recalibrate the Decca navigator and pick up a satellite navigation system. Sat-nav was in its infancy then, but it was still well in advance of the other systems. With an accurate fix on our own position at last, we began another search of the number one area we had already covered. A week later we had searched an area of 130 square miles without a sniff of the wreck and there were still worrying discrepancies between what Ken Knox had told me and what we were actually finding. Ken had been fast in a depth of 122 fathoms – almost 800 feet – in an area where the sea-bed was of clay or soft mud. Our equipment gave us a depth reading of 245 metres – 808 feet – and the side-scan showed that the bottom was hard and stony. To make matters worse, Norwegian trawlers were working all round us, a sure indication that there were no wrecks in the area.

James came to my cabin that night close to tears. The Norwegian crew members seemed more interested in getting home than finding the wreck and he felt that they were laughing at him. He did not know what to do or where to go next. He even suggested trying to obtain the *Edinburgh*'s position from a friend of his in the Royal Navy, who was based at Faslane. According to James, Britain's hunter-killer nuclear submarines hid in the *Edinburgh*'s shadow to avoid detection.

I had no reason to doubt his word. It was a long-established technique for submarines trying to avoid detection, pioneered by German U-boats during the Second World War to counter the threat from the new sonar and magnetic detection systems carried by Allied warships.

While I was all in favour of short-cuts however, I was not

quite so keen on the idea of being on the wrong end of a spying or treason trial. I told James to forget it and stick to surveying.

We had to face the inescapable conclusion that we were searching the wrong area. Reinforced by Ken Knox's story, we had all been guilty of taking the Admiral's position as read. It now seemed certain that he had deliberately falsified it to conceal the true location of the *Edinburgh* and its gold.

After taking off the survivors from the *Edinburgh*, the minesweeper HMS *Harrier* had managed to get an astro-fix during a brief clearance in the weather. The position recorded had been subsequently corrected by the Admiralty. That correction could also have been false.

We had to go back through all the research and look for flaws, something that might give us a clue as to where the wreck was hiding. The naval reports and trawler fasteners showed a daunting range of positions, covering an area of over 1,500 square nautical miles. The lack of accuracy was no reflection on the wartime navigators. Few of the vessels involved in the action were fitted with automatic plotting tables. In any event, in the heat of a naval action, with shells and torpedoes flying about and smoke, snow squalls and violent changes of course and speed, only the coolest navigator would keep accurate track of the ship's movements, particularly as absolute position was far less important than position relative to other combatants. In such circumstances we could only hope that the ultimate navigational error had not been too great.

We began plotting the positions of all the ships involved in the action: the British ships *Edinburgh*, *Forester*, *Foresight* and *Harrier*, the German destroyers *Hermann Schoemann*, Z24 and Z25 and the U-boats U-88 and U-456. It soon became obvious that something was wrong.

We took the two starting positions for the *Edinburgh*: the one given by the U-boat commander when he first torpedoed the ship, and the position recorded by the *Edinburgh* as the site of that first strike. There was a difference of six miles between them, well within the margins of normal navigational errors. A battle cruiser was better placed to maintain an accurate log than a submerged U-boat, so I placed slightly more credence on the *Edinburgh*'s starting position.

Even before she was first struck by the two torpedoes, *Edinburgh* was following a set zigzag manoeuvring procedure which called for her course and speed to vary considerably over short periods. Visibility was poor, and after the ship had been struck she was unable to steer. Towing attempts were largely unsuccessful and to complicate matters still further, the vessel had completely different steering characteristics going ahead and astern. She could not be held on a southerly course while going ahead, so she resorted to a 'falling leaf' progress. As she went ahead her bow swung to port. She would then go astern to bring the bow to starboard, then ahead again.

Going two steps forward and one step back made navigation very difficult from dead reckoning and visibility was too poor to permit an astro-fix. A speed error of one knot and a mean course error of twenty degrees would have been perfectly possible, combining to give an error in position of as much as twenty miles in twenty-four hours.

The vessels which arrived to help *Edinburgh*, both on 30 April and 2 May (the day of the sinking), had also been manoeuvring sharply and were dogged by the poor weather, but the positioning reports from all of them had to be considered. So, too, had the reports from German vessels engaged directly or on the fringes of the *Edinburgh* action. The German surface ships could be assumed to have had the same navigation problems as the British vessels; the submarines were acting independently of the surface ships and had different ideas of their positions.

Matters were further complicated by the German use of the marine quadrat chart, which divides the earth's surface into rectangular areas, the smallest of which covers about five minutes of latitude and twenty minutes of longitude in the Barents Sea. Translating from the German system caused problems, particularly as errors could easily have occurred in the German quadrat coding.

After plotting the *Edinburgh*'s movements during the action as well as we could, we arrived at the dead-reckoning position. Any difference between the plotted DRP and the actual physical position of the wreck on the sea-bed would be due to navigational error – understandable in a situation such as the Edinburgh found herself on that particular morning. HMS *Harrier*'s original, uncorrected astro-fix put the *Edinburgh* some five miles south of our DRP, well within the margin of error. The *Edinburgh* had also drifted half a mile to a mile back to the north after casting off her tow, taking the position even closer to our DRP.

Even though the *Harrier*'s reported position at the time she met the *Edinburgh* differed from the one we'd reconstructed from her reported courses and speeds, the error of longitude could only have been three or four miles. We worked out her latitude from her passage time back to Kola Inlet, reducing her estimated speed to allow for the weight of several hundred extra people aboard.

Before and after the sinking the *Harrier*'s navigation had been accurate. Her departure from Murmansk, her courses and speeds, her departure from the scene of the sinking and her time of arrival at Kola Inlet were recorded. The one vital error in *Harrier*'s accurate reports remained difficult to explain – except as a deliberate falsification.

The total distance recorded by the *Edinburgh* from the

start of the action was some sixty-seven miles. The Admiral's official sinking report also stated that they'd made a good sixty miles, yet his given sinking position was nowhere near the one we plotted, and did not correspond with his own statement that it was some 180 miles from Kola Inlet. If our new calculations were right and the wreck really did lie 180 miles from Kola Inlet, it was some eighteen miles further to the north-east, just to the west of an area Ken Knox had spoken of as a minefield and marked on the chart in red. I remembered asking Ken at the time I got the chart, 'What would a minefield be doing in a position like this?'

I looked at the chart again with mounting excitement. Trawlermen had told me that when they fished that area, they caused explosions on the sea-bed. What if those explosions were caused not by mines, but by depth charges and munitions from the *Edinburgh* or the *Hermann Schoemann*, the German destroyer sunk by gunfire from the crippled *Edinburgh*? According to the German captain's report, it had gone down only two miles away from the *Edinburgh*.

Through an interpreter I talked to the captain of one of the Norwegian fishing vessels. He immediately showed me the position of a large wreck in that area. 'It's in two hundred and fifty metres of water,' he said. 'And the sea-bed is soft clay. It's also very large. It stretches over an area of about three kilometres.' Three kilometres was two miles, the distance separating the *Hermann Schoemann* from the *Edinburgh*. There seemed little doubt that the trawler skipper's one large wreck was actually two, but to find either of them would lead us straight to the other. All the doubts and frustrations from the fruitless search were swept away and even our Norwegian crew showed some enthusiasm as we set course for the new search area, a box of ocean just twelve miles long by five miles wide.

We were racing the onset of winter, however. We

arrived on location on 26 October to find good weather and a calm sea but our luck did not hold. The side-scan had been in constant use in sea conditions well beyond its design limits and it duly broke down after a few hours, forcing an eighteen-hour stand-down while it was repaired. By the time it was ready, the weather had started to deteriorate. The wind was blowing Force 7 and strengthening all the time and we couldn't get a fix on our buoy because of all the radar clutter from the worsening seas.

The Soviet AIG vessel was also deliberately obstructing our search. Every time we tried to manoeuvre, it came in close alongside. It was especially dangerous when we had the high-speed Zodiac out on the ocean with the divers picking up our marker buoys. The AIG kept blanking off our view of the divers and I didn't think that was playing the game, especially as we were all meant to be on the same side. After a few days, I lost my temper and thought, 'Bugger it, if he can play the game, so can we; we'll have a go at him.' I spun the wheel and aimed the prow straight at the AIG.

To this day I'm not sure if I really would have rammed him, but there was a pretty good chance, I was blazing with anger. There was a pregnant pause as the gap between the two vessels shrank at an alarming rate, then I saw the AIG begin to turn away. I still kept after him, changing course every time he did. We had a high-speed chase for a few minutes but he had far more power in his engines than we could produce and in the end I had to accept that we couldn't catch him. Having vented my anger, I swung the wheel around and went back to get on with the job.

Shortly afterwards the captain of a Norwegian destroyer called on the radio. 'What the hell has been going on?' He didn't seem too impressed with my explanations.

'I'm trying to keep the peace in this area,' he said, 'while you're intent on starting another world war. Just cool it. I'll have a word with the Russians, but if you make any more attempts to ram them, I'll sink you myself.'

The AIG kept a respectful distance from then on, but though we had less than half the area still to search, I knew time was running out. The Decca navigator was jumping all over the place and was virtually useless. I could only order a series of random searches, hoping against hope that we would chance on the wreck.

The weather was steadily worsening but I kept the side-scan in the water whenever possible. There was no point in trying to nurse the equipment now. We all felt that we were within a very short distance of the *Edinburgh*, but the print-out from the side-scan remained obstinately blank. By the afternoon of 29 October we began to see a few interesting traces from it, fragments on the sea-bed that could well have been debris from a wreck. That evening it again failed, however, and with a full gale blowing we again had to suspend operations.

After more repairs we continued random searches all the next day and all through the night, still spotting pieces of debris on the sea-bed without finding the *Edinburgh* itself. On 1 November, the side-scan once again broke down and with another storm brewing and another lengthy stand-down in prospect, we received a telex recalling us to Bergen. So near the wreck-site I could almost smell it, we were forced to steam south, leaving the *Edinburgh* still undisturbed in the icy depths of the Arctic.

I'd had many bitter disappointments in the past over missing, dangerous or unworkable wrecks, but 1979 had been the most cruel year of all. I had expended a huge amount of money and effort on the *Chulmleigh*, the *Waziristan* and the hunt for the *Edinburgh*, and all I had to show for it were a lot more grey hairs and a mountain of bills. The only consolation I could take was the negative one that the expedition had at least eliminated the Admiral's position as the site of the sinking of the *Edinburgh*. We now knew beyond reasonable doubt the area where the ship would not be found. The next attempt the following spring would need a far more accurate navigational system than Main Chain Decca, but given that, I saw no reason why we couldn't find the *Edinburgh* within days of our return to the Barents Sea.

As soon as we docked in Bergen, Graham, Jim Ringrose and I flew down to Oslo for a debriefing with Christian Selmer at Seaway. There was a free and frank exchange of views at the meeting. Selmer made clear the company's disappointment that we had nothing to show for a month-long expedition. I expressed the hope that Seaway now realised the importance of ensuring that a survey ship had the right equipment for the task. They couldn't just send a vessel into the middle of the Barents Sea, where the usual navigational aids were all but useless, and expect to find a wreck. We didn't even know where we were to within a few miles, never mind being able to pinpoint a wreck on the sea-bed. And even if we'd found it, we had no transponder on board to mark the site. A buoy would not have lasted the winter.

The frost between us deepened when Selmer told me that the promised new company, Seaway–Jessop had still not been formed.

For the next three months we exchanged an endless series of calls and telexes without advancing the formation of the company at all. It was obvious that the Norwegians were just stringing me along. I knew that I was wet behind the ears when it came to the ways of big business, but I naïvely expected to be dealing with men who would stand by their word. One thought helped me through; all the fine words and fancy agreements in the world would not get the gold from the *Edinburgh*. Only divers like me could do that.

I felt that I needed a sharp lawyer on my side however,

someone who could see the traps hidden in the tangles of clauses and sub-clauses in draft contracts. As a result I went over to Manchester to see a firm of lawyers who'd been recommended to me. Graham and I were sitting at the end of a corridor, waiting for our meeting with the senior partner, when a man came out of one of the side offices. He was pale and thin-faced, with a shock of very dark curly hair, and his eyes appeared to take in everything and everybody as he glanced down his most outstanding feature, his hawk-like nose.

Graham and I came out with the same, simultaneous remark: 'Bloody hell, look at that sharp-looking bastard.' After agreeing terms with the senior partner, the sharp-looking bastard was introduced to us as our new solicitor. Mr David Bona, we were assured, was just the person to help us with our project. He had some time on his hands and would work for us on a 'no cure, no pay' arrangement, but could be recalled to his own work if business picked up.

One of his first tasks was to form a company, Jessop Marine Recoveries Limited. I extracted £10 from each of my children to pay for their percentage of the new company. Persuading my youngest son Ian to part with his £10 was almost as hard as getting money out of Seaway. One of David Bona's next official duties was to come with us to a last-chance meeting with Seaway. Selmer had contacted me at the end of January 1980, to ask for one more meeting in London about the *Edinburgh* project. I had been told that in the meantime, Seaway had invited the Russians to Oslo in an attempt to do a deal with them.

As arranged, we arrived at the Seaway flat in Cambridge Square at 10.30 a.m. Neither Jacob Stolt-Nielsen nor Christian Selmer were there. This would have puzzled me, had I not already spoken to John Jackson at the Salvage Association, who'd told me that they'd also arranged to see him at the same time. Either they were going to be in two places at once or they wanted to make sure we were out of the way while they put a pitch to Mr Jackson.

We waited a couple of hours, then went round the corner for a drink and a sandwich. The two of them arrived soon afterwards with no apologies or explanations, and Jacob made his pitch. They intended to raise $15 million for the *Edinburgh* project: $5 million for the survey and $10 million for the recovery. I was to be on call to Seaway, they wanted my research and planning, and my name was to be on the contract. I suspected that they needed it to sell themselves to the Salvage Association; otherwise they would not have bothered to offer me anything. As it was, they were offering me a deal to stand aside. I would get 9.5 per cent of the returns from a successful recovery of the *Edinburgh* gold, but only after the deduction of all expenses.

I didn't need my sharp lawyer to tell me that Seaway were putting themselves in a no-lose situation. Jacob was effectively telling me that he could raise $15 million with my research, by using it to persuade an investor to put up the money. They would then charge out their ship, divers and equipment to the expedition at the usual exorbitant rate. If the expedition failed they would have the consolation of the profits from the charter of their ship. If the gold was recovered they would draw an even more handsome, no-risk profit.

On the face of it, 9.5 per cent for just sitting on my hands while they salvaged the *Edinburgh* gold was a good offer, but it was net of Seaway's costs. Previous experience had shown just how high those costs could be when Seaway was chartering its ships to its own expeditions. Much more important to me, however, was the fact that the *Edinburgh* was my project. I'd conceived and nurtured it, researched and developed it, at a time when virtually no one else had even thought of it. I was damned if I was going to step aside now.

My mind was already made up at this point, but I told Jacob that my team and I required time to think and talk. Rather than ask them to leave, we'd go outside for a walk. Outside, we talked over the offer. Looking back at all the unpaid money and the broken promises, Graham, David and I came to the same conclusion: we could not trust these people. Before we went back into the meeting, I called Mr Jackson and told him that I was calling it a day with Seaway.

Back inside, it looked like a nice, happy party. Coffee had been brought and Christian and Jacob were arranging all the new paperwork and addendums for me to sign.

'Take it or leave it,' had been Jacob's final words to me. I told him immediately. 'I'll leave it. It's my opinion that Jessops are wasting Seaway's time, and Seaway are definitely wasting the Jessops' time. So I'm calling it a day – and may the best man win.'

There was a deathly silence around the table. I could see disbelief on both their faces. They appeared unable to speak to each other and from Christian's reaction I got the distinct impression that he thought Jacob had overplayed his hand. They had certainly never expected this answer. He started to put his paperwork away as Jacob stalked out of the office. We left without any goodbyes or thank-yous.

I had no regrets at the course of action we had taken. I didn't believe we had any other choice, but I felt a great sense of waste, both of so much hard work and of a lost opportunity. Seaway–Jessop could have gone on to become the most successful salvage company in the world.

Chapter Seventeen

The Royal Connection

I now had just one thing on my mind: I was going to beat those Norwegians to the *Edinburgh*'s gold. But I also knew deep down that they held virtually all the cards. My only advantages were my nationality and my good standing with the Salvage Association and the War Risks Insurance Office. If I could put together an all-British operation, I might have a chance of the *Edinburgh* contract, but it was a daunting, near-impossible task for a penniless salvage man.

David Bona was the first to speak, 'What do we do now Keith?'

I answered with more bravado than conviction, 'We'll just have to start again and find someone else with enough sense and money to help us make it work.'

As soon as we got home, Graham and I sat down to put together a fully costed survey plan for the *Edinburgh*. There was no point in trying to make a detailed plan for the salvage operation until we had found the ship and examined it with an ROV – a remote-operated vehicle.

An ROV was used in the same way as a moon-buggy on a space mission. It contained TV cameras, sonar, floodlights, water jet and mechanical arms, mounted on a pair of supports like skis. Controlled through a 400-yard umbilical and driven by hydraulic thrusters, it could explore the ocean bottom, locate a wreck with its sonar, film it from every angle, blast away accumulations of sand and silt with its water jet and detach and raise small objects with its mechanical arms. It would show us the fine details of the *Edinburgh*'s position on the sea-bed and the condition of the hull around the bomb room where the gold had been stored. Only then would we know the difficulty of the salvage operation – if the gold could be recovered at all. Rear-Admiral Bonham-Carter had stated in his report that the ship had broken in two at the time of the sinking. If so, the gold could be irretrievable, scattered all over the sea-bed.

We also made yet another visit to the Public Record Office at Kew, in search of the track charts that should have been with the Admiral's damage report on the loss of the *Edinburgh*. Even the assistants at Kew were unable to trace them, but they promised to keep looking. A couple of days later, a letter arrived. They were still unable to find the track charts and could only assume that they'd failed to survive. That assumption flew in the face of their own records which listed the track charts as having been included with the Admiral's report.

I'd found in the past that documents of a delicate nature were sometimes put into the Public Record Office under misleading titles or references, making them difficult or impossible to find without inside knowledge. If that provoked trouble at a later stage, the documents could always be discovered again. The PRO could never be accused of obstructing the public's right to see the documents, they had simply been 'misfiled'.

Some time later a contact gave me a file number to check at the PRO. Surprise, surprise, we'd found the missing charts.

My first attempts to build a British consortium to find the

Edinburgh were failures. I wasted six precious weeks with one company, who then decided the venture was 'too speculative'. It was already looking as if we were going to miss yet another season in the Arctic.

I was also in financial trouble. Chasing the *Edinburgh* contract, I was spending money and not earning any. I was starting to get serious earache from Mildred and severe problems with my bank. A letter from the manager pointed out that I'd already exceeded my overdraft limit by £1,000. Unless I put my account in order, he would stop cashing my cheques – even though he held the deeds to my house. The irony was not lost on me. Here I was chasing a multi-million pound deal, and yet I was unable to clear a four-figure overdraft.

There was more bad news in a call from Mr Jackson at the Salvage Association. Risdon Beazley were going to the Arctic to look for a wreck, the *Astoria*, not far from the North Cape. They would also be looking for the *Edinburgh* on the same terms as we had been given: find, look and film, but do not touch.

There was nothing I could do about it, but I was very frustrated and a little annoyed. In a strange way, I felt that I'd earned the right to be given a chance at the *Edinburgh* and I was not impressed when someone else stepped in after I'd rekindled their interest. Risdon Beazley had been give their chance to salvage the *Edinburgh* years before and had turned it down, stating that the gold had probably spilled out all over the sea-bed when the torpedo struck near the bomb room. What had happened now to change their minds?

The news was a blow but the encouragement I was receiving from the Salvage Association, underwriters and the government departments concerned with salvage kept me going. They wanted competition to return to the salvage industry because they wanted a better return than they were getting from Risdon Beazley.

David Bona now felt that we were finished. I could tell by the way he spoke to me that his enthusiasm had gone. I wasn't ready to throw in the towel just yet, but I knew that time was running out. If we didn't put a consortium together soon, either Seaway or Risdon Beazley would beat me to the *Edinburgh*. I sat down and thought hard. All I was short of was capital and equipment. I was beginning to realise that there was plenty of money about if you knew where to look and after the turn-down in the oil industry, there was certainly plenty of equipment available in the oil-fields. The diving vessel I needed for the *Edinburgh* was a very expensive piece of equipment. But rather than having it tied up alongside a pier doing nothing and costing money at the same time, it would surely pay its owners to have it in use on a job that could earn them a fortune.

I rang an old friend, Les Halmshaw, who was doing business with a relatively new, but very successful British diving company, Wharton & Williams, known as 2W for short. Ric Wharton and Malcolm Williams, the owners, were affectionately known as 'the piranha twins' by the divers who worked for them. I had worked for 2W in the past and knew that Ric was a lad with a reputation for having a go. I asked Les to mention the *Edinburgh* operation to him. He called me back within twenty-four hours to say that Ric was very excited by the *Edinburgh* project. We arranged a meeting in Aberdeen later that week.

I found Ric Wharton to be a straight talker and very much to the point. I took to him straight away. He knew his business, I knew mine, and we got down to it with no flannel. I talked him through all my research, explaining why I believed that the gold was still there. There was no doubt that he was very keen on the idea, but 2W had no diving vessels of their own and would have to approach an outside shipowner to join a consortium. If this failed, Ric said he would finance a smaller-scale operation on another wreck for a start, to built the capital for the *Edinburgh*.

He asked the obvious question: 'What will our return be from the *Edinburgh*?'

I told him that I'd advised Seaway that fifty per cent was the maximum I'd ask from the underwriters on a 'no cure, no pay' contract, but to be sure of undercutting Seaway, I recommended that we ask for no more than forty-five per cent. The *Edinburgh* had been carrying ten tons of gold and forty-five per cent of that was more than fair payment for the job. Ric agreed.

A few days later the agreement between 2W and Jessop Marine arrived. Ric had been moving fast and had already arranged a meeting with a German company, Offshore Services Association, who ran a fleet of around 100 vessels. I knew OSA well and had worked off a number of their vessels in the past, but I was concerned that their German ownership might cause us problems. To cover that point David Bona and Ric agreed that the main contractors would be Jessop Marine and 2W, with OSA as subcontractors. The consortium remained all-British – just as long as you didn't look too hard at the small print.

Our first meeting with John Clarke, an ex-Royal Navy surveyor, who was Head of Special Projects at OSA, went very well. I took him through the main research and produced documentation covering the sinking of the *Edinburgh*, the storage position of the gold cargo, and a complete chronological sequence of the naval action including the track charts of all the British and German vessels involved. James Ringrose, whom I had brought back into my operation, helped me brief him on the results of our expedition with Seaway, useful only in that it showed us where to avoid spending valuable time and money on a search.

Before committing themselves however, OSA asked for a

further meeting with the Salvage Association. I suspected that they simply wanted to make sure that what I'd been saying about the *Edinburgh* gold was true.

After the meeting, James told Graham and me that he had been having a word in a 'well-known Royal ear', as he put it, and our consortium was going to get backing from the very top. I didn't know whether to laugh or take him seriously, but if it was true, it could certainly do us no harm at all.

I next spoke to Mr Jackson. I told him that it was impossible for me to step off the merry-go-round now; I was completely committed to the *Edinburgh* project. I was doing what he and his predecessors had been encouraging me to do for years, attempting to bring some competition back into the British salvage industry. I then asked him if the Salvage Association would support our application for the contract to recover the gold. He thought for a while and then answered, 'Yes.'

Any reservations OSA had about the viability of the project were soon resolved by their meeting with Mr Jackson, but John Clarke had one further condition: OSA would only join the consortium if an experienced survey company was also involved. He had no trouble in persuading me on that point; I'd had enough of blundering around the Arctic with inadequate and inaccurate equipment. By good luck John had served in the Royal Navy with Carl Oberman, who was now Staff Surveyor at Decca Marine. He set up a meeting with Decca's Operations Director, John Lucken. He seemed lukewarm about the idea at first, but by the end of the meeting he was pumping our hands and saying, 'You can count us in. Anything you want, you've got.' He had been an Able Seaman on wartime Arctic convoys and, nearing retirement, he was damned if he was going to miss a project like this.

After our problems with the Decca Main Chain, we asked some tough questions about their proposed navigational system for an operation in this part of the Barents Sea. He told us that they'd be using a different system, OASIS, that actually did work in the Arctic.

Decca Marine's enthusiastic participation was great news but it also made James Ringrose's position superfluous. We had no need of our own surveyor when we had the world's leading survey company on board. John Clarke also made no secret of his dislike for him. He was surprised to learn that James said he was a qualified marine surveyor. The world of Royal Navy hydrographers was a small one, and John claimed to know or have heard of every member of it. With that news, the only thing that made it worth keeping him on the team was his alleged Royal connection. He could have been exaggerating his links with the Prince, of course, but it was worth the gamble; a friend in high places could make the difference between getting the contract and watching Seaway or Risdon Beazley sail off into a golden sunset.

I got home to Keighley in a very happy frame of mind. Although there was still a lot of tough talking to be done and the giant hurdle of the award of the contract to be cleared, I was confident that we had assembled a consortium that was well ahead of our rivals – 2W, OSA and Racal–Decca were all leaders in their fields and I wasn't bad in mine either.

My only problem was the traditional one – a desperate shortage of cash. That was partly eased by a call from an old friend on Islay, Tim Epps, who wanted to buy the remains of the *Otranto* from me. I'd always held the wreck in reserve so that I could work it with my sons one day, but my financial position was now so desperate that I decided I had to let it go. We swapped a few old stories and then got down to the usual dead-horse-and-donkey dealing of a bit of haggling. Finally we agreed a price. I'd bought myself a couple more months' breathing space, but I'd sold my last asset, apart from my house.

David Bona was soon on the phone to wipe the smile from my face. My bill from his firm, Linder Myers, was already in the region of £50,000. Even though it would only be paid if the *Edinburgh* operation was successful, it felt like an axe suspended over my neck.

Soon afterwards he asked me to come to his home in Altrincham for a meeting. I found it odd that we weren't meeting at the Linder Myers offices, but I thought no more about it until I arrived and he started to give me the story of his life. I couldn't understand where it was leading until he announced that he was prepared to come and work for me on a full-time basis for the next ten years.

I was surprised and I suppose a little flattered by the offer. He had done a very professional job on my behalf and his expertise would certainly be useful in the negotiations to come. I was also highly relieved at the thought that my massive bill with Linder Myers wouldn't be getting any bigger. I thought about it for a few minutes, then offered him five per cent of my share of the *Edinburgh* returns for his full-time commitment on a 'no cure, no pay' basis, the same deal I had agreed with James Ringrose. We shook hands on the deal. I was not sure just how he was going to work it with Linder Myers, but he was a clever lad, and no doubt he had already given that a lot of thought.

He would have the chance to start earning his corn straightaway, for we were about to make a formal application for the rights to salvage the *Edinburgh*. On 7 July 1980 Jessop Marine Recoveries Limited submitted its application to the Salvage Association. It included one element that we hoped would help us steal a march on our rivals:

Having regard to the estimated total cost of the operation

as a whole, Jessop Marine Recoveries Limited believes that it would be more feasible for a survey and salvage recovery to be carried out in one operation rather than in two high-cost stages. The planning and execution of a one-stage operation would also be significantly easier to achieve. Should the beneficiaries of the cargo agree with this premise, then Jessop Marine Recoveries Limited is now in a position to proceed immediately upon a one-stage survey and salvage recovery operation, with total commitment whilst using the appropriate deep-diving support vessel.

A one-stage operation was not necessarily what we actually planned to do, but we hoped it would force a quick decision and leave the other contenders struggling in our wake to prepare their own detailed salvage plans in time.

A few days later, I received a call from Mr Jackson at the Salvage Association. The Foreign and Commonwealth Office had called him, requesting a letter giving details of the different parties bidding for the rights to recover the gold from the *Edinburgh*, particularly Jessop Marine. The letter was to be delivered to the Foreign Office in Downing Street by hand, not by post. It appeared that the push from Ringrose's friends in high places had arrived.

Mr Jackson also told me that a decision on the *Edinburgh* could be made in the next couple of weeks but that all three contenders would first have to put their case to a panel in London.

Our group was now put on stand-by for this meeting and we prepared the best presentation we could muster. We held a big meeting at the OSA offices to thrash out the remaining details of the plan and satisfy any lingering doubts in the minds of the members. I explained the latest state of play on the award of the contract and talked them through the history of the sinking of the *Edinburgh*. I was then asked, 'How can you possibly work in this area of the Barents Sea with all the snow and ice around?'

'Because the whole of the Arctic becomes a high-pressure zone during the summer. Whilst we were up in Spitzbergen on one trip enjoying twenty-four hours of daylight and flat calm seas, we listened to reports of ships in distress in extreme weather around Britain. Two were even sunk.'

There were no more questions on that topic and we moved to the planning stage, each party giving an input.

A group of us then went down to HMS *Belfast*, the *Edinburgh*'s twin sister, where we met up with Chief Petty Officer Robbjohns. We were given permission to visit parts of the ship, including the bomb room, that were off-limits to the general public. We took many photographs of the approaches to the bomb room and its interior to help the preparations of the dive team.

After lunch James Ringrose and I covered all the research and the results of the previous operation to find the *Edinburgh*. I was given a tough time by Captain Woellert of the OSA, who understandably preferred to trust the positions given by the German craft involved in the action. We argued a few times but in the end he appeared convinced. At the end of the meeting John Clarke was asked by one of his colleagues, 'What do you consider the most difficult and dangerous part of the operation?'

'Keeping my job, if we come back without finding the *Edinburgh*.'

The meeting at which we were to present our case for the *Edinburgh* contract was set for Tuesday, 22 July at Parliament Square House in London. We were second in the running order, sandwiched between Risdon Beazley and Seaway. On the urgings of my fellow board members, the Managing

Director of Jessop Marine had bought himself a sober and respectable grey suit for the occasion.

On the morning of 22 July, a baking hot summer day, the whole team met up at the OSA offices to rehearse the presentation one final time. David Bona, James Ringrose and I would represent Jessop Marine. Mike Stewart, the man chosen by 2W to handle the diving side of the proposed recovery, would speak for them and John Clarke of OSA and John Lucken of Racal–Decca were on stand-by to answer any specific queries on their parts of the operation. The whole presentation seemed pretty impressive to me, but it was entirely possible that I was biased.

After lunch we walked round to Parliament Square, sweltering in the heat. The panel consisted of Joe Evans, Chief Salvage Officer for the Ministry of Defence, Simon Butts of the Foreign and Commonwealth Office, Terry Holden of the Department of Trade and John Jackson of the Salvage Association. David Bona took the chair on our side, and one by one we presented our individual parts to the panel. In a way I'd been rehearsing for this moment for years. I'd already had to convince some of the hardest men in the oil-diving and shipping industry that my ideas were right. We had also formed the strongest salvage company ever put together. If the contract was to be awarded on merit I was certain that we would be chosen.

We were questioned hard on the war grave aspect of the *Edinburgh*. That pleased me. I was sure that by using divers to recover the gold, we could salvage the wreck in a way that would fully respect the war grave. I was equally confident that Risdon Beazley could not. They only ran 'blast and grab' type of operations at these depths and would have to open up the wreck by the crude method of lowering explosives down to it. After the blast they would grab for anything that was left down there. It was a completely inappropriate technique for a small, high-value cargo like the *Edinburgh*'s gold, particularly on a ship that was an official war grave. It was also potentially hazardous. There was a high risk of a sympathetic detonation of some or all of the massive amounts of unexploded ordnance still on the *Edinburgh*.

That the Admiralty could once have considered this method of recovery left me dumbfounded. Nor could I understand what yardstick was used to designate wrecks as official war graves. I found it hard to understand why no merchant ship – and many were lost during both wars – had ever been classified as a war grave. Over 400 servicemen lost their lives on the *Otranto*, yet no mention was made of any war-grave implications when I applied for permission to salvage that. The government was willing to sell it for £200, no questions asked. Yet HMS *Edinburgh* was declared a war grave, after being sunk – by the British – with fifty-seven bodies on board. Perhaps the English class system even extends to shipwrecks and their dead crews. Or perhaps war grave status is a useful way of keeping people away from ships, like the *Edinburgh* or the *Hampshire*, which for various reasons the government does not wish to see disturbed.

I was careful to keep my opinions on such matters to myself in front of this gathering, however, and the presentation went very smoothly. When we compared notes afterwards, we were all very confident, but Graham then turned up and wiped the smile from my face. He had been at the Public Record Office all day and had just discovered a document suggesting that there was only five and a half tons of gold on the *Edinburgh*.

I found this hard to believe. I'd done my sums. The insured value of the gold at the time of sinking was £1,547,080. Dividing that by the value of gold in 1942 – £4 4s 11½d per ounce – gave a total of 364,018 ounces, just over ten tons. Something was wrong somewhere. It gave me the shivers to think that I could have made a mistake of this magnitude. I got James Ringrose to work out the figures as a double-check. To my relief, he reached the same conclusion. The insurance value equated to ten tons of gold. At today's price it was worth £100 million, and the salvors' percentage would be £45 million.

There were still the documents that Graham had unearthed to consider, however. I decided to check them in the morning. The thought of having to tell my consortium partners that we might have lost five tons of gold kept me awake for much of the night. The following morning, heart in mouth, I began to examine the documents. I first rechecked the report by the Russian Admiral, Arseni Golovko, who stated categorically that ten tons of gold had been put on board the *Edinburgh*. Could a Russian Admiral be wrong?

As I studied the new documents that Graham had found the uneasy feeling grew that the answer might be 'Yes'. The official documents showed that only five and a half tons of gold, not ten, had been loaded at Murmansk. As I dug deeper over the ensuing weeks, the true story began to emerge. It seemed that the Russians had indeed shipped ten tons of gold, but only five and a half tons of it was in payment for war supplies from Britain and the United States. That was the shipment that was meticulously documented. The other four and a half tons was private cargo to be lodged in the West for the personal use of Stalin and his inner circle. The documentation for that was less complete.

With the help of the Russians, we eventually traced the movement of the gold from Moscow all the way to Murmansk, and then to the lighter tied up alongside the *Edinburgh*. There the trail went cold. My private prayer was that it had also been loaded into the *Edinburgh*'s bomb room.

If it was anywhere else on the ship it would now be virtually impossible to find. We could not just start searching a 600-foot long sunken cruiser from end to end.

The £100 million of gold we had been chasing was now around £50 million. I tried to think of some way of breaking the news gently to our consortium partners. There was none. I could offer them some good news alongside the bad, however. Mr Jackson rang to tell me we were to be the recommended group to find and recover the *Edinburgh* and its cargo. The other candidates had not impressed the panel at all. I made a number of calls to let everyone know the outcome. For the first time in a long while, we could all relax just a little.

Mr Jackson also told me that he now felt that it would be wise to consider filming the entire recovery operation. He felt that the two losing parties might leak details to the press, who could easily whip up hysteria about the *Edinburgh*'s status as an official war grave. If we put it all on film it would show the measures taken to respect it. I agreed with him, with one reservation. I prayed that there would be no disasters during the filming. An accidental explosion or a diver being killed would make the film a very two-edged sword.

The government's endorsement of the panel's recommendation was expected to be a formality, but we were warned it might take some time. Politicians around Westminster in late July and early August were as rare as ice floes on the Thames. As we waited for news, we carried on with our preparations, but I then found out that John Clarke was starting to interview a number of *Edinburgh* survivors. I was angry that he was doing so. I thought it was clear that research was our responsibility; it was not for him or OSA to go out and do this. Their job was to supply the ship for the survey and salvage. More important, to have news of the project leak out before the official announcement by the

Ministry would not do us any good at all. And talking to survivors could well stir up the war-graves argument. John had to be told to stop.

I then got a call from James Ringrose, who was in the throes of a major panic. Amongst John Clarke's interviewees had been the engineer on the *Edinburgh*. He had told John that all the gold in the bomb room had been shot away by the first torpedo strike. That was all I needed to hear right then, but after a moment's reflection I began to wonder if John was not just winding James up, as part of the feud that now appeared to exist between them.

I reminded him that the engineer's official sinking report had made no such claim. I also told him that after forty years the tale could all be in the engineer's imagination. Previous experience had shown me how the mind tends to remember what it wants to remember. Just the retelling of a story over the years can distort the truth. Without my diaries and records, my own memory would often have led me astray, even on events which were very clear in my mind.

CHAPTER EIGHTEEN

WAR GRAVE

———————•———————

The days drifted by with no official announcement and we began to get impatient. The Arctic diving season was once again starting to slip away. We had even begun seeking legal advice about doing the *Edinburgh* as a salvor in possession or volunteer salvor, when we were finally given official confirmation that we had been selected to recover the gold. Even then, it was indirect. The Ministry told us only that both Seaway and Risdon Beazley had been informed that we were the chosen party.

James Ringrose left no one in any doubt that it was his word in the Royal ear that had brought this about. On my next meeting with David Bona, I was surprised to find James there as well. His opening remark was brief and to the point. 'Keith, the time has now come for you to pay the piper.'

'What?'

'For the Royal help. You're now required to deposit the sum of £100,000 in a numbered account of a Swiss bank.'

I was left to understand that this money was for the private use of Prince Charles. I may be a Yorkshireman and a bit slow at times, but one things was certain, I was not going to swallow this story and let James Ringrose get his hands on

£100,000. The fact that David Bona was nodding sagely in the background made me think that he was also hopeful of a slice.

After a very nasty argument, Ringrose then shifted his ground a little. The money would still be paid through the numbered account but would go to a charity. I laughed. 'I'll tell you what, Jim. I very much doubt if HRH is really involved in this, but if and when we get the contract from the Russians, if and when we find the wreck, and if and when we recover the gold, you can tell HRH that if he cares to nominate a charity, I'll ensure that Jessop Marine makes a donation to it. Until then he's on the same terms as the rest of us: "no cure, no pay". First you earn it, then you spend it.'

By now I was getting a little tired of this team of mine. My own view was that James Ringrose's only usefulness lay in his alleged Royal connections but sceptical though I was about some of his claims, I was not going to rock the boat at this delicate stage by tossing him overboard. I had similar reservations about David Bona, whose sharpness in negotiation and drafting of legal documents – his principal asset as far as I was concerned was very useful. But I would not keep him if I thought for a moment that his energies might be turning towards feathering his own nest. He and Ringrose spent a lot of time together. Both were well educated, but I was beginning to wonder whether they might not become sharp boys with an eye on the main chance. Both were at the start of going through divorces. They'd hit it off from the moment I'd introduced them. From then on, I was definitely the odd man out whenever the three of us were together. At first I began to feel the object of the occasional snide comment about my lack of formal education or one of Ringrose's characteristically oblique hints about my corresponding lack of social airs and graces. Later there was also an undercurrent of something else, less easy to interpret. The patronising remarks were less frequent, but the smiles also seemed much more forced. There were also incidents which were trivial in isolation but taken together left me with a growing feeling of unease.

That left me in a very delicate position. I needed no advice from anyone on salvage, but I was the first to admit that I was a total novice in the ways of big business and in the protracted, government-level negotiations that lay ahead. Bona already knew a great deal about the *Edinburgh* project. A good replacement would take some time to find and even more to bring up to speed. The abrupt departure of Bona and Ringrose might also upset the other members of the consortium.

I thought long and hard about the situation and decided that the only thing to do was to continue with them. They would need watching closely, but it seemed the least bad solution I could find. A public split with them could cost me everything I'd worked for. I had to keep my eye on the ball and what counted most was finding and recovering the gold. As events were to show, I was right to be worried about my position. Their private discussions extended well beyond the attempts to secure the *Edinburgh* contract. They were already hatching a long-term plan to undermine me and wrest my own company from my control.

Had Ringrose never become involved in Jessop Marine, I think Bona might have been content to exercise his sharpness and ambition wholly on my behalf. Ringrose dazzled him, both with his tales of his Royal connections and his claims of great expertise in locating wrecks. Was I imagining things in beginning to get concerned that they might feel with Bona to run the business and Ringrose to find the wrecks, why would they need a thick Yorkshire salvage man as well?

If I had been less absorbed in the pursuit of the *Edinburgh*, I might have been able to deal with the position earlier. Bona had a habit of thrusting documents requiring my signature in front of me at the least opportune moments. On one occasion he shoved a bundle of contracts into my hand only minutes before a vital meeting with the Russians.

'They're straightforward, just as we discussed the other day Keith, but we do need to get them in the post today.'

I scanned through them and there seemed nothing amiss. Bona took them back, shuffled them together and then began laying them down on the table in front of me, open at the pages where I was to sign. I dutifully did so. Only after the end of the *Edinburgh* operation did I discover that among those contracts, was a document making James Ringrose a director of Jessop Marine. I believe that it was step one of a plan to take over the company.

A while later Bona told me, 'I've been thinking, Keith. You really should be paid something for the research that you've put into the company.'

In my dire financial position, I was far from averse to being paid some money, though it seemed a bit like transferring it from one pocket to the other, since it was effectively all my money anyway. It didn't occur to me that there might be an alternative explanation for his unexpected suggestion. Could it have been that he and Ringrose wanted to take a viable company from me and for that reason they wanted my assets – particularly my research files – to be owned by the company, not myself as an individual?

My ignorance of business procedure also made me completely unaware of the importance of the company minute book. In any legal battle, I am told, the minutes are naturally regarded as the best available evidence of what has occurred. I never realised the importance of exercising control over them. As it was I had more pressing problems on my mind and left the recording of the minutes to David Bona. Again, the seriousness of that error only became apparent after the end of the *Edinburgh* salvage operation, when I discovered that Bona had not only written the company minutes from his point of view but on one occasion the minute book referred to a board meeting about which I knew nothing. Had I not had my own diaries to refer to, I would not have been able to show that I was not even in the country at the time.

All that lay in the future, however, and for the moment we resumed our uneasy business relationship.

We'd persuaded the British government to back us; all we had to do now was convince the Russians. Even though the Cold War was at its height, the Thatcher government gave immediate clearance for negotiations to begin with the Soviets. They weren't expected to take long. The Russians were notoriously strapped for cash and here they were being offered the chance of tens of millions, in gold, for no outlay or effort at all.

While we waited for the Soviets to rumble into gear, we pressed ahead with our own preparations. As surveyors to the consortium, the location of the *Edinburgh* was now Decca Marine's responsibility. I plotted on to a chart all the information taken from the logs and charts of all the ships and U-boats involved in the naval action that led to the sinking of the *Edinburgh*, and passed it to Carl Oberman at Decca with all my other material. I also included the information on fasteners from Ken Knox and two other trawlermen, John Gibson and Fred Myers, who had also lost nets in the same area.

Information about the sinking position of a wreck is normally scant, but there was almost a surfeit of documentation about the *Edinburgh*. I knew where I thought the wreck was and had marked the position on my own chart, but Carl would naturally wish to reach his own conclusions. He now had to decide where to start the search. Decca Marine's reputation rested on him making the right choice. He soon made an important discovery when he talked to Ken Knox, who had lent him his logbook of the time he was fast in the wreck. Carl discovered that Ken had been operating on the Consol navigation system at the time but had since converted his position to a Decca reading. In doing so he had compounded an already large navigational error.

Carl analysed the figures and found that Ken had actually been much further north than he thought, right inside the area that was now our prime search area. There were no other sunken British warships in that area of the Barents Sea. He must have been fast in the *Edinburgh.*

As a further cross-check Ringrose accompanied some Decca people to Norway to see if they could get any further input from the Norwegian trawlermen who fished the Barents Sea. He called me from Tromsø to tell me that they'd been given a definite position by the fishermen there, then rang again from Vardø. He now had 'a super fix on the *Edinburgh*', in a completely different position. It appeared to me that every time he was given a new position he immediately fell in love with it.

Carl Oberman was equally unimpressed. He put more trust in the positions plotted by the *Edinburgh*'s British escort vessels, rather than those of Norwegian trawlermen who, like fishermen of every nationality, are close-mouthed and secretive about their fishing grounds, particularly when questioned by strangers.

A search area large enough to encompass all the different possible positions of the wreck would have been bigger than Greater London and Carl's prime task was to narrow it down to the most probable ones. He called to say that his conclusions broadly agreed with my own and that he was looking forward to getting started next year.

'To hell with next year,' I said. 'We're all in the starting blocks to go now. All we need is the acceptance from Moscow.'

'I doubt you'll get that for the next couple of weeks at least, the Eastern Bloc countries are holding naval exercises in that area of the Barents Sea.'

Weeks drifted by without any word from the Russians, despite Foreign Office pressure. Everyone in the consortium was starting to get edgy. I was taking phone calls by the hour, all asking for the latest news and updates. OSA were even threatening to pull out of the operation altogether unless confirmation was received soon. I could understand their problem: the *Stephaniturm*, the OSA salvage ship, was very expensive to keep on indefinite stand-by. It could have been earning them tens of thousands of pounds a week in charter fees.

In the end we ran out of patience and telexed the Foreign Office, telling them that unless we got clearance from the Soviets by the following Monday, we would be demobilising for the season. Monday came and went without word and we reluctantly mothballed the operation until the following spring.

It was yet another disappointment; I was determined it would be the last.

A few days later there was movement at last on the Soviet front. Mr Darling from the Black Sea and Baltic Insurance Company rang to invite us to London for talks about the *Edinburgh* with his directors. We were also to stand by to go to Moscow in the very near future, to do a presentation to the Russians on how we intended to find and recover the gold. Mr Jackson, David Bona, James Ringrose and I met them at their London offices in the last week of October. We were all a little on edge at the thought of meeting the Russians for the first time.

The Managing Director, Novojilov Constantine, did most of the talking. Much to my surprise it soon emerged that his company were very interested in exploring a long-term salvage arrangement with us. It was an exciting prospect, opening up areas of the oceans that held many special wrecks.

After lunch we met Captain John Bannister from the Anglo-Soviet Shipping Company. We'd been warned that Seaway were pressuring Moscow for the *Edinburgh* contract but he assured us that the Russians wouldn't work with the Norwegians and wanted a British company to do it. It was music to our ears.

There were rather more discordant noises after the first press stories about the *Edinburgh* salvage. The first reports appeared in Norwegian and Swedish newspapers, perhaps planted there by Seaway, and simply stated that the British government was likely to give permission for an operation to salvage the *Edinburgh*. The reports produced a Klondyke atmosphere in Oslo. A couple of days later *Navy News* broke the story in Britain, adding that the survivors were far from happy with the situation. There was also a big splash in the *Daily Mail*, headlined 'Race for the £100 million sea gold'. BBC News picked up the story and from then on it was open season.

I was pleased that the story was starting to break, hoping it would force the government into a public confirmation that we had the contract and stop Risdon Beazley's background manoeuvres to get the decision reversed.

But early in November there was a front-page story in the *Sunday Times*.

The wreck of the British cruiser *Edinburgh* with £50 million in gold aboard – it is one of the world's great sunken treasures – has been found by a British salvage company.

311

After frequent unsuccessful searches by British, Russian and Norwegian salvage experts for 25 years, the wreck was found this summer by a Southampton-based company, Risdon Beazley.

'It will be one of the most difficult salvage operations ever,' says the company's cargo recovery manager, Fergus Hinds. 'But the wreck is there, the gold is there and the job can be done.'

Risdon Beazley, a swashbuckling company with a reputation for handling difficult salvages, was given permission by the Defence Ministry to search for the *Edinburgh* on the strict condition that no effort was made to board her. After four months the company search vessel, *Droxford*, which was regularly buzzed by Russian planes and escorted by Russian submarines, quietly headed home.

Yesterday the company told the *Sunday Times* that the *Droxford* search had, in fact, been successful. Hinds, however, refused to give the exact location of the wreck or to release pictures taken of it from a diving bell. Apart from Risdon Beazley two other companies have approached the Department of Trade, which handles salvage contracts on war wrecks. A Norwegian company, Stolt-Nielsen of Oslo, says: 'We feel we have a lot to offer.' The third contender for the contract is Jessop Marine Recoveries.

Although the Department of Trade and the Ministry of Defence say that no decision has been made on whether to allow a salvage attempt, Risdon Beazley believes that an announcement is imminent. 'We could do the job without disturbing the areas of the ship where we think the bodies are,' says Hinds.

The statement that Risdon Beazley had found the wreck

was a joke. Trawler skippers had told me that Fergus Hinds had been in Hull only recently, asking if they could help him find the *Edinburgh*. It was hardly the action of a man who already knew where it was.

The publicity stirred up some strong reactions from the *Edinburgh* survivors. I was delighted when one of them stated, 'Best to get the gold out, then leave the wreck alone,' but he was definitely in the minority. After a public meeting in Warrington on 19 September the *Edinburgh* survivors wrote to the Admiralty opposing any salvage attempt. I understood and respected their feelings but even setting aside my own vested interest, it was no longer realistic to expect that anyone could prevent a salvage operation now. The *Edinburgh* lay in international waters and the gold was going to be removed whatever the wishes of the survivors and their government. Far better for it to be done by a team using saturation diving techniques under the watchful eye of a British government representative, than by a pirate salvor.

There were calls aplenty from 2W, OSA and Decca about the press stories. The only response from the Department of Trade was that it 'wouldn't be wise at this time to issue a statement that Jessop Marine are the party recommended by the British government, as it might appear that we're trying to force the hand of the Russians'. They did agree to send us a telex, however, privately confirming that we were the chosen party.

By now funds were getting very low in the Jessop household. Graham was broke and I was getting regular love letters from my bank manager. When I went to see him, I was told there would be no further extensions to my overdraft – despite the fact that he still had my house deeds. I walked ten yards across the road to another bank and emerged with a £10,000 overdraft. It was good news for my daughter Carol as well as me, I'd just borrowed £200 from her. The over-draft didn't last long. Most of it was swallowed in clearing a few other debts.

We had to find some work to keep us going, but as all our contacts in the oil industry now knew that we were involved in a multi-million pound salvage project, it would have been more than a little embarrassing for us to have had to ask for a job. Fortunately, Malcolm and Ric at 2W under-stood our problems and found Graham some work in the North Sea. It looked as though he was going to be support-ing his dad for a change, but later the same morning 2W put me on stand-by to go out to India as a diving supervisor on the *Pacific Constructor* in the Bombay High Field. I was told to have jabs for typhoid, paratyphoid, cholera and tetanus. Bombay sounded like a nice place . . .

I flew out to India the following week. I'd always wanted to go there but to see the 'Jewel in the Crown' full of such poverty, disease and total degradation of human beings came as a real shock to me. I came down the aircraft steps in the stifling heat and began the endless passage through Immigration, Passport Control, Customs and half a dozen other officials, all asking silly questions. The Indians had obviously absorbed the British love of paperwork in triplicate.

The road to the heliport was lined with people living in absolute squalor, in cardboard boxes or whatever they could find to give them shelter. Even in the depths of the Great Depression in Keighley as a child, we had lived like kings compared to these unfortunates. I saw very young children climbing out of a deep hole in the dark red soil. They scaled rickety bamboo ladders with baskets full of earth on their heads and the mud and slime covered their heads and bodies. Perhaps they were the lucky ones; they did have a job.

Our transport out to the oilfields was a very dilapidated

Russian helicopter. It looked ready for the knacker's yard. Just before take-off a man came out and polished the pilot's seat with a cloth. Next came the pilot, fussed over by his retinue as he strutted to the helicopter. Just before getting into the cockpit he put on an immaculate pair of white gloves and a silk scarf. There were no seats for the passengers, so we just sat on the floor amongst all the diving gear. The rattles and bangs from the engines and the way the rear doors looked as if they could burst open at any time made us very relieved to get off at the production platform.

More shocks were in store. As we made our way down from the platform to a crew boat that would take us across to our work vessel, we came across workers brewing up and making meals on small stoves. It was an area where smoking was absolutely forbidden and would have brought instant dismissal on a North Sea platform. When we at last got on board the *Pacific Constructor* we heaved a collective sigh of relief. In the next few days we twice heard large explosions and saw clouds of smoke coming from the main production platform. We were never told what had happened but assumed that the combination of combustible gases and al fresco catering had claimed another victim.

We soon found that working in this oilfield was very different from the North Sea. I was one of the supervisors running the air spread, responsible for all the air dives down to 160 feet. Below the 160-foot mark was the responsibility of the saturation-diving team.

I'd drawn the short straw and took charge of the night shift, from midnight until noon. The nights out on the deck were pleasant and warm but the sea and its contents were something else. This was my first encounter with poisonous sea snakes. You never saw one during the day, but at night, attracted by the lights, they came to the surface in hundreds. One bite from some of these things was enough to kill. It made the divers who had never seen them before very nervous about getting into the work-basket. Divers being divers however, it wasn't long before the sea snakes were being caught and turned into snakeskin belts. The Australians, who had obviously done that sort of thing before, caught them by the dozen using a length of wire with a loop at one end, pushed through a length of electrical conduit. They killed and skinned them in no time and left them hanging on the line to dry.

Sea snakes were not the only danger. There were plenty of sharks too, encouraged by the stupid policy of throwing rubbish overboard. In UK waters it's either burned or returned to shore. Here it was just tossed overboard.

One night the flare stack was surrounded by a pack of big sharks. I was putting down a new diver, who was very, very nervous about these monsters swimming around. I gave him the usual patter, 'Get a move on, they won't touch you', and we got him into the metal work-basket, with the tools for the job. We lowered him down to 100 feet, but I then had a few problems persuading him to leave the cage and swim the two or three yards to the platform. According to the diver these sharks were the size of killer whales, just waiting to have a go at him. After a few hard words, I finally got him to make the swim to the platform. I could tell by the sound of his breathing that he'd made it and was now clinging to the metal jacket of the flare stack.

After a short wait I said, 'Well, are you going to start work?'

'I can't. I've left my tools in the basket.'

He had to make the swim three more times, but he survived.

Our main project was to repair a damaged length of piping and fix a new set of anodes underwater to stop a flare stack from rotting away. In the North Sea the damaged piping would have been replaced immediately. Here a patch was welded over the hole. I saw many other things that made me glad to get away from the Bombay High. If ever there was an accident waiting to happen it was there.

On our way to the airport in the middle of the night for the journey home, we passed a couple of dead bodies lying in the road. They were being stripped of the few rags they wore.

I arrived back in the UK on 4 December, desperate for news of the *Edinburgh* operation. Graham brought me up to date. The Russians had now given the all clear for the project in principle but they still needed to be convinced that we were the right party to carry out the salvage. As well as Seaway and Risdon Beazley, Swedish and East German salvage companies were also now trying to get in on the act. However, just as the Russians were warming up, the Foreign Office was going cold because of the situation in Poland, where the strike at the Gdansk shipyards was developing into a challenge to the government itself. It seemed as though the *Edinburgh* project was in its usual state – situation normal, all fucked up – and I was fast losing patience.

The Bombay job paid for a decent Christmas, but my financial situation remained desperate. It was good to see the end of 1980. It had promised so much but in the end had delivered so little.

As I was staring out of the window at a grey, cold New Year's Day, the telephone rang. John Baross, an old buddy from *Drillmaster* days, was now working for Oceaneering in Brazil. He had a great shore-based job and said that if either Graham or I wanted a job he could fix up the pair of us. I made my New Year's resolution on the spot. I couldn't face the thought of another wasted year hanging around waiting and hoping for things to happen. If I couldn't get a definite answer from the government within three months, I'd abandon the *Edinburgh* project, dissolve Jessop Marine and go to Brazil. I'd get back to salvage once I'd built up my capital again.

In the event I didn't have to test how genuine my threat was. Later that week came the breakthrough; the Russians were coming to the UK on 19 January. It was electrifying news and all thoughts of Brazil disappeared from my mind. Graham decided to go however. We had one of those father–son discussions about it, and in the end he felt the money and the chance to learn saturation diving were too good to miss. I saw him off at the airport a few days later.

Our first encounter with the Russians took place at 1 Victoria Street, a place used for discreet British government meetings. It was the second meeting of the day for the Russian and British government delegations. I would have given a lot to know what had been said during the first one.

The Soviet party consisted of six people, two legal and four technical. The introductions were very formal and my first impression was that the Russians all looked rather dour and were very heavy smokers. They spoke little English and all conversations had to go through interpreters, which caused a few problems. At one point we were under the impression that the Russians wanted to take charge of the salvage vessel. Tensions were rising to danger point until we discovered that all they wanted was a representative on board the vessel.

The next bone of contention was the handing over of the gold once we had it aboard the recovery vessel. In true civil-service style, that knotty problem was deferred to the next meeting. After that the meeting became more friendly. The ice appeared to have broken.

We rushed down to London Airport for the flight to Aberdeen, where the Russians were to have an inspection tour of 2W and the proposed salvage vessel, the *Stephaniturm*, which was moored at Montrose. After they had checked into their hotel they made it clear that they would not be averse to a drink before departing for their tour. A couple of drinks made them late, but rather less dour.

The delegation was still being shown round the plant when 2W faced a drama. They had a bell fast on the bottom of the North Sea with divers inside it. We kept the news from the Russians, who only learned about it later from the evening news on the television. Mike Stewart, 2W's Project Manager, smoothed their ruffled feathers, explaining that a rescue vessel was now alongside and all was under control. The Russians nodded and went back to the serious business of sampling the hotel's entire stock of malt whiskies.

The following morning we all moved down to Montrose for the inspection of the *Stephaniturm*. The German crew put on an excellent meal and another liberal supply of drink. It was again much appreciated by the Soviets. At one point Mr Zlobin, the vice chairman of Ingosstrakh, the Soviet insurance company, was arm-wrestling with the German first mate. The pause for refreshment lasted so long that the end of the tour around the ship had to be called off, to enable us to get our visitors to the airport in time for the flight back to London.

CHAPTER NINETEEN

THE KREMLIN

The next morning the Russians visited Decca Marine to see the equipment that would be used to find the *Edinburgh*. From their broad smiles on their return it appeared that light refreshments had once more been served and appreciated.

There was then a further meeting at 1 Victoria Street. The frost of the first meeting had now thawed completely. The Soviet delegation pronounced themselves delighted with everything they had seen during their visit and to a man, said they would recommend Jessop Marine for the contract. The signing of the formal contract would have to await the clarification of a few points back in Moscow however. Meanwhile lines of communication would be kept open between the two governments so that any problems could be quickly sorted out.

We drank a series of toasts to Anglo-Soviet friendship and before the Russians left they issued invitations to a reception at the Soviet Embassy the following week, by which time the heads of agreement would be ready for the two governments to sign.

I knew the Russians set great store by punctuality – when not delayed by light refreshments – so I turned up at the Embassy in Kensington Palace Gardens in good time. The entrance to the gardens was closed and I had to convince the copper on duty that I had a genuine reason for wanting to go in. After showing him my invitation card and being checked off on his list, I was allowed through the gates. 'Rather you than me, lad, going into that place.'

I found myself facing a big, dark building with hardly a light showing. I walked up the drive to the front door and gave the bell a good ring. I could hear footsteps approaching and then the door was opened by a stern-faced individual. I showed him my invitation. The only response was 'Nyet.'

After a bit of arm-waving I got the message. The reception was being held across the road in another building. I was feeling distinctly nervous by this time. I was a long way from Keighley and in hostile territory as well.

The door across the road was opened immediately. I was led along a short passageway and into a huge room. I was the first guest to arrive and the place was empty apart from a line of half a dozen Russians, all in what looked like identical dark suits. I was introduced down the line, then paired off with a person introduced to me as a First Secretary, Economics, at the Embassy. He spoke perfect English without a trace of any accent.

'Mr Jessop,' he said, 'would you like a drink?'

Never having tasted vodka in my life, I asked for one.

'May I suggest you try our best Russian vodka, Blue Label Stolichnaya?' He poured me a tumbler full.

After a couple of drinks, and with another in my hand, I was now guided across the room to a table laden down with food. I was feeling just a little on the hungry side and could have got stuck into a meat pie or something more substantial than fancy canapés. There was nothing that would make a decent mouthful. My new-found friend saw my dilemma. 'Mr Jessop, may I suggest you try some of our Russian beluga caviar – you know, the stuff Mr Bond made famous.'

By now the room had started to fill up. I was introduced to the Ambassador and the Military and Naval Attaches, resplendent in their dress uniforms. Captain Zotov, the Naval Attache, had a powerful handshake and looked very much like the Russian actor Oscar Holmolka. A group of other Russians joined us and we started talking about the salvage of the *Edinburgh*. The conversation continued for some time, ranging over all the wrecks sunk in the Barents Sea.

Captain Zotov then asked me if we could meet the next day for lunch as he had a proposal to put to me. Maybe I had seen too many Bond movies, but alarm bells started to ring. It was time to depart. I stood up on my toes to see who I could call to my rescue. To my dismay I saw that my fellow Brits had all been and gone. The whole place was now empty, apart from the group surrounding me. I stammered, 'Sorry gentlemen, I've just noticed the time. I've a young son waiting outside in the car to take me home.'

Outside the Embassy, the air never tasted so sweet. I jumped in the car and told Ian to get under way fast. I learned from newspaper reports that Captain Zotov was later deported for recruiting spies.

The following day the heads of agreement were signed between the two governments. Rather surprisingly I was also told that the Russians wanted a film to be made of the operation and would place no restrictions on press coverage or any book. They were also very keen to examine all the other things that came up from the wreck. Could it be that they were interested in the whereabouts of the missing four and a half tons of gold?

Although it seemed dangerously like counting our chickens, we made the arrangements for the sale of the gold, once recovered. On receipt of an official telex, Rothschilds would pay the daily market price of gold, fixed in London at 10.30 a.m. and 3 p.m. each day, provided that the gold was in mint condition and had all the correct assay marks. Any damaged gold would have to be resmelted at an over-all cost of about £14,000. Rothschilds also wanted to be certain of the provenance of the gold because Tsarist gold was generally of poor quality, but Soviet gold was the best – 999.9 per cent pure.

Our consortium partners were now prepared to mobilise as soon as the main contract was signed. A draft contract wasn't enough. If we were to sail to attempt the recovery operation this spring, OSA wanted to see a signed contract. Having worked in the oil industry, I could understand the pressure they were under. Vessels capable of doing this type of operation were very expensive animals indeed and much in demand at this time of the season in the North Sea. They set a cut-off date of 6 March for a 1 May sailing date. If the contract had not been signed by then, they would have to put the boat out on charter. That gave us only ten days and there was now another reason for speed; the price of gold was starting to fall back from the previous season's all-time high of over $800 per ounce.

For the next ten days a constant stream of phone calls and telexes failed to produce the answer we needed, but the blame for the delay couldn't all be laid at the door of the Russians. It emerged that the British were holding some sort of war game and everything, including our contract with the Russians, had been shunted back into the pending tray until the exercise was over. Finally during the late afternoon of deadline day, 6 March, the Salvage Association called with the answer. We were all to travel to Moscow on 29 March, stay a few days to iron out any final problems and then sign the contract. It was good news, but not good enough; we would not now be sailing in May. Just the same, everyone seemed relieved to have some sort of definite answer, even if it wasn't quite the one we'd been hoping for.

For eighteen long months, I'd been fire-fighting, damping down a series of problems and disasters that could have blown the whole *Edinburgh* project to pieces, long before we got anywhere near the gold. For the first time in my life, I'd begun to feel a few degrees under the weather. The tension was starting to catch up with me.

John Clarke cranked it up another few notches when he called later that day. We were now back to a two-stage operation – first the survey, then the salvage. OSA were making a smaller vessel, the *Dammtor*, available for the survey to find the *Edinburgh*. Meanwhile they had put our proposed salvage vessel, the *Stephaniturm*, out on contract to Comex Diving for a year. He assured me that the vessel was let on the clear understanding that it would be released back to us for a period of up to six weeks on fourteen days' notice.

'I hope you're right, John. I hope you're right.'

Before we flew to Moscow, we were given a briefing on how we should conduct ourselves in the Soviet Union, to ensure that none of the party could be compromised. We were warned that our hotel would be bugged. If we wanted to talk business we were to leave our rooms and talk while walking in the street. We were not to change money out on the street or accept invitations to people's homes. After all the revelations in the press about Soviet spies and British intelligence cock-ups, I found this stress on total secrecy quite amusing. I suspected the Soviets already knew more about our negotiating position than we did.

As we boarded our package-holiday flight to Moscow (the government delegation flew British Airways), there was only one cloud on the horizon – the ongoing troubles in

Poland. We all had the feeling that if it led to Soviet intervention – and it was sounding by the newscasts that it might – the British government would cease all negotiations with the Soviets. That would sink our venture, for the time being at least. I could only cross my fingers and hope.

We landed at Sheremetyevo Airport in the late afternoon of 28 March and were taken by bus to our hotel at the bottom of Gorky Street. I had a quick look at Red Square and the Kremlin from the front of the hotel. It looked very imposing. It also felt very, very cold.

The hotel smelt of stale cigarettes and boiled cabbage. We'd arrived too late to eat in the restaurant and there was no room service. As we were shown to our rooms, I noticed there was a person sitting in a chair on each corridor, taking in all that happened. We were never to be free of the feeling of being watched. The next morning, after a hearty breakfast of one boiled egg, I took a walk down into Red Square and around the Kremlin. There can be few sights in the world to equal it. I wrote in my diary: 'Whatever else happens in Moscow, this alone was well worth the trip.'

I was rather less impressed with the Moscow shops. Everything I had seen and been told about the Soviet Union was true. There were endless queues of pale and pinched-looking people shuffling into shops that seemed empty of anything worth buying. There were also shambling drunks on every corner. They were hustled away from the vicinity of Red Square by uniformed or secret policemen, but elsewhere they were left to lie where they fell. This was still the morning; I shuddered to think what it would be like at night.

The British government delegation held private talks with the Russians that morning. We joined them for lunch, then made our way to the offices of the Ministry, where at last we got down to finalising the contract.

During the preliminary discussions the Russians told us that in addition to the official cargo they were pretty certain that at least another three and a half tons of gold was on the *Edinburgh* and promised a big effort to find the supporting documentation. We were also told that we'd have a Russian vessel on site with us at all times and an escort back to Murmansk once we'd recovered the bullion. All other vessels would be instructed to keep well clear of the area during the operation.

The process of agreeing the final form of the contract was slow and tortuous. By the end of the afternoon we had only managed to cover eighteen clauses. The inclusion of the extra OSA vessel for the survey alone occupied an hour of nit-picking, argument and table-thumping before it was finally agreed.

The following days were entirely occupied by the slow grind through the contract, but finally we'd managed to reach the end. The working party would have to work through the night to produce final printed versions in English and Russian.

We had a rather less arduous evening planned, a trip to the Hall of Congress inside the Kremlin walls, to see the Bolshoi Ballet perform *Icarus*. There were no signs of poverty or shortages there, just men and women in expensive clothes and a lot of foreign delegations and military top brass, judging by their uniforms and medals. Much to my surprise, I enjoyed the evening very much, though I couldn't help wondering what some of my Keighley acquaintances would have made of the sight of Keith Jessop watching a ballet.

The next morning, to no one's great surprise, we were told that there would be a delay in signing the contract. In the meantime, there were to be meetings and yet more meetings. We jumped into the big black Zil limousines for a ride across Moscow to the head office of Ingosstrakh, the Soviet insurance company.

The last problems with the contract were finally resolved early the next morning and the full delegation arrived at 10.15 for the signing. As we should have known by now, it was not quite that simple. The British government representatives and Jessop Marine signed every paper of the bulky contracts and a letter of intent. The Russians kept their pens in their pockets, pending the approval of their Minister.

Our copies would remain at our Embassy in Moscow, and on Monday or Tuesday of the following week, with the approval of their Minister, the Russians would sign and date all the contracts. The British Embassy would then telex Jessop Marine and the UK government to inform us that the contracts were signed and active. On the following Friday a question would be asked in the House of Commons, enabling the Minister to give the House an explanation. Until then we were warned that we were under parliamentary privilege and had to remain silent about the contract.

I'd enjoyed some things about Moscow but I wasn't sorry to leave the poverty, the grey faces and the constant surveillance behind. I wasn't the only one to feel that way. As our plane left the ground to begin the return trip to the UK, a spontaneous round of clapping burst out.

As soon as we were back in England, messages began to flash back and forth between all the interested parties. The question was always the same: 'Any word yet?'

We planned to launch the survey expedition within ten working days of the Soviets signing the contract and there were frantic last-minute preparations to ensure that the *Dammtor* and its crew had everything necessary for success. She would be in Peterhead, in the north of Scotland, by 13 April, ready to sail, but the news from Decca was less encouraging. It was their responsibility to find the wreck. They had all the available research, including my own, and the full reports on the previous expedition. But so far they had been unable to erect their Hi-Fix masts at Vardø and Gamvik on the northern coast of Norway, because of deep snow in the area.

They were vitally needed. The signals from the masts combined with a Global Positioning System would tell the survey vessel its position to within a few feet at any time, in any weather conditions. Once the wreck was found it would fix its position once and for all. Had that sort of equipment been available on our first expedition to find the *Edinburgh*, the gold might already have been sitting in the bank.

While Decca tried to find snow-blowers and snow-ploughs to clear a way to the Hi-Fix sites, we kept waiting for the Russians. I could have read *War and Peace* – in Russian – faster than they could get through a fifteen-page contract. A telex arrived from our Embassy in Moscow to say that the contract had done the rounds of the Kremlin and was now back on the desk of the Chief of the Russian Merchant Marine. 'It should be signed by tomorrow.' The next day came and went, and the next, and the next. Still there was no word from Moscow. The phone lines between myself and my consortium partners were once more buzzing like angry wasps.

Easter came and went and on 24 April, some twenty days past the promised date for the signed contract, there was news of another delay. In the original contract it was agreed that the Russians would keep all the gold. We would be paid in cash, so there would be no VAT problems for the consortium members. They were so short of hard currency, however, that they now wanted us to take our share in gold. There would be a delay of a further two weeks while the paperwork for this was sorted out. At the time this switch appeared to be merely one more tedious delay, but it was to have a much more significant impact later on. We'd negotiated a 'no cure, no pay' agreement with both the UK and Russian governments. We were well aware that we'd have to pay tax on the money we earned, but no mention was made by any British government representative of the fact that by importing gold bullion rather than currency into Britain we would be making ourselves liable for VAT.

As with the copper of the *Johanna Thorden*, we could have sold our share of the gold abroad and just brought cash back to the UK, but we were never given that opportunity, nor the chance to renegotiate the contract. We were simply told that the gold must come back to the UK. Fifteen per cent VAT would make a huge dent in our earnings from the *Edinburgh* and give the UK government an unearned and unjustified windfall.

Everyone's patience with the Soviets was now exhausted. We sent a final telex, indicating our intention to sail the following week. If they failed to sign the agreement for any reason, we would go ahead anyway and complete the operation as volunteer salvors. We assembled at 2W's offices in Aberdeen for the mobilisation meeting. We checked all the research paperwork to ensure that nothing was missing and established a random code procedure for the *Dammtor*. It was no use letting the world know what we were up to by passing messages over the radio telephone.

We then moved up to Peterhead for a look at the *Dammtor*. It was one of the best-equipped survey vessels ever to set sail. OSA, 2W and Decca were doing us proud.

We had returned to Aberdeen and were sitting in Malcolm's office when his secretary put a call through. It had to be important because he'd left orders not to be disturbed. He put the phone down, took a deep breath, then burst into the biggest smile I'd ever seen from him. 'The contracts have been signed.'

The champagne corks were finally popped.

The government press release was issued later that day, setting off a wave of media coverage that would have swamped the *Edinburgh* itself. The press reacted with incredulity to the fact that Jessop Marine – an obscure Yorkshire one-man band – had beaten two giant corporations to the rights. It made a good story to portray us that way, but there was nothing small or obscure about our consortium partners – 2W was one of the biggest diving firms in the North Sea and OSA and Racal–Decca were industrial giants, leaders in their fields.

Apart from fending off incessant press enquiries, our main problem was now to make sure we got the Russian representatives aboard the *Dammtor* before sailing time. If we didn't, the contract could have been void. None of us relished the thought of relying on either the British or Soviet governments to get a visa issued in time, but in the end a simple solution was found; the Russian would be transferred to the *Dammtor* from a Soviet salvage vessel, the SS *Agat*, somewhere *en route* to the site.

I watched the *Dammtor* being readied for departure with mixed feelings. The *Edinburgh* had been my project, my obsession, these last few years. I had battled on, often single-handed, doing the research to establish that the gold was on board and identify the search area. I'd won over the initially sceptical figures in the Salvage Association, the underwriters and the Department of Trade, and the companies that were now my consortium partners. But now my work was largely done. My partners, not me, would be running the operations to find and later salvage the wreck. They were the experts in their fields and it would have been foolish of me to interfere. I knew where I thought the *Edinburgh* was, but

John Clarke, as Project Manager, and the team of Decca technicians would make their own decisions on where to search, based on Carl Oberman's work. OSA's crew would run the salvage ship and 2W's team of divers would find and lift the gold – if it was still there to be found.

It was a bittersweet feeling to relinquish control of the day-to-day running of the operation now that it was finally going ahead, but I had the utmost confidence in my partners in the enterprise. I thought back to a day long before, when I'd visited a factory making neoprene wetsuits. 'You must need to know a lot about diving as well as manufacturing,' I had said to the owner.

'Not a thing lad,' he said blithely. 'I just pay the wages of people who do.'

It was a lesson I'd never forgotten: find the most expert help you can and then let them get on with it. The only difference was that it was not me but the *Edinburgh* that would be paying everybody's wages on this job. I would not even be sailing with the *Dammtor*. John Clarke and the Decca survey team already had all my research so there was no need for me to be there. As the surveyor to Jessop Marine, James Ringrose was the only one who would be on board.

His chase around Norway with some of the Decca team, talking to trawlermen, had as usual left him convinced that he had the *Edinburgh* position pinned down. I couldn't resist having a bet with him about who would be the closest to the actual site. David Bona immediately suggested that I photograph my suggested sinking position to ensure that 'John Clarke doesn't take all the credit for finding it'.

I gave him a hard look. 'I couldn't give a monkey's toss who finds it or takes the credit, just let it be found.' But I did take a picture of my marked position – although I never saw one from Ringrose, just his fishermen's position.

The *Dammtor* left Peterhead on 30 April 1981 – thirty-

nine years to the day since HMS *Edinburgh* had been torpedoed. She had to call at Kirkenes in Norway to collect some
more navigation gear from Decca before sailing for the
Barents Sea.

I returned to Keighley, but my son Ian drove me over to
Manchester the next day for a long-delayed, clear-the-air
meeting with David Bona, whose manoeuvrings behind my
back had continued. At his insistence, we met at his secretary's flat. It was apparent to me that he did not want to have
the meeting at his firm. He was also very insistent that Ian
remain outside in the car.

A number of very heated arguments followed, which
soon developed into some 'eyeball-to-eyeball' situations. At
one point I had him by the tie, up against the fireplace. After
a couple of hours of hostilities we reached an uneasy peace,
agreeing to bury our differences and make a fresh start in the
interests of seeing the *Edinburgh* through to a successful conclusion. I doubted if Bona was genuine in his expressions of
future goodwill, and I was equally false. My intention was to
rid myself of both him and Ringrose as soon as the *Edinburgh*
operation was finished.

Ian was very upset on my return to the car, not only
because of the time it had taken, but because he'd also
missed a near punch-up.

The *Dammtor* arrived at Kirkenes well ahead of schedule and
John Clarke called me from there on 7 May to tell me of a
heated debate he'd had with Ric Wharton about the use of
the ROV, *Scorpio*. Ric had told John in very clear terms that
if he lost it, it would cost him $850,000. ROVs were as rare
as hen's teeth at the time and very much in demand by the
oil industry in the North Sea. John professed to be less worried about the money than the fact that the loss of such a
major piece of equipment could be enough to knock the

whole project on the head. Before we hung up, I gave John one final piece of information about the *Edinburgh*. 'Robbo' on the *Belfast* had told me that the *Edinburgh* had a crest of a castle. If the ROV picked up the crest from the bridge of the wreck, it would establish beyond doubt that we'd found the *Edinburgh*. I wished him the best of luck.

The weather was excellent and the sea very calm, but there were still ice floes in the harbour as they set sail at 2.30 that afternoon.

We received our first operational call from James Ringrose on the *Dammtor* the next day. Bona and Ringrose had devised a secret code, separate from the one that 2W, Decca and OSA were using. It was fiendishly complex, based on numbers, each one relating to a page, line or word in *Roget's Thesaurus*. I interpreted the message with the aid of the *Thesaurus*. They were to begin with a trial search of area one and would then return to Vardø to do Hi-Fix calibrations.

The following day there was a second message from *Dammtor*. They had picked up the Russians at 72.09N, 34.20W. From now on, the *Dammtor* would only make contact with shoreside in case of emergency; there were to be no more signals from the ship, because it would interfere with the Hi-Fix equipment.

All I could do now was wait and hope.

CHAPTER TWENTY

THE HUNT FOR THE *EDINBURGH*

The shore equipment, including the Hi-Fix masts, had been air-freighted to Kirkenes and snow-ploughs cut a path through to the sites. The first installation at Vardø was on air by 10 May. The second, at Gamvik, was in full operation by 12 May. While the two stations were being installed and tested, *Dammtor* carried out trials on the sonar equipment and on 13 May they were ready to begin the search.

The first pass with the side-scan was made at 8.30 that evening. Seas were light but the temperature was down to minus five Celsius, producing light icing on the deck. There had been some dispute between John Clarke, James Ringrose and the Decca representative, Kip Punch, about where to start the search. James remained infatuated with his new position, courtesy of the Norwegian trawlermen, but John preferred to rely on the work Carl Oberman had done using his own and my research notes. The bridge of a large up-to-date trawler was full of electronic equipment which should have guaranteed reasonable accuracy for any reports of fasteners, but even discounting the natural cunning and reticence of trawlermen, the fixes were often single,

unconfirmed reports, with no indication of what positioning method had been used. They were also based on the
position of the ship rather than the net, which was often
three quarters of a mile astern; and once an area of fouled
ground is reported by a fishing vessel (however inaccurately)
that area tends to be widely avoided by other trawlers,
further reducing the chances of good sightings.

Many of the fishing vessel reports were ignored. But one
area attracted James Ringrose and some of the Decca team.
The reports came from different vessels from different ports,
were based on Decca Navigator and were as recent as the
previous year. That five-kilometre-radius area was favoured
as the primary search area by many of the survey team on
board. The final reconstruction of *Harrier*'s position at the
time of *Edinburgh*'s sinking had opened up another search
area with a five nautical mile radius, however. That had
been Carl Oberman's first-choice position. The two areas
were fifteen nautical miles apart.

As Project Manager, John Clarke pulled rank on the
others and the search began in Carl Oberman's preferred
area. He did not have to wait long for vindication. At 2.21
the next afternoon, 14 May, just two hours after full track
control had been established, a large contact was made on
the port trace of the sonar record. *Dammtor* turned for a
second look and picked up the same contact on the second
run. Echo-sounder runs and the deployment of a second,
more powerful sonar established that the contact was a
wreck and that its shape justified an ROV inspection.

The wreck appeared to be around 600 feet long, much
larger than the *Hermann Schoemann*, which had sunk close to
the *Edinburgh*. Before the *Scorpio* could be deployed, however, the weather began to worsen. After waiting for the
weather to ease, John ordered its launch at 3.45 on the
morning of 16 May.

It was the most hazardous time for the ROV, for they had as yet no knowledge of how the wreck was lying. At first the picture was lost in a snow storm of static. Then it began to clear. Through the incessant silent rain of sediment, the outline of a massive warship began to emerge. The first piece of good news was immediately apparent. Though the hull was twisted and pierced in places by the impact of the torpedo strikes, it was still in one piece. Rear-Admiral Bonham-Carter's report had stated, 'She rolled over to port, her back broken.' It seemed that once more he had been a little economical with the truth.

John Clarke and the survey team crowded around the screen, scanning the images and comparing them with the photographs of the *Belfast* laid out on the table before them. A lattice-like structure near the motor cutter was the first piece of the ship to be recognised, quickly followed by the cutter itself. There was no longer any doubt that they were looking at a Royal Navy cruiser. HMS *Edinburgh* had been found.

The wreck was lying on its port side and it was possible to fly the ROV all the way along the starboard side from the cutter to the bow. The bridge superstructure was missing and they made a careful examination for signs of explosives or cutting. After my experience with the *Chulmleigh* we needed to be very sure that no one had been on this wreck before us. There was no trace of any exploration of the wreck and the bridge superstructure was soon found lying on the sea-bed to the stern of the wreck.

After the initial survey of the whole ship, the ROV was then zeroed in on the torpedo damage close to the bomb room. The hole looked extremely close to it, as we expected, but the exact position of the damage was vital. It would indicate whether the gold still lay in the bomb room or had been scattered all over the sea-bed.

From what they could see, the after end of the torpedo hole seemed to coincide almost exactly with the forward end of the bomb room. John was later to confess that he fiddled his report so that it looked as if there was a foot or two to spare. He hadn't come this far to see the project scrapped for the sake of twenty-four inches.

By 9.45 that morning the *Scorpio* had done its work. After completing the survey they retrieved it and laid three Aquafix beacons around the wreck. They would lie dormant on the sea-bed, ready – in theory at least – to be brought back to life by a radio signal from the salvage ship.

Because of the need for maximum security of communications, John maintained radio silence, waiting to inform us of the discovery by landline when the ship called in at Tromsø.

The days had dragged by while I waited for the news from the *Dammtor*. On 18 May, eleven days after they had sailed, however, I finally got the coded message I'd been waiting for: 'Operation 24 via Vardø Radio', followed by 'Operation 60 Charlie – Whiskey – Hotel – Approx.' The translation was less cryptic: 'We have found the *Edinburgh*. It is lying on the port side (gold side uppermost). Conditions around the wreck are good. The wreck is upright in a depth of 243 metres. The wreck has been marked with transponders.'

I also received one of our own private coded messages that added a little more detail. 'We have examined the area of the torpedo damage, and all looks fine. There is a twenty-foot hole about ten feet forward of the bomb room. All the fuel oil from the fuel tank is missing.'

It was a pretty good way to start a Monday morning. If the wreck had been found broken in two, as Rear-Admiral Bonham-Carter had reported, or with a great big hole near the bomb room, I am sure excuses would have been made and the operation called off. Had she been lying on her starboard side, there would have been much soul-searching before going ahead with the salvage, for we would then have had to cut our way right through the ship to reach the bomb room. It looked as if the angels were shining down on me.

I called Mr Jackson at the Salvage Association to tell him the news. We both knew what the other was feeling at that moment. He had had the faith – and the courage – to back my belief that I could find and recover the gold. He had made enemies as a result. I'd now fulfilled the first part of my promise; we'd found the wreck. All that remained to be done was to go and recover the gold. Mike Stewart, 2W's project manager, called shortly afterwards to offer his congratulations. He promised me the best divers he could find for the job, not just the ones hanging around the base.

By 22 May the *Dammtor* was back in Peterhead. James Ringrose had left the ship at Tromsø and flown back. In the intervening few days he had been telling the world that *he* had found the *Edinburgh*. It took some time for him to get around to giving me a call. When he did, I asked him where she had been found.

'I found it in the middle of the rough ground at 72.0N, 35.0E, some thirteen miles north of the Admiral's given position.' I let his use of the first person pronoun pass, though I was sure that John Clarke, Carl Oberman and the Decca Survey team would have something to say about it.

When I checked the position, it was only three and a half miles from the one I'd marked on the chart, not far from the one that we'd worked out all those months before on board the *Seaway Hawk*. My only amendment since then had been to include the *Harrier*'s correction. Had we been able to search for another twenty-four hours with the *Seaway Hawk*, we'd have found the *Edinburgh*. I couldn't help smiling at the thought of what that knowledge would do to Jacob Stolt-Nielsen's blood pressure.

The following day I made my way up to Aberdeen to see the video from the ROV. The ship's crest had disappeared with the bridge superstructure but there could be not a shred of doubt that this was the *Edinburgh*. As the ROV tracked along the starboard side of the ship I could spot the 32-foot cutter, one of the triple-barrelled 6-inch gun turrets and the torpedo tubes. There was also a much more recent addition – a plastic shopping bag draped over a guardrail on the upper deck.

Interesting though these images were, I was impatient to see the ones in the area of the bomb room. I was not disappointed with them. If the ROV's positioning was accurate, the torpedo had struck just forward of the bomb room. The damage report at the time of the sinking had been correct.

It didn't take long for the news that the *Edinburgh* had been found to reach the press. As soon as the story started to break we put out a press release giving the details of the find, though not, of course, its location. One story, by Robert McGowan in the *Daily Express*, was definitely not authorised however.

A British company has won the contract to make a seabed hunt for £45 million in gold – thanks to Royal backing . . .

Prince Philip – who as Duke of Edinburgh shares the British warship's name – and Prince Charles both expressed an interest in the venture . . .

Divers will begin work a few days before Prince Charles and Lady Diana Spencer marry on July 29.

One of the company's operations directors is Mr James Ringrose, an ex-naval officer friend of Prince Charles.

A source from 'official circles' added: 'I think Prince Charles and Prince Philip were interested in an academic sense, and I suspect they preferred that, if anyone, a British company should be involved.'

To have Charles and his father publicly identified as influencing the contract award sent Ringrose and Bona into a collective fit of the horrors, although strangely, when I saw Ringrose later that day he could hardly wipe the smile from his face at the sight of his front-page picture, right alongside his beloved Prince Charles. It didn't stop him getting in touch with the Palace to apologise, however, while Bona sent a telex to the *Express* demanding a retraction, otherwise he would instruct counsel.

They then began a mole hunt, dropping heavy hints that they thought I was behind the story, and trying to get me to stand down from the company while they took over. After a little digging, a journalist friend told me that the main story had come from the Ministry of Defence and the Royal interest had been leaked by the War Graves Commission. 'In other words,' he said, 'any good reporter could have done this, and Bob McGowan is one of the best.'

The *Express* story did not convince Ric Wharton and Malcolm Williams, who remained very sceptical of any claims of intervention from Prince Charles. They just took it as more nonsense from James Ringrose, but I was less certain. Something definitely happened to kick-start the process. It was a time when the Russians were fighting in Afghanistan and relations with the Iron Lady's Britain were close to an all-time low, yet suddenly British government officials – and Mrs Thatcher – were falling over themselves to expedite a deal with the Soviets. It could have been gold fever in Whitehall, but I'd like to think that Charles was involved – not for Ringrose's ridiculous claim of £100,000 in a Swiss bank but just because he wanted to help out a former shipmate and play a part in a great British adventure.

I was more concerned by a report in the *Navy News*, once more raising the temperature about the war-grave issue.

> Many members of the *Edinburgh* Survivors' and North Russia Association remain firmly opposed to any salvage attempt . . . The association's Honorary Secretary Bill Daly said, 'I would say that 90 per cent of our association remain strongly against a salvage attempt.
>
> 'I have sent a telegram to the Queen saying "We beg of you to stop this salvage of HMS *Edinburgh*. Leave our shipmates in peace." I am also writing to the Archbishop of Canterbury.'
>
> A motion that pressure be brought to bear to prevent 'deliberate desecration of HMS *Edinburgh* by salvaging her cargo' was being tabled by Kendal branch of the Royal Navy Association at the RNA's annual conference on June 13.

The best way to head off any further opposition from that quarter would have been to have begun the salvage operation at once, but there was no sign of the *Stephaniturm* being available; 2W were keeping the pressure on OSA for a release date but inevitably it wasn't quite that simple. OSA could not get the vessel back from the French diving company, Comex, because Comex in turn had chartered it to Union Oil. They were threatening to sue for $5 million if OSA took the vessel back before the completion of contract date.

To add to the confusion, although Comex were not prepared to release the *Stephaniturm*, they were offering us not one but two other vessels capable of doing the *Edinburgh* recovery. I'd have snapped their hands off, had it not been for the breach of contract writ we'd probably have been hit with by OSA.

The only firm date that could be given for the *Stephaniturm*'s release was 31 August. It was starting to look as if we could easily miss the diving season in those northern latitudes and I was beginning to get a feeling of *déjà vu*.

Telex messages kept flowing between ourselves, 2W and OSA, but meanwhile we got on with the job of preparing for the recovery. John Clarke had a great stroke of luck when he went to look round HMS *Belfast*. As he stepped out of the bomb room he met an old naval friend who was now the Technical Officer of the *Belfast*. John immediately asked him if he had any plans of the ship. 'Plans?' he said. 'I've two compartments full of them. MoD Bath have just sent them to us in case we want them, otherwise they're to be thrown away.'

Invoking the 'old shipmates' act', John persuaded him to let him trawl through the plans. Over the next couple of weeks he found all the ones showing the area around the *Edinburgh*'s bomb room. They included the frames, longitudinals, armour-plate sections, the limits of the bilge keel and detailed drawings of the bomb room itself, including the bomb racks where the gold had been stored. John put together a booklet of the plans for each chosen diver and 2W constructed a scale model of the bomb room area, to help familiarise the divers with the lay-out of the wreck.

The next morning I took time out to go and pick up Graham from Heathrow on his return from his long stint in Brazil. I stood looking for him as the bleary-eyed passengers straggled through Customs. The stream came to an end with still no sign of Graham. By this time the airport reception area was just about deserted. I was beginning to wonder what could have happened when a stranger came staggering out of Customs. He had a very dark complexion, mirrored sun glasses, an Afro hairstyle, a string of beads and bits of coloured string tied around his wrists. He was wearing an extremely vivid red shirt, bright canary yellow trousers and sandals. The travel bag he was carrying as he lurched towards me gave me my first and only clue. My boy had come home.

He was the herald of some good news; we finally got a release date for the *Stephaniturm*. It would be returned to us between 23 and 30 August. It was late in the season, but providing we were fully prepared for a swift departure and had reasonable luck with the weather, the job could still be done that year.

Word had come through that while the British principals weren't too concerned by the delay in starting the salvage operation, the Russians were very upset. I found this a bit rich after the delays we'd endured while waiting for them. None the less, as part of a pacification programme, Mr Jackson, Graham and I met Mr Shuravin from Black Sea and Baltic Insurance Co, one of the leaders of the Soviet delegation, and one of his colleagues at the Small Boats Club on the Thames. On the way to the bar, I asked him what he'd like to drink.

'A good viskey, Mr Yessup.' I sent Graham to the bar for two large single malts.

He was back in seconds. 'They haven't got any good whisky, Dad, only blends.'

Mr Shuravin leaned over to me, put his palms horizontally together over his stomach and then opened them. 'I meant a good viskey, Mr Yessup.' I got the message. Several 'good' whiskies later, we parted on a tide of goodwill. I had the distinct impression that the Russians would be more than willing to work with me on other wrecks in the Barents Sea and other oceans. All we needed to set the ball rolling was a successful recovery from the *Edinburgh*.

To do that we first needed the salvage ship of course. Another couple of weeks had slipped by before I received a confirmed departure date for the *Stephaniturm*. It would be arriving in Peterhead on 25 August and we would be sailing four days later. It was an immense relief. I could now get on with my preparations for departure. I began collecting and checking all my papers – research, ship's drawings, photographs of the appropriate sections of the *Belfast* – anything that might be of use during the recovery.

I held a final meeting with David Bona the day before I left, at a service station on the M62. He produced the customary sheaf of documents for signing. Amongst them was a power of attorney. I didn't know one of those from a hole in the ground. 'What's this?'

'Oh it's just a form you need to sign in case I need to sign letters or anything on your behalf while you're away.'

I hesitated, then shrugged and signed it. What harm could there be in it? In a second envelope was a two-page agreement apparently drawn up by Ringrose. Bona was even more keen that I should sign that straight away, which aroused my suspicions, but I was careful to keep my tone warm and friendly. I looked at my watch. 'I haven't time to read it now, David. Tell you what, I'll take it home and either read it and sign it tonight, or I'll do it in Aberdeen before I leave. Okay?'

'You won't forget?'

'You can count on me.'

When I got home I tossed it in the back of a drawer. No way was I signing it without having its full implications explained to me by someone other than David Bona or James Ringrose. It was just as well. As I later discovered, the document would have handed the two of them control of the company and all its assets.

Mildred was very subdued. She didn't say anything, but I knew her well enough to realise that it was more than just the normal anxiety when I was going to be away for some time. I could tell she was deeply troubled. As we got ready for bed that night, I set out to try and reassure her, even though I couldn't avoid the feeling that I might be whistling in the dark.

I sat her down next to me on the bed and took her hands. 'This is it, Mildred. After all the years of research and hard work, it's now pay-off time at last. After the next couple of months we'll either be very rich . . .'

She waited, impassive. 'Or?'

'Or we'll be bust.'

She was silent for a few moments. 'Will we lose the house?'

I hesitated, then took a deep breath. 'We might.'

She started to speak again, but I held up my hand. 'The overdraft's £12,000 and it's secured against the deeds, but I'm sure it won't come to that.'

My words didn't even convince me, let alone Mildred. 'But even if it does all go wrong, I can go back to the North Sea and start working to pay off the debts. I've done it before, I can do it again.' I paused, trying to assess her mood. 'It's a small gamble—'

She exploded at once. 'It's not a small gamble if it costs us everything we've worked for all these years, including the roof over our heads.'

I tried to ignore the interruption. '—but if it pays off, we'll be millionaires. Can you imagine what a million pounds looks like?'

She shook her head. Nor could I, but I wasn't going to let that stop me. 'If everything goes right, we'll never have to worry about money again. We can buy ourselves any house you want and we can all have a decent car apiece. It'll make up for all the times I've been away from home and all the hard times you've had to put up with.'

She nodded doubtfully. She would not have been human

if she had not harboured doubts. She'd struggled to make ends meet, eking out our dwindling cash while the weeks and months dragged by and the salvage operation never seemed to get any nearer. At times the gold on the *Edinburgh* must have sounded as much of a fairy story to her as it did to most of the people around Keighley.

I gave a helpless shrug, trying to instil a confidence in her that I didn't altogether feel myself. 'We're nearly there now. Just keep with it for a few more weeks and things will be fine.'

After I'd turned out the light, we lay for a long time in the darkness, pretending to be asleep, but both wide awake, staring at the ceiling. Despite my reassuring words, I knew that there were a thousand and one things that could still go wrong with the *Edinburgh* operation and dash my dreams of riches. I turned my head to look at her profile. In the faint light from the window, I thought I could see a tear glistening on her cheek.

When we got up in the morning it was obvious that neither of us had slept much. As ever, she tried to put on a brave smile as I kissed her and said goodbye, but I could still see the doubt in her eyes as I drove away.

I arrived in Aberdeen expecting a pleasant reunion with all the heads of the consortium, together with the Department of Trade representative, Stan Holness, and Mr Jackson of the Salvage Association, at the offices of 2W. Instead I was shown straight into the boardroom, where a very hostile group of people were waiting for me.

Ric Wharton opened the meeting almost before I'd sat down. 'On no account whatsoever, will I or any members of this consortium ever again work with Jessop Marine, as long as David Bona and James Ringrose have any association with the company.' He went on to explain the reasons. One of them was their anger at Ringrose's claim that he'd found the *Edinburgh*. I could only agree with him on that point; it was an insult to 2W, OSA and Racal–Decca, who'd done a superb job of locating its final resting place.

Worse followed. Bona had arranged that the consortium's share of the gold would be returned to the UK and put into the Bank of England under the name Jessop Marine, for later distribution to the consortium members. He had led me to believe that was their wish.

Ric soon disabused me of that. He explained that he was speaking on behalf of all the consortium members. Unless they had their share of the recovered gold, sorted and stacked under their names whilst on board the vessel, and transferred to the Bank of England as such, they would call a stop to the whole operation even at this eleventh hour.

I was left in no doubt that he meant what he said. I could tell by the expressions of the others that they were in full agreement. I would have wrung Bona's neck had he been there – as he should have been. Instead I called him in Manchester, leaving the phone on speaker, so that everyone could hear the conversation. I made it clear to him, in tones that left no one in any doubt, that the gold would be shared out on board the vessel, and that he'd better make sure that his paperwork fully covered that. Then I slammed the phone down. 'Right, sorted. Now let's go and get the bloody stuff before we start falling out over spending it.'

After the strained atmosphere in the boardroom, it was a relief to set off down to Peterhead, where the *Stephaniturm* was waiting.

My cabin was normally reserved for clients – the representatives of the big oil companies. It was on the same deck as the captain's, very private and quiet, and quite a change from what I'd been used to in the past. I felt a small pang of guilt at taking the best cabin, for until the gold began to come aboard I'd be little more than a bystander, watching and checking that my partners fulfilled their contracted roles in the operation. As I explored my quarters, I tried not to think of the others having to share cabins. I consoled myself with the thought that if it hadn't been for me, none of us would have been there at all and set off to explore the ship. In all my time I'd never seen such an excellent collection of diving gear on one vessel.

There were new hot-water suits to enable the divers to work in relative comfort at the bone-chilling depths, remote and hand-held TV cameras, oxy-arc cutting gear and a high-pressure water jet, so powerful that it could sever a diver's leg or arm like a hot knife through butter. In addition we took on board the maximum amount of diving gas that the *Stephaniturm* could carry. The gas-storage system was fully charged and we also had four 25-ton gas Kelly trailers, sixteen oxygen quads (racks holding a dozen oxygen bottles) and five therapeutic gas quads – a staggering 1,131,085 cubic feet.

We would have needed even more, but for a revolutionary gas-reclaim system designed by an American called Don Rodocker. A diver at depth breathes a mixture of helium and oxygen, the percentages varying with the depth. On this particular dive the mixture would be ninety-seven per cent helium and three per cent oxygen. Divers normally used an open-circuit system and the gas exhaled was lost into the surrounding water. Don had devised a closed system. The exhaled gas was returned to the surface, cleaned of its carbon dioxide, replenished with oxygen and then recycled back to the diver.

The gas we'd taken on board had cost around £75,000. Don claimed that his system could save up to ninety per cent of the gas used. Apart from this saving, it also meant that the vessel could stay on location longer, without having to do long runs to shore for more diving gas.

Alongside the ship's normal navigation equipment, Decca had supplied a satellite navigator, survey main chain equipment, and Aquafix to help in the relocation of the wreck. We also had side-scan sonar as a back-up, just in case.

With the possible exception of the US Navy search for their lost atom bombs off southern Spain, this had to be the best-equipped operation ever to set sail. Thanks to Ric and Malcolm of 2W and the two project managers, John Clarke for OSA and Mike Stewart for 2W, the operation was being given every chance to succeed. The equipment was the best that money could buy and the divers were hand-picked, some of the best in the business.

The following morning I was up bright and early. I didn't want to miss anything. Many of my old friends in the diving fraternity started to arrive on board. First was Geoff Reudavey from Australia, who'd been on my last expedition to find the *Edinburgh*. Pete Croft had been involved in salvage out in New Zealand and was so keen to join this team that he'd stepped down from Diving Superintendent to diver. Dave Keen was next; I'd worked with him on the *Northern Protector*. Banjo West and John Diamond had been with me out in India. There were many more old friends. It was great to see them all coming on board.

As well as the ship's crew and the divers, we also had to make room for a few other people. Don Rodocker was sailing with us to run his gas-reclaim system. We also had a reporter and photographer from the *Sunday Times*, which had the exclusive rights to cover the operation. I knew very little about the reporter, Barrie Penrose, other than that he had been involved with Simon Freeman on the Jeremy Thorpe case for the 'Insight' page. I was to learn a lot more about him and his ways of working over the next few weeks.

We also had to accommodate the government representatives. Two Russians arrived, Igor Ilin, whom I'd already met many times, and a new face, Leonid Melodinsky, a big, tough-looking guy. I formed the opinion that Melodinsky was KGB; while Ilin was keeping an eye on us, Melodinsky was keeping an eye on Ilin. The British government had only sent one man, David Keogh, but he was a man of many parts. He worked for the Ministry of Defence, but was also representing the interests of the Department of Trade and the Salvage Association. He later filled in as ship's chaplain as well.

David shared a cabin with Sidney Alford, a small, wispy-haired man. At that time I didn't have a clue who he was or why he was there, but I knew that anyone on board must have had a very good reason for being there, because the vessel was absolutely full. I soon discovered his speciality. He was an explosives expert, charged with the delicate task of making safe any unexploded ordnance that the divers encountered when working on the *Edinburgh*. He also had another function, but that was only to be revealed much later.

Because of the war grave, we'd been compelled to give undertakings that no explosives would be used in gaining access to the bomb room. I understood the reason why they had been banned – explosives generate an emotive reaction among the uninitiated – but conventional cutting techniques were potentially more dangerous than the use of purpose-designed, controlled, shaped explosive charges. And from a diver's point of view it was a bad decision, exposing them to needless additional risk. Explosives were just another tool, to be taken out of the bag and put back after use. Would anyone send a mechanic out to repair a car without half his tools? Yet instead of using a very small shaped charge to cut a small keyhole through the bomb room bulkhead, a diver working in horrendous conditions and at massive depth would have to burn a small hole with a cutting torch. Every precaution would be taken to ensure that there were no bombs on the other side, but in the end the diver would just have to steel himself to make the cut. If there was a fully loaded bomb on the other side of the bulkhead, the torch would cut straight into it and it would explode. It had happened before, even under carefully controlled conditions. Divers had once been killed by a sympathetic detonation on the *Hampshire*.

The *Edinburgh* was one of those jobs where Nelson's blind eye should have been turned, the job done quietly, and that would have been the end of it. In fact, even though we had given an undertaking not to use explosives, the *Stephaniturm* was carrying a selection of shaped charges. If we faced a situation where there was a strong likelihood of our divers having to cut near live ordnance, then I for one was willing to ignore the ban on explosives and give the go-ahead to use a very small shaped charge. It might upset the two governments and outrage the relatives of the *Edinburgh* dead, but it would stop more names being added to the already long death toll.

Our equipment checks were nearly complete, but before we left I had one more thing to do. I went into Aberdeen to pick up a wreath to leave on the *Edinburgh* at the end of the operation, whether or not we found the gold. It was a mark of respect and remembrance for the poor men who had gone down with the ship, and for all the other sailors who gave their lives on the wartime suicide run to Murmansk. I imagined that my wreath would be just one of many. In the event, it turned out to be the only one.

I said a final round of goodbyes and best wishes before reboarding the ship. My sons Graham and Ian knew they couldn't go with me this time; there was no room for anyone not directly involved in the operation. We didn't speak much, but the looks we exchanged said it all. When we next met I'd either be a rich man or a broken one. They shook my hand, turned and walked away.

The *Stephaniturm* slipped quietly out of Peterhead harbour at 2.30 the next morning, 29 August 1981. It was time for the most dangerous diving operation ever to begin.

CHAPTER TWENTY-ONE

THE FIRST DIVE

———— • ————

I awoke that first morning to find the sun shining and a
calm sea as the *Stephaniturm* ploughed its way through the
North Sea, past giant oil platforms stretching from horizon
to horizon.

Free of oilfield work, we had better things to do today.
We were on our way to do what all divers dream about, but
never really expect to happen – dive on a wreck full of gold.

We took the scenic route, the inside passage, up the west
coast of Norway and past the Lofoten Islands. We had
Tromsø on our beam at midnight on 30 August. After passing through Mageroy Sound, the diving team chosen for the
first part of the operation were now ready to enter the
decompression chambers for the blow-down to commence.

I wanted to speak to them first, not because they needed
a pep-talk – they were twelve of the best deep divers in the
world, after all – but to remove any trace of gold fever from
their minds. Like us all, they were working on 'no cure, no
pay' terms. They stood to gain tens of thousands of pounds
each if we found the gold; if we didn't, they wouldn't get a
penny. I knew how they felt; I'd get millions if we found the
gold, but if we didn't, I'd be bankrupt. Every penny I had
made from over twenty years' hard and dangerous work
would be gone. I could almost hear the mocking laughter

from some of my acquaintances in Keighley ringing in my ears.

Strangely the most important thing on my mind wasn't the money, however. The Arctic wasn't the North Sea. If anything went wrong, a doctor, a rescue bell or a rescue ship, were hours and even days away. We were on our own, venturing into the unknown. No one had ever dived to such depths, in such waters, for such a length of time before.

I tried to impress on them that safety came before anything else. I wanted the gold so badly I could almost smell it, but I didn't want it stained with yet more blood. If the choice was losing a diver or losing the gold, I'd see it go back to the depths without a second glance. I wanted the gold but I wanted a full dive team back with us as well. I listed a few of the things that could go wrong, though they knew them better than me, then wound up the talk with a joke. There were a few strained smiles. The tension had got to all of them. Even the most experienced diver is nervous before his first dive on any new job, and this wasn't just any job.

The shift supervisor, Derek 'Cyclops' Hesketh, gave them a terse briefing on the technical details of the dive, then they were blown down to a depth of 500 feet, a five-hour journey, where they were held for six hours for stabilisation before the pressure was increased again. Then followed the long slow compression all the rest of the way until they reached the holding depth of 750 feet. Barring accidents, injuries or illness, they would stay there until the operation was complete.

The team had entered the chambers at 10.43 on 2 September, but they did not reach their holding depth until just after midnight. The slow descent was to ensure that they did not suffer high-pressure nervous syndrome, which can be caused by a too-rapid compression.

Amid rising tension, we finally arrived on location –

72.06N, 35.09W – at 10.35 the next morning, 3 September. It was the anniversary of the day the last war broke out and the day I joined the Marines. I wasn't sure if those were good or bad omens.

Not content with their two men on board, the Soviets had also sent out the usual trawler to shadow us. It was like meeting an old friend again. It was obvious from the myriad of aerials protruding from it that this was no ordinary fishing vessel, but another Advanced Information Gatherer. We'd been warned that it could intercept any messages sent from the ship. I would have given a lot to know if they could make sense of Bona's precious *Thesaurus* code.

I walked to the bow and stood alone, looking out over the grey ocean swell rolling away on every side to the horizon. I did what I always did on my first arrival at a wrecksite – casting my mind back for a few moments to the day of the action, trying to imagine what those men must have suffered in the battle that had seen the *Edinburgh* and the *Hermann Schoemann* sunk. What a waste of young men's lives it had been. And now other young men's lives were on my conscience as we began the first dive.

I looked back at the cables still unwinding from the drum, as the bell made its long, slow descent, then walked back to the dive shack. The crisis was soon upon us.

'Danger level!'

I stared blankly ahead of me, not daring to raise my eyes to the gauges again. Were those divers to be lost on the first dive, it was inconceivable that the exploration of the wreck could continue. A normal salvage dive remained secret until it was over. This one was being carried out in the full glare of world-wide media attention. If there was a disaster it would be public knowledge around the world within twenty-four hours. The wreck would be closed down and all I would have left to show from my twenty-year quest for the *Edinburgh*'s gold would be a mountain of debt.

I sat motionless, silently willing the men on as they laboriously coiled the umbilicals back into the cramped space inside the bell. They had to get it right first time, for I was sure they were too weak with CO_2 poisoning to drop the umbilicals back out and begin again.

The gauges remained in the danger zone, dropping slightly each time the bell was flushed with gases, then inching remorselessly back up. I stole a glance at the clock. Twenty agonising minutes had ticked by since the first warning of danger. Finally I heard Banjo's thick slurring words. 'Umbilical stowed.'

'Close top door. Diver! Close top door.'

Once more the long, terrifying silence, then the faint reply. 'Top door closed. Seal acquired.'

Derek yelled the order to begin raising the bell from the depths. We were not yet out of the woods. It would take twelve minutes to haul it back from 750 feet, still ample time for the men inside to lose consciousness and die, for with the top door shut, they could no longer flush the accumulating CO_2 from the bell.

Unable to bear just sitting in the control shack, I went out on to the deck and paced up and down by the moon-pool, constantly peering into the depths for the first sign of the returning bell.

At last there was a glimmer of orange and shortly afterwards the bell broke surface. Men sprinted to secure it and connect it to the trunking. There was a blast of inrushing gas as the pressure was equalised between the trunking and the bell. I ran to the window of the main compression chamber and peered inside.

There was a long pause, then I saw Banjo's head appear in the mouth of the trunking. As he crawled into the chamber the other divers rushed to him and carried him over to his bed. John came next but there was a final heart-stopping pause before Brian appeared, moving in slow motion. As soon as he was inside the chamber he pitched forward on to his face. As the divers picked him up, I sprinted back to the control shack. Derek seemed to have aged ten years during the course of the dive. He turned a haggard face towards me as I rushed in, but then broke into a smile of pure relief as we heard Banjo's voice on the intercom. 'We're all okay, shagged out, but okay.'

The clock showed 6.59, almost three hours since the dive had begun. It felt like three weeks.

Chapter Twenty-Two

The Bomb Room

***

Eight hours later the bell was back in the depths, but this time with only two divers aboard, my old mate Geoff 'Ru' Reudavey and Pete Summers. After the near fatalities of the first dive, a lot depended on this one. I watched the TV monitors as it again made its slow way down to 750 feet. Once again the divers experienced a CO_2 build-up, but it was nothing to compare with the first dive. This time they were immediately aware of the problem and gave the bell a good flush through.

Ru was the diver nominated to do the first shift on the wreck. He dropped out of the bell and sat on the big weight suspended a few feet below it. Last-minute instructions passed between the surface and the diver. It was then time for Ru to leave the weight and drop down to the wreck, but he remained motionless. I could see him sitting there, a small, very lonely figure in the dim pool of light that surrounded the bell. Below him was nothing but an inky blackness. In those situations and conditions divers, like parachutists, sometimes freeze. It happens to every diver at some time.

Tension began to mount; was Ru going to descend that extra fifty feet to the sea-bed, or was he just going to sit there? Finally he let go of the weight and sank out of sight into the blackness, dropping down to the ocean floor. He stood by the massive wreck towering above him, faintly illuminated by the dim light cast down from the bell.

Unprompted, he now let the surface know that he was going to observe a two-minute silence for the brave lads whose bodies had been trapped down there in the dark, cold waters forty years before.

His gesture had a powerful effect on all of us in the control shack. We remained motionless and silent until his Australian twang came back from the sea-bed. 'Right, let's get on with it.' He began to move purposefully towards the wreck.

I knew what he was experiencing in that cold, dim, dark, lonely place. The only sound would be the harsh rhythm of breathing, the noise loud in his ears. On open circuit he would hear the bubbles rattling away on their long journey back to the surface. On gas reclaim he would lose even that friendly sound.

The Arctic is rich in sea life but the diver sees none of it. All he is aware of is the endless rain of sediment blurring the outlines of the massive wreck ahead of him. He is focused only on the iron, steel and debris that have to be removed before the gold can be won.

The work began in earnest. Ru positioned the two Aquafix buoys and fixed recovery lines leading from them to the area of the bomb room. A black-and-white pan-and-tilt camera was lowered down to the wreck so that we on the surface could observe the area of work. At this depth, everything was done in slow motion. Every movement was an effort. The energy expended just in moving about was many times that of a miner hewing coal at the coalface. Even drawing breath was a struggle. As one of the divers said, 'Breathing the gas is like breathing soup.'

At change-over time, Ru went back to the bell and Pete

Summers came out to complete the workload for the dive. He gave us an excellent description of the torpedo hole and the surrounding area and also reported that he could see boxes. The excitement was not damped down until the next dive, when they were identified as boxes full of ammunition, not gold bars. The dive finally ended at 11.29 p.m., eight and a half hours after it had begun.

The silt suspended inside the wreck had caused problems, reducing the diver's vision to less than a foot at times and making the inspection of the inside of the hull very difficult. The only other problem was with the hot-water system. It was pumped down from the surface, via the umbilical, to the divers' suits, where it flowed all around the body, down the arms and legs, before being vented outside the suit. It had to travel a distance of 750 feet down the main umbilical to the bell and then a further 150 feet before it reached the diver. He controlled the flow by a valve on the side of his diving suit. In theory it was just like working in a bath of hot water, but working at these depths and in such icy water – only one degree above freezing – the temperature was very difficult to control. Too much of a flow and the hot water coming into the suit caused nasty blisters, but if he cut down the flow too much, he froze. The problem was never solved and hampered the divers right through the operation.

Night and day now meant nothing. Diving continued around the clock, stopping only for bad weather or mechanical failure. As dive followed dive, we made slow progress. On Dive 3, Brian Cutler and Jim Tucker reported that the provisions room forward of the small-arms magazine was badly damaged. One of the ship's outside plates was bent back on itself, blocking their view towards the bomb room, but the small-arms magazine just forward of it was intact apart from some moderate damage to the starboard corner.

This was excellent news, more confirmation that the bomb room was intact.

The ship's fuel-oil tank separated the bomb room from the outside hull of the ship. Fortunately it was empty of oil. After examining the inside as well as they could in the murk, the divers began to cut through the hull into the fuel tank. Once inside the tank they could begin working on the bulkhead separating them from the bomb room, cutting an opening just below the number nine armour-plate that had shielded it from the worst effects of the blast.

We first lowered the high-pressure water-jet to the divers, so that the area to be cut could be cleaned. The oxy-arc cutting gear was then sent down and secured on the wreck, but on the next dive, Scouse Cooper was sick in the bell because of the surge from the surface. The bail-out bottles were also found to be leaking and the dive was aborted.

Diving operations were then suspended because of bad weather. I cast an anxious eye to the north. I knew to my cost how early winter could come in these latitudes and we still had a very long way to go to reach the *Edinburgh*'s gold. Each delay or problem ratcheted up the tension another notch, but we were all powerless to do anything but wait for the weather to ease.

I had little to occupy my time. The bosun's store on the *Stephaniturm* had already been prepared for its precious cargo. We had emptied it of all the ship's equipment and tools, and welded steel uprights in place to ensure that the shelves didn't collapse under the weight of the gold I hoped would soon be there. We'd also moved our high-tech weighing scales into the store, ready to weigh the gold bars as they came aboard. They were so sensitive that a breath on them caused a fluctuation, and we soon found that even the ship's movement caused wild variations. We put them back in the box; we would have to rely on the weights stamped on the bars.

The weather eased enough for diving to resume and bell run followed bell run. It was hard graft for the divers: eight hours on the bottom, four hours each out on the wreck, then sixteen hours back in the deck chambers, before their next shift began. They were living at a depth of 750 feet, approximately 24 atmospheres absolute. The pressure inside the chamber was a staggering 352.8 pounds per square inch, enough to blow your car tyres off the wheel-rim many times over. The pressure was maintained by nothing more than rubber O-seals. If any one of the seals had failed, the divers would have been dead in seconds. The massive amounts of gas their bodies had absorbed would expand them like balloons until they burst.

Precautions had to be taken when sending anything through the medical lock on the side of the chamber. A corked bottle or sealed tin would have imploded and polyurethane cups of tea would shrink so much under the pressure that three-quarters of the tea would be spilt. The medical lock was a steel tube about two feet in length, and eighteen inches across which passed through the walls of the main chamber. A steel door at each end of the tube was locked in place to prevent any loss of pressure from the chamber. To pass anything in or out of the chamber, the person on the outside asked to be 'given the lock'. The diver inside ensured that the hatch door at his end was fully secured and clamped in place, and the bleed nut was fully closed. The high-pressure gas inside the lock was gradually released by opening the bleed nut and the door was then free to open. It was always wise to stand upwind of the escaping gas. So many divers confined in a small space inevitably ensured an over-ripe smell. A similar system was used to remove body waste from the toilet system. Without it the escaping gas would have been even more overripe.

It was not the only reason why scrupulous hygiene was vital inside the chamber. Bacteria could thrive in warm, moist conditions and in those cramped quarters any infectious illnesses or viruses were certain to spread like wildfire.

The divers were looked after by a team of saturation technicians, who controlled the environment and did the multitude of other jobs required to ensure that they were safe and well. I could only admire the fortitude of the lads living inside the chamber like trapped birds in a cage, day in, day out, for weeks on end.

Work progressed slowly but surely, despite regular halts for bad weather. The ship's heading also had to be moved constantly to minimise the effect of the waves and make life for the divers down on the wreck more comfortable.

In between halts, the task of cutting through the *Edinburgh*'s hull went on. After completing the preparation work for the cut into the fuel tank, the first arc with the cutting gear was struck at 12.45 on 7 August, but bad weather meant it was two days before a piece of the armour-plate was cut away and sent to the surface. That rusting bit of plate was examined by almost everyone on board. It was our first physical contact with the wreck, the first confirmation on the surface that things really were moving down below. It was carefully stored away and later incorporated into the new HMS *Edinburgh*, which was being built for the Royal Navy.

Although the work was progressing steadily, the next crisis was never far away. While using the cutting gear, Pete Summers suffered a severe blow on the chest after a blowback from the oxy-arc gun. It was a not unknown occurrence and could easily leave a diver with fractured ribs – or worse. There was an ominous silence in the dive shack, the only sound the hissing of static from the communications. Then there was a burst of vivid swearing in Pete's unmistakable accent. We all breathed a sigh of relief. They made those South Africans tough.

On the next dive Scouse Cooper reported that one of the massive plates in the ship's armour had moved. It was suspended just above the area where the divers were working. If it slipped again, it could block access to the bomb room, or injure or even kill a diver. After a close inspection, the divers thought that it would not move any further, but it was another source of tension over the next few days, until it was secured.

On that dive I got my first glimpse on camera through the hole that had been cut in the ship's side. I could see little inside the hole because of the amount of silt floating in the water, but the effect the waves on the surface were having on the camera and crew below was very clear. There was virtually no movement of the water at these depths – less than half a knot of tide – but the movement of the vessel on the surface often caused problems. Sometimes the upward and downward movement of the bell was as much as ten metres. One minute the camera was rushing down towards the hole, the next beating a hasty retreat from it. It showed how difficult and uncomfortable the conditions were for the lads working in the bell.

The strain they were all under was suddenly increased when three of them – Banjo West, John Diamond and Brian Cutler – all went down with an ear infection called pyo, one of the banes of divers working in saturation. It can be treated by ear drops, but it's highly infectious and to avoid the other divers becoming infected we decided that the best treatment was to isolate them. They were transferred into a lifeboat chamber to begin the seven-day, fourteen-hour journey of decompression before they could step out of the chamber to join us mortals on the surface and be treated by a doctor brought from shoreside.

Our good planning and forethought meant we were in a position to blow down extra divers to replace the ones coming out of saturation. Without them the operation would soon have ground to a halt under the extra workload the remaining divers had to face.

The next day the three pyo victims were joined in the lifeboat chamber by 'Swift Eddie' Wilde, who had gained his nickname from his expertise at acquiring other people's money in card games. He was also suffering from an ear problem, though his was more serious, a suspected perforation of the eardrum after an accident when he was getting back into the bell, caused by its violent up-and-down motion in a rough sea.

Two extra divers went into compression, John Rossier from Rhodesia, the youngest Sergeant to serve in the Rhodesian SAS, and Dougy Matherson, the hero of the remarkable rescue in the North Sea during the Russians' visit to 2W in Aberdeen. Dougy had recovered a diver in distress from one bell and transferred him to a second one sent down for the rescue, and had received an award from the Queen for his bravery.

The operational diving team had now been reduced to six divers – just enough to maintain the twenty-four hour shifts. We could only hope there were no more casualties before the replacements were blown down. It put a lot of extra pressure on the remaining divers but they coped with it remarkably well.

A check on the on-board gas now showed that we had enough mixed gas left for a further twenty-one days' diving, plus one more blow-down. The new gas-reclaim system had really started to play its part, with gas recovery on some dives reaching ninety-eight per cent. The divers had been suspicious of it at first and Mike O'Meara had been forced to read the Riot Act at one point to stop them from switching to the traditional open circuit, but they were now convinced of its safety and its value.

The weather was still causing the divers serious problems. Nasty, short, steep seas were causing cables and lines to the wreck to get twisted and snagged, and this in turn caused delays while lines were cleared.

The one bonus of operating at these latitudes was that the wind rarely stayed in one quarter for any length of time. It tended to swing around the compass, preventing any really big seas from forming. Used to the weather patterns further south, I found it amazing to watch a sea beginning to get up from one point, only to be flattened again as the wind changed.

The Soviet trawler still shadowed us and Russian reconnaissance planes made regular flights over us as well. They did a couple of turns around the vessel to let us know we were being watched and then disappeared in the direction of Murmansk. If nothing else, it appeared to cheer up Ilin and Melodinsky.

I was much more interested in the sights below the waves. The access hole to the fuel tank had now been completed and the plating and beams pulled clear. For the first time we could now see into the fuel tank. It wasn't a pretty sight. Instead of an empty tank and a clear path to the bomb-room bulkhead, all the camera showed was a mess of twisted and tangled scrap metal. The diver holding the camera explained the cause. The torpedo strike had caused the deck-head above the fuel tank to pull away from the side of the vessel, curling down and in and virtually blocking the way to the bomb room. Equipment and machinery from the deck had also tumbled down the hole, littering the fuel tank. All this would have to be removed by the divers before they could proceed.

A couple of days' hard work later Scouse Cooper was able

to show us a glimpse of the bomb room bulkhead and the small-arms magazine next to it. I felt my excitement mounting as I peered at the small monitor screen. All that now separated me from the dream I had nurtured for so long was an inch of steel plate.

As they cleared the mess the divers had found some of the everyday things used by the sailors on the *Edinburgh*. They were sent to the surface in the work-basket. David Keogh and I picked them out and examined them. There was an old teapot, a tin still full of Brasso and some naval message pads. I still have the Brasso tin today, a reminder of the life of the sailors on the *Edinburgh*.

The naval message pads were a little tatty around the edges but still legible. Sidney Alford did a good job on reclaiming them until other, more dangerous souvenirs started to come up, and took first priority on his time. The trolleys used to move bombs and shells around the ship turned up in large numbers and live ammunition and pom-pom shells were also raised, still in their boxes and as bright and shining as the day they were made.

Most of the ordnance was loaded on to a Zodiac and dumped back into the depths a safe distance from both the wreck and the *Stephaniturm*, but Sidney also showed his expertise by removing the cordite and caps and rendering a number of the shells safe. These all later disappeared and no doubt are now shining bright in someone's living-room – just like mine.

Everything removed from the oil tank and later the bomb room had to be sent to the surface to be identified and made safe if necessary. The last thing we wanted was any accidents or underwater explosions. It was a terrible job for the divers, working in virtually nil visibility, groping among the tangle of metal for objects covered in heavy fuel oil.

It was distressing, but almost inevitable in these conditions, that one day the basket was found to contain a couple of human bones. The divers had unknowingly put them into the basket. They came up from the bottom mixed with the rubbish and so covered with oil they were almost unrecognisable. The two men sifting the debris had dropped them back over the side before they even registered what they were.

That involuntary action was later used by the *Sunday Times* reporter to stir up a controversy about the war grave. A few more bones were accidentally sent to the surface during the remainder of the salvage operation, but on each occasion, as soon as they were identified, a memorial service was held by David Keogh and the bones were then returned to the sea.

Down on the wreck, the divers found larger and larger items blocking their way. I watched on the screen as the *Stephaniturm*'s crane hauled a large and very heavy compressor out of the fuel tank and dropped it away from the wreck. It was a sight that caused me some amusement. A few years earlier I would have been wild with excitement at the thought of the non-ferrous metal that compressor contained. Now it was just a useless obstruction barring the way to some infinitely more precious metal. On later dives an eight-ton lathe and a large electric motor were also dragged out of what we had hoped would be an empty fuel tank.

The diver first had to check that the object was free to move. That was a lot easier said than done, working in zero visibility. He had to feel his way round the object to check that it was clear to lift, and it was always very difficult to be sure. The crane wire was then sent down from the surface, with its glowing light sticks attached so that the diver could locate the hook and lifting strops. He would take them inside the tank and secure them to the object to be lifted.

The diver then moved well to one side before the lift in case something went wrong. On the surface Gunter, the German bosun, took personal charge of the crane.

The message to commence the lift was relayed to him from the dive-control shack and the struggle would begin, not helped by a message from the diver, 'Get a move on, surface.'

Up above Gunter had the maximum strain on the cable and the cabin alarm bells ringing in his ears told him that he had reached the lifting capacity of the crane. The compressor was far from free to move and Gunter was trying to move the whole of the *Edinburgh* with his crane. I could hear him cursing those 'mother-fucking sons of fucking bitches' down below.

After some further work with the oxy-arc gear and a certain amount of lifting and lowering, the compressor was again declared free to move. The crane again took the strain. All I could see on the monitor was an occasional wisp of silt from the hole, counterpointed by another stream of Teutonic swearing from Gunter. Then the object suddenly exploded out of the hole, streaming a vapour trail of silt and falling debris behind it. It was quite a sight. The compressor disappeared beyond the circle of light into the darkness surrounding the whole scene, where it was lowered to the seabed, never to be seen again.

Once the silt had settled, the next diver, Jim Tucker, went back into the wreck. He reported to the surface that he'd found a wooden box. The writing on it was illegible, but it matched the size of the gold boxes we were looking for. Jim tried to show us the lid on camera, but we failed to get a clear picture and in the end the crane wire was lowered to bring it to the surface. A crowd gathered on deck as the object broke surface, but a quick examination was enough to show that it was only the lid of an ammunition box. Excitement was over for the day, but gold fever now had a firm hold.

The divers expected to gain entry to the bomb room within the next four days. This was great news – the end could be in sight – but I tried to damp down any excitement. There had already been too many false dawns, too many dashed hopes, during my diving career. I was not going to start counting my gold bars until the last one was safely stowed away on the *Stephaniturm*.

There was more drama during the next dive, Bell Run 18, but it was unconnected with the gold. Diving operations were stopped because of loud, unidentified sonar noises. They caused the divers on the bottom a lot of pain in their ears. The bell was brought to the surface for over an hour until the noises ceased. The surface was clear from horizon to horizon. The only thing visible was the Russian AIG vessel. Scouse had to return to the bell on a subsequent dive because of extremely loud engine noises, in the very close vicinity of the wreck. Once again there was nothing to be seen on the surface. The noise could only have been caused by a passing Soviet submarine – or was it one of the British submarines Ringrose had told us about, looking for shelter?

During Dive 18, Doug Matherson and John Rossier, now working fifteen feet inside the fuel tank, began to cut a small window measuring one foot by one and a half feet into the bomb room bulkhead. It was one of the most dangerous moments of the whole operation. Until an opening had been made, we had no way of knowing what lay on the other side of the bulkhead. It could have been more silt and debris; it could have been gold; it could have been an unexploded bomb.

A small shaped charge could have cut a hole no bigger than a penny in the bulkhead. There would have been no risk to anyone's life and the divers could then have checked if it was safe to start cutting. Explosives had been denied to us because of the war grave, however, and they would now have to cut blind through the steel plate of the bulkhead. If the oxy-arc torch detonated a bomb, a single explosion would kill the diver operating it; sympathetic detonations of other ordnance could conceivably spread outwards like the ripples on a pond, blasting the wreck apart and shredding the gold ingots like confetti.

I paced around the deck, unable to bear the gnawing tension in the dive shack as the two divers cut into the bulkhead, inch by inch. At last there was a whoop of triumph from the shack. The observation hole had been completed and the divers were safe. Before they began cutting an entrance-way into the bomb room, they could now check that the area to be cut was clear of unexploded ordnance.

The divers pointed the video camera through the hole in an attempt to show us the interior of the bomb room, but we could see virtually nothing for the clouds of silt suspended in the water. A water-lift was sent down to help clear the silt and on Dive 20 we got our first clear view inside the bomb room. We were the first men to lay eyes on it in forty years. I now had absolute confidence that what had been loaded into that bomb room all those years before was still there. It was obvious that no one had been on this wreck before us.

Even so, the sight was not exactly encouraging. 'Like a cellar full of junk', in Scouse's words. The bomb room was on its side, starboard side uppermost, and was over two-thirds full of silt and debris. But somewhere amongst all the junk and unexploded bombs were at least 465 bars of gold.

Barring accidents, entry into the bomb room would be made in the next few days. Our goal was now within reach, if not in sight, but problems were looming. That dive, Bell

Run 20, was cut short by a failure of the hot-water system. The divers faced immediate problems with the intense cold at those depths, exacerbated by the fact that breathing helium caused them to lose body heat far quicker than breathing air.

We had more to worry about than temporary equipment problems however. We were now not only racing the onset of winter, but hurrying to complete the recovery before diver exhaustion forced us to stop. The absence of the four sick and injured divers – now at a depth of 279 feet on their long journey back to the surface – was being keenly felt by the remainder of the team. The extra workload was making them more and more exhausted. They were working under extremely hazardous conditions, up to their armpits in debris, including live ordnance. The more tired they became, the higher the chance of a mistake or accident that could still jeopardise the operation, even at this advanced stage.

On Dives 21 and 22, the divers steadily enlarged the hole in the bulkhead until it measured some four feet by three. When the silt had settled Scouse took a good look into the bomb room and reported that he could see the H-beam that had been used to move the bombs around. A moment later I heard his excited voice again. 'I can see boxes.' His description of them appeared to match that of the gold boxes. The excitement and tension on deck was cranked up a few more notches, even though the boxes remained tantalisingly out of reach.

We sent a coded signal back to shore to let them know that entry into the bomb room was imminent so that the insurance of the gold could be activated. We had no intention of finding and then losing a fortune because of another disaster at sea.

Three more dives followed, as the hole was carefully

enlarged and the silt and debris removed. On Dive 25, the hole was completed. It had grown to nine feet by seven — big enough for divers to enter the bomb room.

CHAPTER TWENTY-THREE

GOLD!

A t the surface, the tension was now at breaking point. We made our final preparations to receive the gold bars. The special keys and locks to secure the bullion room were issued by David Keogh. The Soviet representatives had one key; David, on behalf of the half-dozen British ministries he represented, had the second and I had the third.

During Dives 25 and 26, the divers entered the bomb room for the first time and began the painstaking job of clearing the mountain of silt and debris by hand.

I knew that we had to strike gold soon. I stayed awake all night, haunting the dive shack and pacing the deck, pausing to watch for the glitter of gold as each basket of oil-soaked debris was raised from the depths. Four more sack barrows were raised, along with piles of twisted and tangled metal, but there was no trace of any gold.

In the late afternoon of 16 September 1981, I stood on the top deck chatting to Mike Stewart and John Clarke. I'd already been awake for almost thirty hours, anticipating the finding of the gold. Rain had been falling steadily all day, but it had eased to a fine drizzle and pale autumn sunshine was breaking through. I pointed to a large rainbow that had formed in the sky to the west. 'That has to be our sign of good luck. There really is a crock of gold at the end of that one.'

Bell Run 27 started at 8.40 that evening, with John Rossier and Doug Matherson as the divers. As the bell began its descent, I decided to grab a couple of hours' sleep before I dropped. I went to my cabin and lay down on the bunk.

John Rossier left the bell at 9.25 and swam down to the wreck and in through the hole into the blackness of the bomb room. The water lift was lowered and John began clearing the silt and feeling among the accumulation of oil-encrusted rubbish. He sent another set of barrows and some live shells to the surface. Then his groping fingertips touched something solid, but softer than iron and steel. He had found a wooden box.

What seemed like seconds after I'd closed my eyes, some-one was shaking my shoulder. 'Something's happened. You'd better come down to the control van.'

His expression was neutral; I couldn't tell if I was being summoned to a disaster or a triumph. By the time I'd rubbed the sleep from my eyes, he'd gone. I hurried to the dive shack, unsure whether the gold had been found or a diver lay trapped or killed on the bottom.

As soon as I opened the door to the control van, I knew that we'd hit the jackpot. Dave Keen, the dive supervisor, was talking over the headset to John, urging him on. The tension and excitement of the moment had got to both of them and John was having difficulty cutting through the rusting metal bands around the box. There was a long silence, broken only by the sound of John's rapid breathing as he struggled with the box. Dave could stand it no longer. 'What is it John? What is it?'

Then his helium-fuelled, Minnie Mouse tones burst over the loudspeaker, shouting again and again, 'I've found the gold. I've found the gold. I've found the gold. I'VE

FOUND THE FUCKING GOLD.' The control van erupted and even the two Russians were smiling for the first time since they'd joined the ship.

I glanced at the clock, wanting to freeze this instant in my memory and savour it again and again. It was 10.48 on the evening of 16 September 1981. I would remember this moment for the rest of my life.

Dave Keen was trying to make himself heard. 'John, you're screaming like hell at me.' He gestured at the monitor. The figure of John Rossier seemed to be doing a slow-motion victory dance. 'He's flying down there. Flying like a doll.' He glanced down at his own hands. 'Christ, my hands are shaking.'

He made a visible effort to get a grip on himself. 'John, what are you going to do with it? Make sure you put it safely in the basket.'

A few moments later I heard his reply, 'Okay. One bar safely in there. Raise the basket.'

It was pitch black outside, but I hurried out on to the deck to wait for the basket to reach the surface. Gunter was back on the crane for the most important lift of his life.

Virtually everyone on the ship was now on deck, staring in silence at the waves slapping against the side of the ship. Several agonising minutes later the basket broke surface. At first I could see no sign of the bar, but as the basket was lowered on to the deck in the harsh glare of the arc lights, I thought I caught a glimpse of gold amongst the muck and oil-stained debris. The diving superintendent, Mike O'Meara, stepped forward and dug deep into the basket. Then he turned and handed me the dull gold bar. I had never held anything as dense and heavy before.

Someone shouted, 'Well done Keith' as I cradled the bar in my hands, holding it as tenderly as a baby – a very heavy one. It had arrived on the surface in almost pristine condition, unmarked apart from one small scratch. I vowed to myself that this bar was going to be mine. I would keep it as part of my share of the proceeds, a reminder of the day when the council-house scrap man found the richest treasure in the history of the sea.

That one bar's value was around the £100,000 mark but it was worth far more than that to me, hard proof that keeping the dream alive through so many years of frustrations, hardships and disappointments had been worthwhile.

There was another shout, 'Hold it up Keith, so we can all see it.'

As I did so, there was a barrage of flashes as everyone snapped their souvenir pictures. Despite the whirl of emotions in me, I still had the presence of mind to hold the bar so that my Rolex watch was in shot, thinking, 'Maybe Rolex will give me a gold one.'

I passed the bar to Igor Ilin.

'Is it genuine?' David Keogh asked. Ilin studied the Cyrillic markings on the bar, KPO 620, and then nodded, beaming like a proud parent at school speech day. Even better, there was a hammer and sickle inscribed on it, rather than the Tsarist double eagle. The gold was absolutely pure.

He handed the bar back to me and I set off around the ship, parading it like a captain at Wembley with the FA Cup. I took it down to the Mess Room so that everyone could have a look and a feel of the bar and have their pictures taken with it. It was a team effort and they all deserved to share the moment. Next I took it into the dive shack to let the dive supervisors, Dave Keen and Derek Hesketh, have their chance to hold it. Dave told the divers in the bell far below us, 'I've got a gold bar in my hands and it's beautiful.'

I then took it out to the decompression chamber and held it up to the tiny portholes so that the divers who'd laboured so hard and so long in such dangerous conditions could all share in the moment.

Finally I went to the bullion store with David Keogh and the two Russians. We each turned our key in our lock to open the door. I was reluctant to part with the bar – I'd rather have taken it back to bed with me – but I turned it over to be formally logged in. The details of gold bar KPO 620 were carefully recorded in the log, its numbers and marking recorded, and the bar signed for by Keogh, Ilin and myself. Then it was locked away in splendid isolation, a solitary gold bar on shelves that would soon be groaning with them.

I went back to my cabin, lay down on my bunk and stared at the ceiling, wanting to savour the moment alone. I'd put everything on the line, including my house, to pursue the *Edinburgh*'s gold. Failure would have meant bankruptcy. Even so, my thoughts in those first heady moments were not of the money I was about to make, but the vindication of my dreams. I could count on the fingers of one hand the people back in Keighley who had taken me seriously when I'd talked of the fortune in gold waiting to be won from the ocean depths. They'd be taking it a bit more seriously now.

Despite my fatigue I was far too excited to sleep much and was up early the following morning. The same two divers had found several more gold bars which were now on their way to the surface to be cleaned and logged in.

First the news had to be broken to the consortium partners. At 7.20 that morning David Keogh contacted David Bona, who would have the job of passing the news on to the other principals. The rest of us gathered around the loudspeaker on the bridge, listening to the ringing tone.

David Keogh still passed the news to Bona by the agreed code: 'Keeper to Kennel, Greyhound zero-zero-one, Henry zero-zero-one, Foxtrot' – one gold bar now on board.

When we'd got over the initial excitement, we got back to work, cleaning and logging the gold bars. The recovery would have gone quicker if the bars could have been raised in their wooden boxes, but sea-worm had eaten away at the wood and the boxes simply disintegrated if they were moved with the gold inside them.

Dives 28 and 29 recovered a further twenty-three bars, along with the inevitable debris: seven more sack barrows and stacks of live ammunition. The gold bars came up separately in a large metal basket specially made for the job, with a lid that could be closed and locked. We had no desire to have the basket snag, tip up and spill its load, sending £2 million of gold bullion tumbling back into the depths.

The basket was too big to be taken inside the ship, however, which entailed a long swim from inside the bomb room carrying the heavy bars, which took time and sapped the diver's energy. As a result, the first basket was soon discarded for a smaller model that could be lowered right into the fuel tank. That in turn was replaced by a very stout nylon bag like a services kitbag, which was much easier to manhandle.

When the first few loads of gold bars came on board, we had no lack of volunteers to help us and the arrival of the basket on deck was greeted by a crowd wanting to see and handle the gold. As they got used to seeing it landed the number of people watching dwindled away to nothing.

We soon perfected our system for handling the growing number of bars in the bullion room. I'd volunteered to be the one to clean them. David and the two Russians had the job of recording and stacking them in the order in which they had arrived. A card recording the number of bars in each load was then placed between them. When we were called to make the random checks of the bars at any time of night or day, we could quickly make sure that none was missing.

Most of the bars came up in a fairly clean condition, but some had a coating of fuel oil and sawdust stuck to them. By trial and error I found the best way to clean them was to stick them into a plastic bucket full of diesel. This softened the coating of oil and then I tapped and brushed the bar with a cleaning brush until it was clean, without leaving a mark on the gold.

After the *Sunday Times* photographer had wired back some pictures of me cleaning the bars, I received a message from an official at the Bank of England: 'You should not treat gold bars in this fashion.'

I sent a prompt reply: 'You want them treated differently, you dive for them.' There was no further message.

The bars were now coming up thick and fast. On Dive 30, Doug Matherson and John Rossier managed to put forty into the basket – £4 million in one load. Dave Keen in the dive-control van told them, 'They're complaining up here. You've only got forty bars in the box and that's just a million quid an hour. You'll have to do better.' Dougy's answer was unprintable. Everyone gathered on deck for the arrival of that basket of bars. To see them all glittering in the ship's powerful arc lights as I bent down to open the basket was some thrill. A wag had hung a notice on the outside of the basket: 'Safe Working Load £4,000,000.'

Geoff Reudavey and Pete Summers were the next divers to go down. They installed a mercury vapour light which gave us a better view, but more importantly, it also improved the working conditions inside the bomb room. They sent up more loads of junk and nasties, including some unexploded bombs and yet another couple of sack barrows, but they also recovered another forty gold bars.

Every time I came out of the communications room after

the daily coded exchange with base, I was now asked the same question. 'What's the gold price today, Keith?'

Despite the euphoria produced by the mounting stacks of gold in the bullion room, we still faced a number of problems. The water lift was constantly becoming tangled with the TV cable and sometimes got itself fastened around the diving bell itself.

More seriously, our pool of fit divers was shrinking still further. The four divers in decompression had now arrived back on the surface after their seven-day trip, but a number of the others were suffering from nasty hot-water scalds caused by their inability to maintain the correct temperature in their suits.

The fatigue that they were all feeling also made mistakes and accidents almost inevitable. On Dive 32, while stacking gold bars on a convenient beam, Jim Tucker dislocated his finger and had to return to the bell in some pain. Acting as doctor, Scouse Cooper gave it a good tug and it popped back in. Scouse then left the bell to put the gold bars into the cage, but had to return almost immediately with a swollen ear. The dive was aborted and the bell returned to the surface, with Scouse now another suspected pyo case.

On the next dive, Number 33, Doug Matherson got the basket stuck. After a struggle he managed to free it, but in doing so he got himself in a tangle and was caught fast. I remembered the terror of being caught in the copper wire on the *Johanna Thorden*. How much more terrifying it must have been in the icy blackness at the bottom of the Barents Sea. I sat in silence watching Dave Keen's strained face as he talked to Dougy over the head-set, trying to keep him calm. After several tense minutes he managed to free himself.

Undeterred, he went back to work and was soon reporting that he had twenty-eight gold bars stacked. Then disaster struck. Returning to the bell for a diver change-round with John Rossier, he slipped climbing into the bell and badly dislocated his shoulder. As John tried to put the shoulder back into place, Dougy's curses, grunts and yelps came over the communications loud and clear. The attempt failed and the dive was aborted. The bell was brought back to the surface and Dougy was given pethidine to ease the pain. We immediately signalled for a doctor to be brought to the ship to treat him, but it would be seven days before his journey back to surface pressure would be complete.

Two more divers on the surface were immediately put into the chamber to be pressed down. Brian Cutler, who had been in the bell on the first abortive dive that nearly ended the whole operation, was now recovered and going down for the second time. With him was Dave Hardy, making his first trip down to the wreck.

The next pair of divers collected Dougy's twenty-eight bars and added a further eighteen of their own, but problems kept occurring. Once again the hot-water machine broke down and another dive was aborted. Then the big basket used for the removal of debris from the bomb room became hopelessly fast. The burning gear had to be sent back down to cut it free. This all ate into our precious remaining time. Fully loaded with debris, the basket was then sent to the surface. While it was being cleared of high-explosive shells and other live ordnance, two more human bones were found. The remains were quietly returned to the sea by Mike Stewart and Sidney Alford after a brief memorial service which we all attended.

That evening, 21 September, I had an urgent telephone call from Graham. I could tell by his voice and the way he was speaking that something was up. We had a rather more simple system of codes than that devised by David Bona. Graham was using a very broad Yorkshire accent to ensure that anyone listening could not understand a word we were saying. We'd used the same system many times in the past, especially when working with the Norwegians.

Graham asked me one question. 'Did you sign the agreement that Bona gave you on the M62, just before departure?'

'No.'

'Thank God for that.'

I was desperate to get more details from him, but I couldn't risk it on an open line. The explanations would have to wait until we had docked back in Britain.

I put my personal problems behind me and concentrated on the job in hand. The gold, the ammunition and the inevitable sack barrows continued to come to the surface despite the continuing problems with the hot-water supply to the divers. On Dive 37, Geoff Reudavey had to abandon his dive because of very bad scalding. Pete Summers continued to remove debris and ammunition for the rest of the dive without suffering the same problem, but on the next dive, there was a further breakdown of the hot-water pump.

Despite the interruptions, gold was still being landed, though not at anywhere near the previous rate. On Dive 39 another problem recurred with the discovery of three skeletons inside the bomb room. They were carefully moved to one side by the diver but once again, because of the minimal visibility, some bones found their way into the debris basket. I spoke to the divers concerned to confirm that it had happened by accident and not design. A simple burial service was again held at the stern of the vessel and the bones quietly recommitted to the sea, using a red ensign.

The next dive brought us close to catastrophe once more. Two heavy coils of wire had been removed from the bomb room and were being brought to the surface when one slipped. It fell back into the sea and dropped all the way down to land on top of the diving bell. It was pure good luck that the bell sustained only minor damage and the divers suffered nothing worse than a severe shock. It took one of them a considerable amount of time and effort to untangle and clear the wire from around the bell.

Two hours later, one of the divers, John Rossier, had a rather more pleasant surprise. We received a telex from Malcolm Williams telling us that John had become a father for the first time. Derek Hesketh took the precaution of waiting until John was back in the bell before passing on the good news. From John's shout of delight, we gathered that he was quite a happy man.

On Bell Run 43, Geoff Reudavey again remained inside the bell, unable to do his lock-out because of his blisters. Pete Summers went into the wreck and we used his kluge to check how far the divers had penetrated the bomb room. The kluge is a rubber pipe within the diver's umbilical. To find the diver's depth, the dive supervisor turns a valve on the control panel, allowing air to flow into the kluge line and expelling all the water. The pressure created as water comes back into the line tells the dive supervisor the exact depth of the diver. It revealed that the divers had only penetrated the bomb room to a depth of some ten feet. Pete then took soundings to discover how much silt remained inside the bomb room. The answer was equally depressing. The silt was nine feet deep at one end and seven at the other. Somewhere amongst it was the remaining gold, perhaps including the missing four and a half tons. We now knew the size of the task that still remained.

By now, I should have been a happy man. I had already achieved the goal I set myself, the recovery of most of the gold from the *Edinburgh*. But I was too preoccupied with the ongoing problem of recovering the rest without jeopardising the safety of the divers to spend much time daydreaming about what I would do with my share of the money.

Like David Keogh, I also had my hands full trying to keep the peace between the warring parties on board the *Stephaniturm*. As the contract holder, it was my responsibility to ensure that the Russians received all the co-operation and information laid down in the contract. It was not an easy task, for there was open hostility to the two Soviet representatives from some quarters.

It was obvious that in addition to making sure that none of the recovered gold went missing, they had also been given a remit by their government to find out as much as possible about the new diving techniques being used. With the Cold War still at its height, to have the Soviet AIG vessel watching our every move and two Russians actually on board the salvage vessel in close personal contact with the crew and divers — many of them ex-Royal Navy — was very hard for some of them to take.

The *Sunday Times* reporter, Barrie Penrose, was also causing a lot of friction by poking his nose into everything. I suppose he thought he had a right but divers are like anyone else, they don't like being asked personal questions by a complete stranger. One of them came up to me and complained that Penrose had been asking them how much they expected to get out of the job, whether they were working on 'no cure, no pay' and a load of even more personal questions. On behalf of himself and the others, the diver had given Penrose a succinct answer: 'Piss off.'

Penrose was soon belabouring my other ear. 'Come on Keith, I have the right, I have the exclusive on behalf of the *Sunday Times*. You've got to make these people speak to me.'

He was wrong. As far as I was concerned, I didn't have to make anyone speak to him. His problems were of his own making. He simply made himself unacceptable to most of the people on board, The atmosphere between us grew increasingly poisonous and that was to have long-term consequences, but for the moment it was a very minor problem beside the continuing risks involved in the diving operation.

The most important thing was the safety of the divers. They were now all very tired, and in those circumstances, accidents could easily happen – a fatality amongst the divers was still a very real possibility. Despite the haul of gold glittering in the bullion room, there were still no grounds for complacency. We could not afford to relax one iota until the last bell run had been completed.

The gold bars were still coming up from the depths, but the unglamorous work of clearing the silt, debris and live ordnance was just as vital. Dive 44, commencing at 11.59 p.m. on 23 September, was fully occupied with removing and dumping live ammunition but that cleared the way for the next team of divers, John Rossier and Jim Tucker, who sent another twenty-eight gold bars to the surface, one of the biggest hauls in days.

The two divers in decompression, Scouse Cooper and Doug Matherson, had reached 254 feet when Scouse suffered a hit – a bend – in the knee joint. The pressure in the chamber was increased in an effort to relieve the pain. At 288 feet he reported that he was starting to get relief, and at 304 feet, the pain had completely disappeared. They were held at that depth for a further six hours to ensure all was well, then the slow journey back to the surface was restarted. It was to be another four days before they could step out of the chamber and back into the surface world.

By 26 September we had recovered 315 gold bars, all cleaned and safely stored on board the *Stephaniturm*. There was still a fair way to go to get the 100 per cent recovery we all wanted and the time left available to us on site was starting to run short. One limiting factor for the expedition, the amount of helium for the divers that we could carry on board, had been alleviated by the use of the gas-reclaim system. But other problems were less easily solved. It was late in the season in these latitudes. The weather had been exceptionally kind to us so far but that could change at any time, without warning. Plans for the *Stephaniturm* to run inshore and take on extra supplies of food, fuel and water were scrapped. That would have used up too much of the precious diving time before winter put a stop to the whole project. Instead we made arrangements to take on fresh supplies at sea.

A doctor, Mike Childs from Aberdeen, arrived on the same vessel. He had his hands full immediately, setting Doug Matherson's dislocated shoulder and treating the painful ear infections and hot-water burns suffered by the other divers. I looked in on one of his treatment sessions and the blisters caused by the scalding water were something to be seen. There were big, raw, red patches of flesh where the skin from the blisters had been rubbed off inside their diving suits. It was painful just to look at them and my admiration for the bravery and fortitude of this diving team went up a few more notches.

There was more friction with the Russians, however. As Dougy and Scouse came out of decompression, Igor Ilin entered the chamber to check that no gold bars had been hidden there. He looked ill at ease doing it, but said, 'It's in the contract, so I have to do it.' If we failed to make 100 per cent recovery, the Russians would have to stay with the vessel all the way back to the UK, to search the chambers when the last divers had cleared decompression. It showed a lack of trust on the part of the Soviets and left a distinctly bad taste in the mouth. If we'd wanted to acquire half a dozen bars for ourselves, we could have done so without any trouble. I felt a little sorry for Ilin however. He'd made a big effort to get to know the divers and now he was back to square one with them.

The doctor's arrival had been timely, for another problem now showed itself. Dave Hardy was taken ill with what appeared to be flu symptoms. An outbreak of flu in the chambers would have put a end to the whole operation, but we managed to isolate him, and though he never dived again on the *Edinburgh*, the other divers remained unaffected.

The doctor could do little about the seasickness that the divers experienced in the diving bell, as the surface weather conditions deteriorated. At times it was rising and falling ten metres. It also got itself entangled in some of the extra service cables and hoses we had running down to the wreck from the surface. Freeing it caused more delays.

The dwindling dive team was boosted on 28 September, when two more divers were compressed to help out the fast-tiring team on the bottom. One of whom was Pete Croft – dive superintendent with Seaway. Swift Eddie Wilde was also going down for the second time. We were now down to seven fit divers, and even with two fresh men we had to start closing down the diving system for short spells to give them their full rest period.

Our luck with the weather now ran out and the full weight of an Arctic storm hit us. It grew in intensity until we were forced to suspend operations and pull off site on 1 October, with storm-force winds of Force 10 and 11 battering us from the north-west. I stood on the bridge looking out at the grey, wind-blown sea. Massive waves lined up to charge straight at us. The bows of the vessel first rode up the wave and then dropped over the edge with a sickening motion. It looked as if the bow would bury itself deep in the oncoming wave, never to rise again, but somehow it rose back as a torrent of water streamed from the deck. There was a momentary respite and then the next giant wave engulfed us. I felt for the divers locked away in the chambers. At least on deck we could walk around and get ourselves involved in something to take our minds off the weather and sea conditions. The only good to come of it was that they had a chance to grab what rest they could and regain a little of their strength.

As I waited for the weather to break I took stock of our situation. The last four dives before the storm broke had sent another forty-seven bars of gold to the surface. The total recovered stood at 386. If we were to get 100 per cent recovery, seventy-nine bars remained to be found.

Another forty-eight hours elapsed before we got back on to station and it was not until 4.45 on 3 October that we began diving again. The dive team was now even more depleted, for Brian Cutler and Dave Hardy, both suffering medical problems, had entered the lifeboat chamber to start their long journey back to the surface. Before the clearance and recovery work could start again, all the service lines needed on the wreck, like the video lights and pan-and-tilt camera had to be repositioned and the water lift and water-jetting equipment had to be rerigged.

Almost five hours later, clearance of the bomb room restarted. We were still hopeful of getting 100 per cent recovery, but it was obvious to all on board that the good weather had now left us. The weather and sea conditions were such that diving was only just possible. We were working near the limits of safe diving, which made everything just that little bit harder. Hoses and cables continued to get tangled in the bell wires and the sea swell was still causing motion sickness amongst the divers. They were very tired and needed extra concentration just to ensure that they didn't get into difficulties.

I became obsessed with the fear that something would go

wrong and a diver would be trapped or killed outright. I had been a diver virtually all my adult life. I did not want any diver to lose his life on this operation, no matter how much gold we recovered. I would rather leave the rest behind than risk a death. Mike Stewart, the project manager for 2W, with ultimate responsibility for the dive team, was of exactly the same mind. At eleven o'clock on 5 October he called a meeting of the Russian and British principals on board and said that all diving would be suspended for the season at ten o'clock on 7 October. I completely agreed with the decision; it was the only one we could have made. Quite apart from the deteriorating weather, we were now down to two fit working divers, with no more on deck to send down.

It was very appropriate that the last dive, Dive 67, was made by my old mate Geoff Reudavey and Pete Summers. They had made the first dive on the wreck, when Ru had called for a two-minute silence as he stood in the icy blackness alongside the *Edinburgh*. They had gone into the chamber on 2 September and would not emerge from decompression for another seven days, a total of thirty-eight days in saturation. If ever an award from Her Majesty's Government was merited, these divers deserved one. I know what it took for all those lads to do the job and I took off my hat to the whole team.

With another gale forecast and the sea starting to get up once again, forcing the vessel off station, that final dive had to be aborted. We had recovered 431 gold bars. A further thirty-four, worth almost £4 million, still lay inside the bomb room – enough to finance another recovery operation one day, in the hope that by that time the hiding place of Stalin's other, private shipment could be identified.

So quick was the deterioration in the weather that both the pan-and-tilt camera and the water-jet had to be cut free before we could move off site. By this time the wind had already reached storm Force 10. We spent most of the day steaming east, riding out a storm that at times reached Force 12.

The next morning the weather had eased a little. We returned to site and before departure for Murmansk, a service of remembrance was held. It was a simple ceremony led by David Keogh and open to all on board. It was obvious just by looking at the faces of the people there that they were remembering all those brave men who died in action back in 1942. Finally the wreath of poppies and lilies that I'd brought from Peterhead all those weeks before was committed to the sea in remembrance of the dead. The *Edinburgh* and her crew would now be left to rest in peace.

At 11 a.m. on 7 October we departed for Murmansk to deliver the Soviet share of the gold. I was now sailing back into waters I knew little about, back into the hands of the politicians and the dry-land sharks.

Chapter Twenty-Four

Murmansk

That night we were making about fifteen knots and were still some distance from the Kola Inlet and Murmansk when I heard the engines slowing down. I went up on deck and was told that an engine pressure test was about to take place. I thought no more about it until I saw Melodinsky rushing about, red in the face. The cause was Sidney Alford, the wispy-haired old gentleman who had been dealing with all the live ordnance that had come on board over the past few weeks.

He was an explosives expert of great experience, and having rendered all the live and sometimes dangerous ordnance from the wreck safe, he had, in my book, more than earned the right to be there. Whether that also gave him the right to carry out curious experiments in Soviet territorial waters was another matter. But he had persuaded someone on the bridge to stop the vessel for a short time while he tested a small explosive charge by lowering it to the sea-bed. Whether it was as innocent as he claimed, or whether he was actually carrying out some test of the Soviet anti-submarine defences on behalf of the Ministry of Defence is an open question. The Russians were far from pleased with the episode and no doubt reported it to Moscow, but nothing came of it. Perhaps the Soviets preferred to look the other way, delighted to get their hands on the gold.

We entered the Kola Inlet on 8 October, picking up our pilot at 06.15 GMT. On our way into Murmansk we passed the might of the Russian fleet at anchor in Polyarnoe on our port side, including the vast aircraft carrier, the *Kiev*. Most of the people on board appeared on deck with their cameras, and started clicking away taking pictures. The Russians didn't like this, and attempted to get me to put a stop to it. It was a hopeless task. The feeling on board was, 'Look, we've just recovered all this gold for you, what's wrong with us taking a few pictures?'

As with the explosives incident, wisdom prevailed and nothing further was said, but I got the uneasy feeling that had we not been bringing in the gold, it would not have been such a happy ending.

Murmansk was not exactly the Venice of the North, a sprawl of drab, grey buildings surrounding the enormous dockyards. As well as the Soviet Navy, it was also home to a massive fishing fleet and an all-pervading stench of fish hung in the air. I was told that Russian workers had to be paid extra money just to go and work in Murmansk. I could see why; it looked a grim, bleak, windswept place.

After clearing Customs and Immigration we tied up alongside Pier Eleven at 11.50. Waiting for us was a fine collection of officials, both British and Russian, and a number of Russian reporters and cameramen. Our divers noticed that a Soviet diving vessel was tied up alongside us. We were sure that at some time during the night the underside of our vessel would be examined by the Russian divers, just to make sure all the gold was where it should be. Quite a bit of banter passed between the two vessels.

I welcomed the Russian and British representatives on board, including Mr Zlobin and Mr Korolyov, whom I knew from earlier meetings. They were delighted with the outcome. As the negotiators of the contract, it would do them no harm with their bosses back in the Kremlin.

Naturally the first thing they wanted to see was the gold in the bullion room. It was already divided and documented into the appropriate shares: 45 per cent to the consortium, two-thirds of the remaining 55 per cent to the Russians and one-third to the British, the way the gold had been insured at the time of the sinking.

The allocation of gold bars to cover those shares took hours. An exact split was impossible because, much to our surprise, we'd already discovered that the weight of the individual bars could vary by as much as two kilos. There was an endless round of calculations and recalculations as gold bars were pushed to and fro across the bullion room like gambling chips. Finally we gave up. Without resorting to a hacksaw – which would not have gone down too well with a certain Bank of England official – the weights were as close as possible to the desired split. Any discrepancies would be made right at a later date. Jessop Marine's share – including the first bar, KPO 620 – was a modest-looking pile alongside the stacks for the two governments, but it was still not a bad sum for a ragged lad from Keighley to have earned.

The Russians' faces certainly lit up as they entered the strong-room and saw for the first time all the gold laid out ready for inspection. Over £40 million in gold is enough to make anyone smile.

A reception had been laid on for us all that evening. Only the handful of crewmen needed to guard the boat and the divers still in decompression were unable to attend. It was held in a workers' hotel, the best in Murmansk according to our Russian hosts. The tables were bowed down with food and there was no shortage of drink either – vodka, Russian champagne and a stack of cases of red and white Russian wine.

I sat down next to Mr Korolyov, but recalling my previous experience of Russian hospitality, I said to myself, 'Take it steady, Jessop.' After the meal the first toast was proposed by our host. I drank half the vodka in my glass and then sat down. I received a nudge from Mr Korolyov, who told me quietly, 'The custom in Russia is for the vodka to be taken back in one.' I thanked him for his advice.

A long series of speeches and toasts followed, interrupted by one of the divers, now three sheets to the wind, who started to spray the whole of the top table with champagne. It took a lot of diplomacy and tact to explain to the drenched Russians that the antics of this one diver were the result of him having spent so much time under pressure recovering the gold.

Just after this incident, I noticed that Mr Korolyov was now only taking half of his vodka back after a toast. I gave him a nudge and enquired about the Russian custom of taking it back in one go.

David Keogh and I left the hotel with Mr Zlobin and Mr Korolyov. We were quite a happy little bunch. As we walked down the pathway, a magnificent display of the aurora borealis was lighting up the night sky. I paused to gaze at it and when I looked round, David had disappeared. A moment later I heard a groan from beneath my feet. He'd wandered off the path and fallen into one of the massive drainage ditches. He was unharmed and lying on his back admiring the wonders of the night sky.

The following morning, badly hung over, we watched a spectacular green railway carriage pull up alongside the vessel. It looked like something from the days of the Orient Express, but was the ultra-secure carriage that would transport the Russian gold back to its starting place in Moscow. We all moved down to the bullion room, where the three of us produced our individual keys and started to open the locks. Ilin and I opened ours without trouble but David Keogh was having problems. It wasn't the after-effects of the previous night; his key just wouldn't go into the lock. We then discovered that someone had filled the lock with super-glue during the night. It did not go down very well with the Russians at all. Had I found out who had done it, I would have broken his neck. Two years later, I was told the name of the culprit. It was not a diver or a member of the crew. One day I'll meet him again and until then I will keep the name a secret.

When we finally got the lock open, the gold – 159 ingots weighing 1,880,834.4 grams – was loaded into two green metal boxes, then transferred to the waiting railway carriage by the ship's crane. The boxes disappeared inside the carriage and the doors slammed shut. In front of a bank of Soviet television cameras, Mr Zlobin for the Russians, David Keogh for the British government and myself for the contractors, all signed the completion documents. We shook hands with the Russians and prepared to cast off. The Cold War could now resume.

We left Murmansk at 6.50 that evening and cleared the estuary by ten o'clock, although we had a slight problem in getting rid of the pilot, who had been having a drink or two with his Russian friends on board, Ilin and Melodinsky. As expected, they were returning to the UK with us to inspect the diving chambers once the last divers had finished their decompression.

At last we were on our way home, but our exact destination was a closely-kept secret and radio silence was being maintained to make it difficult for anyone to plot our position. Marine piracy was a real possibility, particularly after the massive world-wide publicity surrounding the salvage operation. The *Stephaniturm* was a slow and unarmed vessel, passing the entire length of the Norwegian coastline, where the fjords and rocky inlets could hide a multitude of possible aggressors. We had no wish to have our prize snatched from us by pirates or terrorists.

The British government had promised coverage of our voyage by a Nimrod reconnaissance aircraft but given their own substantial financial interest, we felt that it wasn't unreasonable to expect them to provide warship protection for us as well. The government obviously disagreed however, and we sailed on alone. The tension slowly ebbed away as we steamed south and west, nearer to home.

Despite the nagging worries about piracy, it was a tremendous relief to be able to relax and forget all the troubles and pressures that had been my way of life for so long. I no longer had to worry about the success of the operation, nor the safety of divers working in very deep and dangerous conditions, nor the wheeling and dealing of competitors and consortium members, nor the activities of the men who I thought had tried to take over my own company and my share of the *Edinburgh*'s gold from me.

After months and years of tension, I had fulfilled all that I'd vowed to do. But all I wanted now was to get back to my family, relax and recharge my engines. I didn't even think about the money I'd earned. I just wanted to get away from it all.

As we entered British territorial waters we received our final, coded instructions. We were to proceed to Peterhead to unload the remaining gold. It had been the starting point for the operation, and it was fitting that we should complete it there.

The last divers finally came out of the chambers at 6.30 the evening before we reached Peterhead, after a mind-numbing seven days of decompression. It was great to see all of them now back amongst us, safe and sound, and suffering no ill-effects. They were still exhausted, but not too tired to join in the celebrations that followed. Along with those of the rest of the crew who were not required to keep the ship pointing in the right direction, we all got pleasantly legless. Even the Russians joined in. We had all earned a last-night party.

We eventually tied up alongside the pier at Peterhead at 7.15 on the morning of 15 October. Including sailing time, it had taken the consortium just forty-seven days to complete the most hazardous recovery operation ever. For security reasons, the pier had been blocked off by the police. The *Stephaniturm* was tied up right at the seaward end. Even at this early hour I could see a small crowd of people behind a makeshift barrier at the other end. I took a stroll along the pier. Waiting behind the barrier were my daughter Carol, my eldest son Graham and a couple of close family friends.

There were also two waiting vehicles, a Brinks-Mat Security van that would take the gold down to London and a silver Porsche. Graham told me it was mine. We had talked many times about what we would do, 'when our ship came in' and I'd often talked about getting a Porsche, but I never expected to see one standing there on my return. Although I'd become an instant millionaire, I hadn't forgotten where I'd come from nor how hard I'd fought to get where I now was. My company now had millions in the bank, but the Porsche was second hand, not brand new.

Bona and Ringrose appeared, smiles all over their faces. I soon got rid of the smiles. Mr Jackson from the Salvage Association arrived shortly afterwards. I greeted him with considerably more warmth. In the early days he'd had the foresight to give me his support, as someone who could be trusted to get a job done. I was delighted for him as well as me, that his judgement had been proved right.

Ric Wharton and Malcolm Williams were the next to arrive. They had been the first people to put their money where their mouths were and the success of the operation was largely down to them. I'd conceived it and formed the original plan, but 2W had persuaded other vital members of the consortium – OSA and Racal–Decca – to come on board and their meticulous preparation and execution of the salvage had made the operation a success.

As the British government press notice said, however:

> Above all the success of the operation is attributable to the courage, tenacity and endurance of the team of divers who operated on the bed of the Barents Sea in extremely arduous conditions and at the limit of free-swimming diver technology.

Once the gold had been unloaded and driven away in the Brinks-Mat van, Ric and Malcolm threw a celebration party on board the *Stephaniturm*. In commemoration of their achievement Ric gave each diver a small gold ingot on a golden chain. The ingots were engraved 'HMS *Edinburgh*'. The party started to break up not long afterwards as all our thoughts turned towards the homes and families we had not seen for so long.

There were many goodbyes to be said: to the two Russians, Ilin and Melodinsky, to David Keogh and the inscrutable Sidney Alford. I shook hands with the two project managers, OSA's John Clarke and 2W's Mike Stewart, who had made a massive contribution to the success of the operation, and the two diving supervisors, Derek Hesketh and Dave Keen, who had ensured that the price of £40 million of gold from the *Edinburgh* did not include any more human lives.

Finally, just as I had done the day the dive team entered the compression chambers, I shook hands with each of the divers in turn as they filed past me. I could see in their faces the toll the work had taken on them, but there was no mistaking their pride in their achievement. They were all very much richer, but I had the feeling that most of them would have done it for nothing, just to have taken part.

I shook hands with Banjo West, John Diamond and Brian Cutler, the three men who'd almost died on the first bell run; Geoff Reudavey, the first man to dive the wreck, and his dive partner Pete Summers; Doug Matherson, still with his shoulder strapped; and John Rossier, the diver who recovered the first gold bar and who now had a new baby to see for the first time. Last in line, just as he had been on the deck of the *Stephaniturm*, was Jim Tucker. I winked at him. 'Shame about those last few bars, Jim. I thought I told you not to leave any down there.'

He smiled. 'Like I told you, Keith, you always leave ten per cent as a tip.'

CHAPTER TWENTY-FIVE

THE OLD BAILEY

On the way down from Peterhead, Graham explained why he had asked me about the M62 agreement over the radio telephone while I was on the *Stephaniturm*. He had gone to Manchester for a meeting with David Bona. Believing that I had already signed the M62 agreement, Bona had used the power of attorney he had asked for 'just in case I have to sign a letter or something', to borrow £630,000 from Rothschilds, using our share of the gold as collateral. The money had been used to pay Ringrose, Bona's firm and his cronies, without my knowledge.

Most of the money had gone on Bona's own enormous interim bill – it was later heavily reduced after I challenged it in the courts – but £100,000 had allegedly been paid to a charity. It came as no surprise to learn that Bona would not reveal which one.

When Graham challenged him on why he'd borrowed the money from Rothschilds, Bona had ignored the question and treated him with thinly veiled contempt. 'We control the company now, so you and your brother had better start looking for new jobs.' I was furious but also relieved. The pair of them had played their hand too soon. I would have news for both of them very soon; it wasn't Graham and Ian who were about to be out of work.

I was determined that nothing was going to spoil my first weekend home with my family, however, and shelved all thoughts of dealing with them until the next week. When we stopped for petrol, I phoned Mildred. 'Don't come back home. There's a hundred press men camped on the front lawn, driving me mad.'

I needed a couple of days' peace before we started on that lark so I got Mildred to book us in at the Craiglands Hotel in Ilkley under an assumed name, then drove straight there. The deception wasn't entirely successful; the manager recognised me straight away and was snapping away like a paparazzo on speed, but I persuaded him not to contact the press until after we'd checked out; that way he got his publicity but I got my peace.

Mildred was waiting for me in our room and had already started on the celebration champagne. She threw her arms around me and gave me a hug that almost cracked a few ribs. Then we sat holding hands as we talked each other through the events of the past few weeks and tried to imagine all the ways that our lives might change for the better now that we were rich. If only we'd known.

I took a long hot bath, slept for a couple of hours and woke feeling more relaxed than I had in two or three years. The rest of the family and a few of our friends and supporters were meeting us for a celebration booze-up in an Ilkley pub that evening. It was in full swing when I was summoned by the landlord to take a phone call. James Ringrose was on the line. 'I've heard that Barrie Penrose is running a story in the *Sunday Times* tomorrow, accusing the divers of desecrating the war grave.' The last sight I'd had of Penrose was when he left the *Stephaniturm* at Peterhead, threatening 'to get my revenge'. His threat had taken less than forty-eight hours to put into effect. I ranted down the phone for a couple of minutes, threatening to rip off Penrose's head and do other equally terminal things to him. Part of my tirade duly appeared verbatim in a subsequent Penrose article. He wasn't the only one getting his revenge; the only explanation I had was that Ringrose must have been taping the call.

I went back to the bar in no mood to carry on the celebrations and when we got back to the hotel I lay awake for a good part of the night worrying about what was going to be in Penrose's story. It was every bit as bad as I feared. The *Sunday Times* ran a banner headline splashing the claim that our divers had been desecrating the war grave and putting light sticks inside the skulls of dead British sailors. The Ministry of Defence promptly announced an official inquiry into the allegations.

Knowing they were completely false, I tried to brush the story aside. To take our minds off it, Mildred and I decided to celebrate our new-found fortune by going house-hunting. In many ways I'd have liked to stay in our old former council house, where we'd been very happy, but just from seeing friends and acquaintances the previous night, I had already realised that the money would change things irrevocably. Some were just the same with me as before, but for others – the majority – the money was already a barrier between us. A couple tried to tap me for a loan, others looked at me with suspicion, bordering on hostility, as if they'd already convinced themselves that I thought myself too good for them now.

If we were going to move, I fancied a farmhouse with some land and a barn where I could store diving equipment. Mildred and everyone else in the family had a different idea of our dream home, however, and in the end we settled on a stone detached house on a hill above Keighley. It had fabulous views over Ilkley Moor and right down the Aire Valley; on a clear day I could see every hole of three different golf courses from our windows.

I had already decided that the house and the Porsche were the only luxuries I would allow myself; the rest of the money would be reinvested in diving equipment and expeditions to find the next rich cargo on my research list. All my adult life I had dreamed of owning my own salvage company. The *Edinburgh* had given me the capital to make the dream a reality – or so I thought.

I had planned to have a couple of weeks off before getting back to work but in the event, that one weekend was all the respite I had. Despite being awash with gold bullion, Jessop Marine's financial affairs turned out to be a disaster area.

One of my first meetings was with Oscar Goldstein, a senior partner at Price Waterhouse in Manchester. Bona was still at my side, for even though he now knew that the M62 agreement remained unsigned, he appeared to believe that he could oil his way out of trouble, and I didn't want to alert him to his imminent dismissal until I had a new solicitor in place to deal with the inevitable legal flak.

While I was concentrating on the salvage operation, Bona and Ringrose had been tasked with doing the necessary tax planning for Jessop Marine's huge windfall. Bona had postponed it, however, claiming that Oscar had told him to start making tax plans when we'd actually recovered the gold. Staring at him with a mixture of disbelief and disgust, Oscar told me that Bona had lied to me. Oscar had actually told him that the time to start tax planning was well before the recovery. After the event, with the gold already landed in the UK, our room to manoeuvre was minimal. I was going to be hammered for tax. After that bombshell, Oscar turned his attention to the alleged charity payment of £100,000, demanding to know the identity of the recipient. Bona repeatedly refused to answer the question.

I went to my next meeting alone. As I told my new

solicitor the story of Bona and Ringrose's actions, I could see the disbelief in his eyes. He later confirmed that, in time, every word had proved to be true. Sacking Ringrose and Bona was easily achieved but their legacy could not be expunged so easily. The third member of the unholy trinity, Barrie Penrose, was also far from finished. The M.o.D inquiry into his allegations completely exonerated me and the divers of any wrongdoing. The only people ultimately hurt by Penrose's stories were the surviving relatives of men lost on the *Edinburgh*. Undaunted by one public reverse however, Penrose resumed the attack in a further article, claiming that I had reneged on promises to pay part of the *Edinburgh* proceeds to three charities – St Joseph's Hospice in the East End, the RNLI and the Mary Rose Trust. Given the identity of its royal patron, I felt the mention of the latter bore the fingerprints of James Ringrose.

Despite the apparently convincing detail of the article, letters to and from each of the three charities revealed that they knew of no promises from me or Jessop Marine to pay them anything. Equally significantly, none of them had ever heard of James Ringrose or David Bona and had never received any of the missing £100,000.

Penrose still wasn't beaten. His next story, 'The Mole That Showed the Way', claimed that Mr Jackson at the Salvage Association had been bribed by me to leak information on our rivals' bids for the *Edinburgh* contract. He repeated and expanded on his allegations in his 'quickie' book on the *Edinburgh*, *Stalin's Gold*.

The article was raised in a question in the House of Commons the next day, provoking a Fraud Squad inquiry. Having examined the evidence, the police concluded that I had no case to answer, but the Director of Public Prosecutions, under heavy pressure from someone, gave the go-ahead for a prosecution. If James Ringrose's friends in high places had indeed helped to win us the contract, they were now out to nail me to the wall.

I was charged with conspiring with Mr Jackson to break Section Two of the Official Secrets Act and with conspiracy to defraud Risdon Beazley and Stolt-Nielsen Seaway but it was another two years before the case came to court. In the meantime I was a pariah, unable even to pursue my chosen career. Fresh from the *Edinburgh* success, I'd been besieged with offers of fantastic contracts from around the world, but once the charges were levelled, no one would work with me. Over and over again I heard the same message: 'Until you clear your name Keith, we can't work with you, it's as simple as that.'

A flood of offers for me to do advertising and product endorsements also dried up overnight. While I fought the charges and set out to prove my innocence, even my own research files on lucrative wrecks had to be set aside and all salvage work stopped for three years. My dreams of buying my own salvage boat and getting my own team together to work on some of the contracts I had lined up had been dashed.

The old-boy network was obviously not working at maximum efficiency however, for while the friends in high places were pursuing their campaign against me, out of the blue Mildred and I received an invitation to the Buckingham Palace Garden Party. I was dying for Prince Charles to turn up so that I could test the truth of some of James Ringrose's claims, but sadly I never got the chance.

It was one of the few moments of light relief in two years of torment. Then at last I heard the words I'd been waiting for all that time.

'What is your verdict?'

'Not guilty.'

'And that is the verdict of you all?'

'It is.'

It had taken the Old Bailey jury the time it takes to have a cup of tea and a cigarette to return their verdict. The ridiculous charge that I had conspired with Mr Jackson to break Section Two of the Official Secrets Act had already been thrown out by the judge a few days previously. All the jury had to do then was find on the remaining charge of conspiracy to defraud Risdon Beazley and Stolt-Nielsen Seaway. The prosecution had tried to suggest that I'd bribed Mr Jackson with a slice of the gold money to ensure that we won the contract. As the evidence showed quite plainly, there was no bribe and no conspiracy. The whole trial had been a waste of time and taxpayers' money.

The way I saw it was that having failed in their own conspiracy to take over my company David Bona and James Ringrose had done their best to make the charges stick. But what I believed to be the truth had been exposed in court.

I had the last laugh on Ringrose and Bona however, and on the *Sunday Times* reporter, Barrie Penrose, whose claims had also been shown to be wrong. I knew I was innocent, but after standing in the dock at the Old Bailey for the best part of a fortnight, to see the judge look up, smile and say, 'Not guilty Mr Jessop' was still one of the biggest adrenalin shots I ever had in my life.

As my counsel rose to ask for costs to be awarded against the prosecution, I let the feeling of pure relief wash over me. It suddenly struck me that I was now free to leave, but there was one thing I wanted to do first. I grabbed a piece of paper from my notebook, then walked through the well of the court to the table where Barbara Mills and the other prosecuting counsel were sitting. I slapped the piece of paper down on the table in front of them and looked them all in the eye, one by one. 'Would you people mind signing your names, so there's no way I can ever forget who you are?'

Nobody moved. They all stared back at me blank-faced as if this had never happened before. Maybe it hadn't, but that's the way I felt.

I walked out of the court. In the corridor outside, the police team came over to me, wanting to shake my hand. 'I hope there's no hard feelings, Keith?' I took their hands mechanically but I didn't speak to them. One thing was for sure: I didn't have any good feelings towards them. They shared the responsibility for my years of hell.

Once outside the Old Bailey, surrounded by my legal team and my family, but confronted by a wall of pressmen and photographers, it all became a bit too much for me. I felt close to tears. All I wanted to do was to go away and walk by myself for an hour or so, to give me time to reflect and settle my mind.

I mumbled something to Graham, Ian and Bruce Buchan, my solicitor, and walked away. For the next hour and more I paced the streets of London, not looking or caring where I was going, just trying to rid myself of the horrible thoughts that had been going through my head. I had an awful lot of hatred inside me towards the people that had put me through all this. I had lost two and a half years of my life because of those fictitious charges. The stress had almost destroyed my marriage and my family. I had also lost virtually all of the fortune I had made and been deprived of every chance to make another one.

The years of waiting before the case came to trial cost me and my company millions of pounds; it also cost the Government a fortune in lost taxes. I had masterminded the recovery of £45 million in gold bullion from the *Edinburgh*, earning the British government well over £10 million in the process. Had a British-based consortium not salvaged the wreck, the gold would have been taken by another salvor and they would not have had a penny. My reward was to be

408

vilified, dragged through the courts and then hounded by the Inland Revenue, for the friends in high places hadn't finished with me yet. As soon as I was acquitted, the Inquiry Branch of the Inland Revenue was let loose on me and my company. Someone was obviously very determined to bring me down.

My accountants had had the very difficult job of preparing accounts with all these charges hanging over the company. They worked closely with the tax authorities and if there had been no criminal charges pending, the tax would have been paid on time. The Inland Revenue had agreed to delay any settlement of my tax affairs until after the conclusion of the court case. I had been told that a payment of around £200,000 would be necessary.

By the end of the case, on the advice of my lawyer, I had retained a new firm of accountants, and I sat facing the Inland Revenue men across the dining table in my house, flanked by my new advisors from Cooper, Lybrand and my old ones from Price, Waterhouse. I was not anticipating any difficulties.

I could not read a balance sheet to save my life, but my accounts had already been turned inside out and upside down by the Fraud Squad. They had forced me to account for every penny I and the company had spent over the previous three and a half years, as they searched for missing money that would supply evidence of a bribe to Mr Jackson. The Fraud Squad had concluded that there was no missing money. Despite this history, one of the tax men announced that they were not happy with my accounts. I counted to ten but then exploded anyway.

'Two of the top accountancy firms in the country have passed these accounts. They've been pored over by the Fraud Squad for two years and they couldn't find a thing wrong with them. Then you come to my house and tell me that you've still got doubts about them.' I was so angry I could hardly speak. 'I want this settled now. What's my tax bill?'

They exchanged a glance with each other. 'We'll need a payment of a quarter of a million pounds.'

'And that's the end?'

He spread his hands. 'Not a penny less, Mr Jessop, not a penny more.'

I took out my pen, wrote a cheque for £250,000 and threw it across the table at them.

It was far from the end. My eventual tax bill was close to £700,000. Including accountancy fees, I finished up paying over £900,000 to settle the tax affairs of Jessop Marine. They had almost cleaned out the company.

I needed to get back to work in a hurry, but first there were two pieces of unfinished business. I would be going back to the courts again, but this time as the plaintiff, not the accused.

I was eager to sue Einar Hovding over what I considered to be the theft of the *Chulmleigh*'s cargo. The case was open and shut. I was the official contract-holder with the British and Soviet governments and we had eye-witness accounts of Hovding's men removing the cargo. While I was prepared to fight the case in the Norwegian courts, however, neither the British nor the Soviet governments, which had also been robbed of their share of the proceeds, would stand up and be counted.

I had more luck with my other court action. With my name cleared by the Old Bailey trial, I sued Barrie Penrose for the libels contained in his articles and book about me. The *Sunday Times*, Granada Publishing and Barrie Penrose preferred to settle on the steps of the High Court in London, rather than have the whole truth about the affair come out in open court. Penrose's book was ordered to be pulped and

I received a substantial out-of-court settlement and all my costs, but it was peanuts compared to the money I could have earned by following my career instead of fighting to clear my name. Instead of the millions I had earned from the *Edinburgh* and the millions more I stood to make on the back of that success, my name had been blackened to the point where no underwriter or wreck-owner would give me a contract and my money had by now been swallowed in legal fees, VAT and taxes.

The one thing they couldn't take from me was my knowledge and my ability, and everything that had happened to me since I stepped ashore at Peterhead had just hardened my resolve to go out and prove that the *Edinburgh* hadn't been a fluke; that I could do it again on another wreck.

I was sick of the sharks in pin-stripe suits however, and desperate to breathe some clean air again, well away from the country that I felt had betrayed me. I had seen more than enough of Britain for a while. I left England in 1986, with the grand total of £13,000 to my name and separated from my wife. I was back to square one, but I was now more determined than ever that the bastards were not going to grind me down.

AUTHOR'S NOTE

For the sake of narrative clarity my discovery of the plunder of the *Chulmleigh*'s cargo has been brought forward in time. In reality I did not discover the theft until a couple of years after the salvage of the *Edinburgh*.

With that single exception, everything in this book has been recounted exactly as it happened.

ACKNOWLEDGEMENTS

I began my professional diving career picking up scrap metal from the sea-bed with my bare hands. My journey from those modest beginnings to the successful salvage of £45 million of gold from a warship at the bottom of the Arctic Ocean was a long and arduous one. It could not have been made without the help and encouragement of countless people.

First and foremost, my thanks to my wife Mildred for giving me the chance to fulfil my dream, and to my children, Graham, Carol and Ian. The demands of my chosen career meant that I saw much less of them in their formative years than I would have liked. If I have one regret from my life as a diver, it is that.

Amongst the many people who helped me with information, advice and above all friendship, I must single out Ruth and Bobby Ramsey from Cadryne Farm on the Mull of Galloway, and my good friend from the island of Islay, Harold Hastie, now sadly deceased.

The Salvage Association in London gave me much help and advice in the early years. I'm grateful to Mr Smith, then Manager in the Salvage and Sales Department, who gave me my first real break by pointing me in the direction of the *Johanna Thorden*. After Mr Smith's retirement, Mr John

Jackson and his assistant Mr Jack Nichols proved equally helpful. They deserve the highest praise for the way they carried out their work; without their diligence the British government would have been many millions of pounds the poorer.

When working in the offshore oil industry it was always a pleasure to hear the lilting tones of 'Wee' Val Reekie down the phone, offering a contract, starting yesterday, in yet another outlandish part of the world.

My thanks also to my old mate from the Marines, Alan Richal, now Val's husband, and to John Patterson for all the hours of amusement listening to his stories and jokes. We were once stuck on a rig in the Indian Ocean for six weeks before he began to repeat himself.

Ric Wharton was prepared to listen to the plans of a Yorkshire salvage man with hardly a pound to his name and then had the nerve and foresight to back them. Without Ric and his partner at Wharton and Williams, Malcolm Williams, there would have been no salvage of the *Edinburgh*.

The late Ian Hunter, manager of the old National Westminster Bank in Keighley, also showed the foresight and trust to give me financial support at a time when I had little but dreams to offer as collateral.

People in my home town who believed I could recover the *Edinburgh*'s gold were as rare as hen's teeth. The small band of true believers included my favourite sister-in-law Barbara, Aunt Ellen and Uncle Bill and my old friend Marcus – now Sir Marcus – Fox. I was relieved and delighted for them – as well as me – when that first gold bar had been recovered and they could say to the many doubters, 'I told you so.'

The team on board HMS *Belfast*, the identical twin of the *Edinburgh*, gave invaluable help in the planning of the operation and I spent many hours sharing a tot with the late Chief Petty Officer Robbjohns and his friends Ted and Bill Roper.

David Keogh, 'Our Man from the Ministry', wore many hats at different times, acting for the Ministry of Defence, the Department of Trade and the Salvage Association, as well as taking charge of the remembrance services for the brave men who died on the *Edinburgh*. His efforts in often difficult circumstances deserved wider acknowledgement.

Mike Stewart and John Clarke, project managers for 2W and OSA respectively, also made major contributions to the success of the operation.

Last but far from least, the divers and back-up crew on the *Stephaniturm* deserve nothing but the highest praise. Like me, they took the risk of working on the *Edinburgh* project on 'no cure, no pay' terms and they fully earned their rewards. The success of 'the salvage of the century' ultimately depended on them.

I have had space to mention only a few of the hundreds of people who have helped me over the years. Others are referred to in the course of the book, but my heartfelt thanks also go to those who have not been mentioned by name. You know who you are and you have my undying gratitude.

Like a salvage operation, a book is a team effort. My sincere thanks also go to Neil and Lynn Hanson, my agent Mark Lucas at Lucas Alexander Whitley, my editor, Martin Fletcher, and all the team at Simon & Schuster, particularly Nick Webb, Bob Kelly and Keith Barnes.

Appendix

———————•———————

Report prepared by the Ministry of Defence in response to the allegations of disrespect to the HMS *Edinburgh* War Grave, made by Barrie Penrose

It has sometimes been said that the M.o.D should never have allowed access to the wreck. But this would have left the war grave unprotected. The choice before the M.o.D was, therefore, whether to leave the war grave to the depredations of would-be salvors, or to forestall them by permitting recovery of the gold under controlled conditions. In the interests of the war grave there could only be one answer, a controlled salvage.

The recent successful salvage operation by Jessop Marine Recoveries Ltd/Wharton Williams Consortium has clearly demonstrated that, with the advantage of present day diving techniques and equipment, recovery of the gold from the wreck was feasible. It was only a matter of time before a pirate operation would have been mounted, with scant regard for the war grave. It was to pre-empt such an attempt that permission was given to salvage the gold under conditions strictly controlled by a contract.

In the planning, preparation and execution of the operation considerable care was given by all concerned to the war grave status of the wreck. An M.o.D representative was on board the recovery vessel *Stephaniturm* throughout the operation. The salvage was meticulously planned and very well executed with the divers operating at remarkable depths in appalling conditions.

The cargo of gold had been carried in the bomb room of HMS *Edinburgh*. Entry into the wreck was made by a precision cutting operation, and through a fuel tank into the bomb room, by direct route where human remains were least likely to be encountered. Throughout the operation the divers had to work in the wreck in conditions of almost nil visibility due to the presence of fine silt which the slightest movement disturbed.

Despite the route chosen and the visibility conditions under which they were working, the divers reported the presence of a few scattered remains in the fuel tank. These were carefully moved aside to a place well clear of the work area. Further bones were reported in the bomb room; these too were carefully removed and placed in the same area of the oil tank as the first remains.

Allegations have been made that other bones were brought on board the *Stephaniturm* and then casually tossed back into the sea, with a hasty burial service conducted by the M.o.D representative only after complaints had been made to him. What actually happened was as follows.

Before the gold could be reached a passage had to be cleared through the debris of all kinds, including ammunition and stores, the whole congealed in heavy black fuel oil. As a safety measure, fused high explosive shells which could have endangered the lives of the divers, had to be taken to the surface to be checked for sensitivity. Recovery baskets brought to the surface contained refuse of all types, broken pieces of wood, pieces of canvas, sediment and other material including HE shells in a congealed oily mess.

Two members of the salvage crew working up to their elbows in the thick mess in one recovery basket were searching, as they had done previously in other similar baskets, for HE shells. They had no reason to expect that human remains might be in the basket. Material other than HE shells was dropped straight over the side. Regrettably, two bones were inadvertently returned to the sea at the same time.

We have investigated this incident and are satisfied that the actions of these two people were almost instinctive, bearing in mind the dangerous task in hand, and certainly not premeditated. In fact, one said that he hardly knew that he had a bone in his hand until he released it. This was the only instance when human remains were returned to the sea without a proper burial.

There was one other occasion, about two days later, when a bone was brought to the surface, again inadvertently, and in a similar manner. Having regard to the proposed method of entry into the bomb room, it had been considered unlikely that human remains would be encountered in the wreck. Nevertheless, during the planning and preparation stages, the Chaplain of the fleet was consulted about the arrangements which should be made and the form of the burial service to be used should any human remains be brought to the surface.

The M.o.D representative, who is qualified to conduct a naval burial service, was briefed accordingly. This bone was, therefore, carefully set aside and a naval burial service, such as is performed by the Naval Chaplaincy Service, was conducted by the M.o.D representative in accordance with the contingency arrangements made before the operation commenced.

The second allegation made concerning unseemly treatment of human remains was that lighting sticks were placed in skulls in the wreck and that skulls were arranged so as to startle the next diver down.

An investigation has been carried out by the salvors and we have been assured that there is absolutely no evidence to suggest that these things happened. Those on board responsible for monitoring every dive in great detail have no knowledge of such incident or incidents occurring. Operating at the limits of technology, it is unlikely that the divers would have indulged in activities which might have placed their colleagues' lives at risk.

Allegations have also been made that explosives were carried on board the *Stephaniturm* for use on the wreck. It was most certainly not intended to blast open the war grave. At no time were explosives used on or near it. The method of entry to the wreck, as agreed beforehand by the M.o.D and D.o.T, was by means of conventional oxy-arc cutting equipment. A precision cutting device, which would have used ounces of explosives to melt metal, was taken on board for use if normal methods would have been dangerous. M.o.D and D.o.T had given prior approval to its use, if necessary, but in the event this sophisticated equipment was not required.

The allegations concerning the skulls, and the isolated but regrettable instance when bones were returned to the sea without a proper burial service, contrast markedly with the general attitude of reverence and respect for the war grave shown by the divers. The first diver of his own accord and without any prompting observed two minutes' silence, 800 feet down, as a mark of respect for those men who had perished with HMS *Edinburgh*.

At the end of the operation the divers, many of whom were ex-Royal Navy, asked for a special Remembrance Service to be held over the war grave, and a wreath of red poppies and white lilies was laid on the sea. Divers still in the saturation chamber asked for the Remembrance Service sheet to be shown to them. This included the Remembrance Day Prayer and the Naval Prayer.

Thirty-four bars of gold, currently valued at about £3.5 million, were not recovered when Jessop Marine Recoveries Ltd/Wharton Williams Consortium, in accordance with the contract, gave notice of intention to suspend operations for the season. This consortium has the option to continue with the salvage next year and although no firm plans to complete the recovery have yet been made they have successfully demonstrated that they have the expertise to do so. It remains the prime concern of HMG to have the gold removed, under controlled conditions, so that the war grave may thereafter rest in peace.

PERMISSIONS

The majority of illustrative material used in this book is the property of Keith Jessop.

With thanks to the following for kind use of other photographs and material:

Mull of Galloway/Landing raft © *Scottish Daily Express/* © *Scottish Daily Mail*
'Yellow Submarine' © *Scottish Daily Express*
The sinking HMS *Edinburgh* © Imperial War Museum
Map of HMS *Edinburgh*'s final battle © Public Record Office
Cross-sections of ship © M.o.D.
Keith cleaning gold © *Sunday Times*
Keith with bar round neck © *Sunday Times*
Keith with diving helmet © *Daily Express*

With thanks to the *Keighley News* for permission to reproduce from their newspaper Saturday, March 2 1968 and Friday, May 30 1969 and to the *Daily Express* for permission to reproduce from Robert McGowan's article of 1 June 1981.

Also to the Department of Trade for reproduction of their press notice on HMS *Edinburgh*.

Permissions

Where it has not been possible to trace copyright holders, the publisher will be happy to credit them in all future editions of this book.